ANTHROPOLOGICAL PAPERS OF
THE UNIVERSITY OF ARIZONA
NUMBER 12

JACK O. WADDELL

PAPAGO INDIANS AT WORK

THE UNIVERSITY OF ARIZONA PRESS
TUCSON 1969

THE UNIVERSITY OF ARIZONA PRESS

Copyright © 1969
The Arizona Board of Regents
Library of Congress Catalog
Card No. 68-58960
Manufactured in the U.S.A.

PREFACE

This study has been conceived with two major objectives in mind. First, it has been my intention to contribute to a greater understanding of contemporary Papago social life by becoming intimately acquainted with a very few individuals and observing how they interact with the social environments in which they find themselves. Secondly, I have sought to discover a few of the ways in which individual Papagos and their families reconcile the demands of their cultural heritages to the social requirements of occupations away from their reservation homes. In short, I have sought to reveal the social structures that are meaningful in Papago lives and to assess changes taking place in individual personalities as a result of the interplay of differing cultural values.

Dr. William H. Kelly, Director of the Bureau of Ethnic Research, first stimulated my interest in off-reservation Papago employment and kindly gave his time and advice during the "feeling out" process of formulating a sound research program. After a period of familiarizing myself with the Papago literature and the Papago demographic records in the Bureau of Ethnic Research, the next step was to conceptualize a social universe and to define a spatial domain within which to confine my research.

I wanted to get to know individual Papagos and how they were coming to terms with the occupational environments in which they were living. Restricting my efforts to Papagos residing and working off-reservation and limiting my field work to southern Arizona, I went into the field with a potential informant list of about 80 Papagos and a crude interview schedule designed to elicit preliminary data. By the end of the first summer's work (1963), I had visited many different rural towns, farm camps, jails, and other places of Papago settlement in southern Arizona. In addition to recording descriptions of these different social and occupational environments, I succeeded in contacting and interviewing fifteen Papago men who represented different age categories and who varied somewhat in terms of their occupational activities, educational backgrounds, language usage, and extent of off-reservation, non-Papago social experiences.

With the aid of revised instruments, a better knowledge of the social fields, and a list of informants, I set out in the subsequent field research to develop more intimate and prolonged contacts with some of these informants, with the final intention of building a few case studies and life histories. From these few cases and the many observations that have resulted from work in the field have come the data that provide the basis for this study.

The initial phases of this research were carried out while I was a graduate assistant in the Bureau of Ethnic Research, from June, 1963, through August, 1964. Beginning in September, 1964, I was able to continue my research with the aid of a two-year fellowship from the United States Steel Foundation. I am indebted to both organizations for their financial backing and for the freedom they have allowed me to develop and pursue a problem of my own interest.

I am especially grateful to Dr. E. H. Spicer for the time he invested and the insights he provided during our many sessions. I wish to thank Dr. William H. Kelly for his continued interest in my research and particularly for his critical insights concerning some of my

theoretical formulations. I am indebted to Dr. Malcolm McFee for his role in the first stages of problem formulation. Dr. Harry T. Getty gave much time in critically reading the manuscript.

I wish to thank Dr. Harland Padfield, Research Associate in the Bureau of Ethnic Research, for the use of some of his field research materials and for his authoritative comments on Papago employment. Mr. Peter Hemingway, Research Assistant in the Bureau, generously aided my research by helping run off an IBM deck containing the off-reservation, southern Arizona Papago universe.

The cordial assistance of Mr. John W. McLean, Employment Agent for the Phelps Dodge Corporation at Ajo, Arizona, is greatly appreciated. Many other individuals, too numerous to mention, in many areas, shared opinions, knowledge, and observations.

The debt I owe to my Papago informants cannot be adequately expressed. They were extremely patient and friendly; they shared their problems, joys, sentiments, and moments of grief.

To a loving and understanding wife, who is blessed with enviable secretarial skills, I owe a special kind of gratitude. Carol spent long hours in typing and assisting with the final version of the manuscript.

JACK O. WADDELL

TABLE OF CONTENTS

LIST OF ILLUSTRATIONS

LIST OF TABLES

ABSTRACT

Case studies of five Papago Indian laborers are used in this investigation as a way of demonstrating how social roles are perceived and enacted in four different kinds of occupational environments. These environments or complexes constitute environments of adaptation in which Papagos are accommodating culturally learned roles to the roles demanded by their involvements with Anglos and within Anglo institutions.

The off-reservation occupational complexes are established on both an impressionistic and a quantitative basis. The temporal and spatial dimensions of these complexes are investigated in order to provide an understanding of their historical developments and an understanding of some of their ecological and demographic features. In addition, social structural features of the different occupational environments are discussed. The temporal, spatial, and social structural data are presented in order to provide a background for appreciating the broader patterns of Papago off-reservation employment as well as to establish an appreciation for the patterns revealed in the individual cases presented.

Sentiments, attitudes, and observed behaviors having to do with the performance of certain social roles are presented and analyzed, using the five Papago cases as specific examples. By analyzing the compatibility of roles, the study reveals some of the factors that seem to be functionally related to occupational adaptation. This type of cultural analysis, using role theory and the theory of institutional behavior, seeks to contribute to general acculturation theory by identifying adaptive processes at work in individual Papago personalities straining for new kinds of roles and abandoning or modifying Papago cultural behaviors.

1. OCCUPATIONAL ACTIVITY AS A LOCUS OF ACCULTURATION PROCESSES

SOCIAL STRUCTURE, ACCULTURATION, AND SOCIAL MOBILITY

Available data indicate a positive relationship between social mobility and the assimilation[1] of ethnic groups in the United States (Spiro 1955: 1243). In this country, as in many parts of the world where there is complex cultural or ethnic contact, the social system functions to encourage assimilation. As Weinstock (1963: 148) observes: "The process of acculturation is functional within the social framework since one of the main objects of social systems is to assure cultural conformity and minimize conflict." Since the social framework is a stratified one, however, acculturation functions to orient different levels of the social system to some degree of conformity to the normative goals. This conformity is never completely assured because of the different orientations of the various strata and cultural groups, but integration of the different levels and groups is achieved as individuals are oriented to new values, new reference groups, and new statuses and roles. Where the aspiration to conform to the general orientations of the social system is highly distributed throughout the strata, where there are means whereby individuals can assimilate these orientations, and where there are opportunities to move from one status to another, a certain kind of cultural conformity and integration exists, although the differentiated strata and cultural groups remain.

At the same time, however, assimilation and social class mobility may endanger the social solidarity of cultural or ethnic groups and status categories and, ultimately, threaten cultural survival of certain segments of a society. Situations of cultural contact may actually stimulate reactions that intensify cultural or ethnic group solidarity and thus impede assimilation and upward mobility. While the Anglo value system essentially encourages both assimilation and social class mobility, the actual class structure in America

prevents the upward mobility of the unassimilated (Spiro 1955: 1244). When individuals use a social class or a particular occupational status as an object of identification and aspiration, the ethnic or cultural community with which they are identified can no longer remain as a reference group, without some form of conflict, unless the class/status structure of the community is similar to that of the larger society, or unless the community supports the identification of its members with these new statuses. If the reference ingroup does support outgroup identifications, it invites competition for the loyalty of individuals. This may be the first step toward the assimilation of individuals into a dominant system. Becoming assimilated, in this sense, means shifting identification from the cultural group to a particular status in the dominant Anglo social system — that is, adopting the behavior and the symbols of a desired occupational status. Assimilation of ethnic individuals is not, therefore, an incorporation into a monolithic Anglo culture per se but an incorporation into any one of several achievable statuses within it. Upward mobility aspirations are strongly encouraged in an open class system and constantly challenge the integrity of culture-bearing units or ethnic groups, thereby tending to speed up the assimilation process (Spiro 1955: 1244).

As Spiro notes, acculturation and social mobility are quite distinct processes, for social mobility is not necessarily assured for those who are in the process of acculturation. Assimilation, or the acquisition of the culture of the dominant society by individuals of a subordinate society, depends on the desires and capacities of individuals to make such an acquisition. In addition, assimilation of individuals into the dominant system also depends on the consenting behavior of individuals belonging to the dominant system (Spiro 1955: 1244). In the course of acculturative change, the extent to which the desired statuses of the dominant system are achieved depends, in part, on the members of the achieving cultural or ethnic

---

[1]Spiro (1955) uses the more comprehensive term acculturation. Assimilation is here used as a more exact term to denote the final processual phase that sometimes occurs in the course of acculturative processes (Redfield, Linton, and Herskovits, 1936: 149).

group. That is, even when the dominant social system tends to encourage assimilation and social mobility, the integrity of an ongoing cultural or ethnic entity may be threatened, in which case processes may be set in motion to ensure its survival. Eaton (1952) has called these regulatory processes "controlled acculturation" — that is, the institutionalization of techniques for dealing with the pressures of acculturation, or the controlling of the rate and the extent of changes that threaten social solidarity and the psychological order of individual members. When assimilative change is encouraged and directed by the dominant society, individuals of a subordinate society still have some measure of control over the kinds of reactions they will express as they confront these forces: whether they will try to acquiesce, resist, or ignore.

Occupational statuses are extremely important variables in the social class structure of the United States. Therefore, occupational activity is considered to be a vital locus whereby processes of acculturation might be understood. The particular "subordinate" society for purposes of this study is the Papago Indians of southern Arizona and northwestern Mexico. Since Papagos are affected by certain aspects of Anglo social structures, and since they do participate increasingly in certain occupational statuses and related activities, certain processes of acculturation should be identifiable by focusing on the occupational activities of Papago individuals. Occupation is not the only significant variable. However, a theoretical framework will be developed by which occupational activity can be used as a means for gaining insight into the acculturative processes affecting individual Papago personalities.

PERSONALITY AND CULTURE

As Spiro (1961a: 459) expresses it, with the modern developments in all of the subfields of the discipline, anthropology cannot really claim a holistic outlook, largely because the dimensions of human behavior have been widely studied; and some aspects of human behavior have incited little interest on the part of anthropologists. Further, the holistic approach of anthropologists in describing exotic or primitive cultures is not adequate in situations involving culture contact. As Beals (1951: 4) and Mason (1955: 1264-5) point out, anthropologists have tended to avoid using the same critical standards of observation when dealing with the larger, more complex societies and have sometimes naively assumed that there is sufficient agreement as to what constitutes, say, Anglo culture. Demonstrating cultural holism at a less complex level of organization is no basis for assuming it at a more complex level of cultural integration.

This caution in treating either the Papago or the Anglo cultures too holistically is not a denial of the culture concept, nor is it a denial of discrete cultural orientations for different peoples. It simply admits that while there are a number of descriptions of Papago institutions and cultural activities (Underhill 1939, 1940, 1946; Joseph, Spicer, and Chesky 1949; Tooker 1952; Kelly 1963; Bahr 1964), Papago acculturation (King 1954; Williams 1956; Fontana 1960), and Papago demographic arrangements (Dobyns 1950; Tooker 1952; King 1954; Hackenberg 1961; Padfield 1961; Kelly 1963), there is currently no adequate descriptive base for dealing with Papago culture as a whole. This study does not intend to end up with any such description or even an approximation. The approach pursued in this research circumvents the holism that has characterized traditional ethnography.

Along with the descriptions that do exist pertaining to aspects of Papago culture, it is necessary to assume that there are normative or regulatory dimensions operating in Papago societies that are generationally transmitted and incorporated by individuals through enculturative processes in primary social units (Spiro 1961b: 94). There is, in other words, a prescribed cultural order that becomes the individual heritage of each personality socialized within it. Because of the dynamic aspect of personality, here defined as a biosocial system of need-motivated behavioral tendencies, and due to the fact that a culture is shared by many personality systems, no sociocultural system has a perfectly reliable mechanism for the replication of a cultural heritage in individuals (Wallace 1961a: 28). This study is based primarily on personality investigations, employing the collection of life histories, depth interviewing, projective techniques, and extended observation, both participant and nonparticipant. At the same time, significant social structures and cultural behaviors are seen operating in the lives of individual personalities. Of major concern is how social systems and cultural norms function in the dynamic personality systems of a few Papago individuals.

OCCUPATIONAL ACTIVITY AND ACCULTURATION

Since the express concern in this study is to discover features of the employment situation having major bearing on the adaptation of Papagos to non-Papago values and behaviors, occupational activity establishes itself as a central area of investigation for bringing culturally established attitudes, values, and behaviors into contrastive focus. For Anglos, the most significant instrumental activities — "those activities that an individual engages in for the achievement and maintenance of a life style and status in the social groups of which he is a member or aspires to be a member" (Spindler and Spindler 1965: 1) — are those represented in the occupational structure. The ways that individuals participate in the occupational structure and how they engage themselves in specific kinds of instrumental activities, as compared to traditionally espoused instrumental activities related to native society, are basic in identifying processes of change (Spindler and Spindler 1965: 9).

Considering that Papago culture may hold before the individual normative avenues of recognition and status that are not occupational activities in the Anglo economic sense, the contrasts in these normative orientations may become difficult for an individual to bridge. In other words, the individual may remain unassimilated in the sense that he has not attached the same value or recognition to occupational statuses characteristic of most Anglo Americans.

Papagos, like individuals of other ethnic groups, are finding it necessary to accommodate to certain aspects of the dominant structure if they are to survive. However, individuals sharing the same culture respond differentially to social forces even in similar social situational fields. Hence, Papago individuals participating in the dominant Anglo sociocultural system should be classifiable into distinct categories which broadly account for different kinds of cultural behavior. There have been several attempts to classify persons of the same culture at different levels of acculturation (Hallowell 1952; Voget 1952; Spindler 1962; Spindler and Spindler 1965).

While perhaps not totally adequate for the Papago case, Voget's effort seems to be the most helpful. Voget (1952: 88) is interested in dealing with the sociocultural heterogeneity of reservation populations in order to define groups and assess contemporary roles of individuals. He suggests that the depiction of the variety of groupings must be in terms of numerical proportions, the extent and kind of cultural integration and content, and the kind of interactions which characterize each distinct grouping. His groupings are based on recurrent types of individuals which can be observed in the population at large.

The four categories or groupings Voget (1952: 89-92) identifies among the Crow are as follows:
1. *Native*, consisting of rank conservatives of the more aged segment who hold themselves aloof from current activities and who live in a verbal and mental world of past or vanishing native values.
2. *Native modified*, consisting of those of the middle-aged generation who adhere to primary values rooted in the aboriginal culture as a result of their socialization in essentially native kinship groupings but who have made some adjustments due to intensive socialization in schools, churches, and other nonnative institutions. They are the active native core working to preserve or revitalize what is perceived to be the identity of the culture.
3. *American modified*, consisting of those who retain their identification with their cultural group but who base that group life on the fundamental values of American culture as gained through active participation in the nonnative Anglo tradition.
4. *American marginal*, consisting of those whose cultural identification is thoroughly non-Indian and who seek to de-identify with Indian culture although their ancestry may bar full participation in Anglo culture.

These groupings are seen by Voget (1952:93) as being developmental stages in situations where two cultures of different complexity are in contact. The last grouping falls short of complete assimilation.

Since the majority of Papagos working in the off-reservation contact situation are still linked to the reservation population through kinship, social events, sentiment, and early socialization experiences, it would seem that some such system for identifying individuals in categories depicting stages of assimilative change could be useful. Classifying a few Papago individuals can be done only impressionistically since there are no descriptions of Papago subcultural types which would permit a typological grouping according to numerical proportions, the kind and extent of cultural integration, or discrete kinds of interactions. Use of Voget's terminology in typing Papago cases is only an attempt to utilize some base for drawing comparisons between the individuals with whom I have worked and to accentuate the need for such a scheme.

Occupational status is significant in the American class/status structure, and the dominant system does directly encourage aspirations for acculturation and social mobility on the part of individuals belonging to the cultural or ethnic units participating in that structure. Indeed, the values of the dominant system make occupational activity necessary for newly induced standards of economic livelihood. Therefore, occupational activities and the way occupational activities are cognitively perceived would seem to be essential for establishing the extent of adaptation and acculturation to the dominant structures and their underlying values.

The study proposes to reveal certain qualities present or absent in certain Papago individuals and their families and how these qualities stand as aids or as impediments in achieving the values and behaviors necessary for participation in an essentially non-Papago economic and social orientation. The cultural heritages of these Papago men are reconstructed in order to understand their activities in terms of the sociocultural contexts in which their life styles have operated.

The individuals selected represent a variety of occupational activities throughout their work histories. They also currently participate in distinct occupational complexes. Since the kinds of occupations represented by the individual cases to be presented are known to be shared by many other Papagos (Papago Employment Survey 1965), certain social structures of particular occupational complexes are also shared, to some extent, by those who operate within them. These structural features would be expected to reveal certain uniformities in occupational and other behaviors, while the individual cases would be expected to reveal individual differences, such as motivation, basic orientation to value systems, intelligence factors, balance of training with motivational features, and other idiosyncratic forms of behavior. The emphasis in this study is on the motivational systems of individuals (personalities) and how individual needs and motivations respond to regulative and normative demands (culture) as they operate in a contact milieu — the occupational complex.

Occupational activity is the variable selected as a manageable locus of individual behavior which can be linked to social structural and cultural contexts of behavior. Other variables will be discussed but only as they relate to occupational activity. The significance of this emphasis for acculturation study is justified by the recognition given to occupational activity by the dominant social system. The extent to which Papagos aspire for and adhere to the structures and values supporting a strong emphasis on occupational status should provide an impressionistic way of locating Papago individuals on an assimilation continuum.

There are identifiable criteria or evaluative assessments by which individuals in the dominant Anglo structures (i.e., government agencies, missions, schools, farms, industries, and employment services) measure the adaptability of individuals. These expectations are by no means uniform among the different structures and are not experienced in uniform ways by individuals confronting these structures. Nonetheless, in terms of the underlying value system which links these structures together, occupation becomes a socially structured index for determining the "progress" Papagos are making in becoming an integral part of the dominant system.

Government agencies, educational institutions, employment agencies, and churches seek to instigate programs in order that Indians might "upgrade" themselves. Institutions of the dominant society have normative directions, supported by the underlying economic, national, humanistic, and religious values characterizing our cultural system, and Papagos as well as individuals from other ethnic groups are encouraged to pursue them. Both the Papagos' own "best interests" and the interests of the various institutions of the dominant society are thereby believed to be fulfilled.

Certain occupational institutions may also have their own interests in which case upgrading may actually hinder the exploitation of traditional Papago work roles. Such institutions may thus have no design to assimilate transitional peoples, for in so doing they might well eliminate an available supply of exploitable labor. Generally speaking, however, gaining access to occupational statuses which are more rewarding in terms of both income and prestige is deemed to be not only economically necessary for Papagos in a practical sort of way, but it is considered necessary in order to put Papagos into communication with the larger social system.

Assimilation of Papagos and other ethnic groups into the prevailing "way of life" is, obviously, an ideal of the dominant cultural system. In reality, the social structure of the United States does not function to ultimately make available a total assimilation to a prevailing way of life. Rather, the class system of the United States actually provides a hierarchy of statuses, largely based on recognition given to occupations, which are more or less accessible. Only limited or controlled social mobility actually occurs, not only because of vested interests and other social restrictions to status which characterize particular statuses, but because there are usually more people competing for certain statuses, particularly the lower ones, than there are statuses available.

There are also resistances from the other direction. Social mobility, as prompted by the class structure, threatens the solidarity and the integrity of unique culture bearing units, particularly if these units are motivated by different normative systems than those which characterize the statuses of the dominant structure. Hence, acculturation is controlled and, thus, assimilation and social mobility are impeded by selective features within the subordinate culture itself.

Considering these features of the class structure which have bearing on acculturation processes, the significance of occupational status becomes paramount. The proclamation that Papagos need to have their own doctors, lawyers, and professionals is an admission that they have not yet perceived the values underlying the United States ideal culture. But it is not proclaimed that the lower class needs its own doctors, lawyers, and professionals. In other words, Papagos, as members of a discrete culture, are not simply a lower class. Ideally, they are encouraged to have access to the range of statuses representing our entire status structure and thereby have access to a number of class positions. Individuals are actually expected to be distributed throughout the entire status structure. This is essentially what assimilation in the United States implies – the access to the whole range of statuses and corresponding identifications and behaviors which characterize our society. Once assimilation is in process, there will be increasing identification with the symbols of the anticipated or achieved class and statuses rather than identification with things Papago, other than self-ethnic identification through knowledge of ancestry. Occupational activity is a significant feature of social identification, which is likely the reason for the kind of occupational self-typing that Papagos are known to do in employment offices (Fitzgerald 1955: 24). Certain occupations provide the familiar roles and the sociocultural contexts for a whole range of behaviors. Occupational activity is therefore considered an important locus for assessing the extent of assimilative change.

TOWARD A MODEL OF OCCUPATIONAL STRUCTURE

The tradition of cultural anthropology has been oriented toward conceptualizing discrete cultural wholes, usually those of nonindustrial or primitive cultures. Conditions in contemporary industrial society have created a need for a different kind of emphasis. As Inkeles (1960: 1) points out, larger segments of the world's population are living or will come to live in "industrial society" and the "standard complex of institutions" associated with this system. He further suggests that ". . . people have experiences, develop attitudes, and form values in response to the forces or pressures which their environment creates" (p. 2).

Sharing the structural features of such an environment does not, however, deny individual variation, nor does it refute the effect of particular traditional cultural ways on behavior. But such an environment can be treated as a force in and of itself despite the influences of individual variation or the effects of traditional cultures. This industrial environment, or what Caplow (1954: 100) refers to as "occupational culture." has shaping and standardizing features all its own. It is this idea, that a particular structure of experience, attitude, and value takes its form from the particular occupational structure, which will become the basis for developing the theoretical model of this study.

To posit an analytical model commits the investigator to defining precisely the elements and the interrelation of elements comprising the model (Hagen 1961: 144). The features of the occupational complex model need to be held constant and insulated from change in order to provide the magnitudes or parameters of our particular system of analysis and the elements of the system. With the system "closed" for purposes of identification and definition, it can then be "opened" to observe changes.

OCCUPATIONAL COMPLEX AS A SOCIAL SYSTEM

A particular occupational structure can be viewed as an environment which, through its particular structural features, structures the experiences of individuals and groups of individuals. In this sense, the occupational structure or complex is conceived as a social environment or a social system in its own right. This implies that, as a social system, the occupational complex consists of "some orderly combination or arrangement of parts into a whole, which in turn, is more than a conjunction, aggregate, chance assembly of parts, and more than a mere sum of the parts" (Hertzler 1961: 4). As a social system, an occupational complex can be broken down into smaller components as well as be related to other components of a still larger social system. As a social system, an occupational complex must exhibit the characteristics or features which characterize social systems in general.

First, while a social system does not provide a uniform orientation for all who share the network of social life, there are some central, dominant institutions which provide the normative directions for the individuals and groups within it. Because there is a central economic or occupational institution around which other institutional activities cluster, an occupational complex can be said to have a general orientation which is more or less shared by all those participating in it. Participation in these institutions is not uniform because the general normative orientations are not uniformly perceived and the motivations of individuals are so diverse.

There are several cultural and subcultural orientations that are represented in the complex through individual participants. These cultural orientations usually must be modified by individuals as they are motivated in the direction of the general orientation. At the same time, institutions and activities embodying these cultural orientations may provide counterorientations that operate to preserve their integrity. In the ensuing chapters, the attempt is made to enumerate some of these central tendencies or the general orientations of specific occupational complexes to see how individual Papago workers have oriented their individual and cultural behaviors to them.

Second, there are also certain capacities or resources available to a social system. Hertzler (1961: 11) refers to "the elemental arena of the natural physical and natural biological environments" that is vital to a social system. In other words, the occupational complex is a spatial entity, encompassing a geographical space, and composed of a complex of natural, man made, and man induced features of the landscape lying within the spatial limits. This implies that there is a means for exploiting the natural and the man made features of the complex, namely, an organizational or social structural means.

Another characteristic of a social system is that it has social structures or a hierarchy of statuses and roles — that is, organizational features oriented to the functioning of the social system that utilize the resources of the complex. There is a "demographic structure" (Hertzler 1961: 12) in that within the limits of the complex there is a population, distributed spatially and consisting of a complex of social relations. The natural arrangements and those historically induced by man in exploiting the natural area provide the basis for a central occupational activity on which the population within the limits of the complex directly or indirectly depends. The population is distributed in space largely in relationship to the central economic activity which makes the complex possible. In other words, remove the major occupational activity and there will be a drastic realignment, if not a major disintegration, of the demographic and social structures. The demographic structure provides the manpower and the social arrangements necessary to support the central occupational activity.

There are individuals representing a variety of distinct cultural systems and social structures who come to participate simultaneously in an occupational complex and its social structures. Individuals from different cultural backgrounds who come to participate in the larger system may have distinguishable demographic arrangements as well as distinguishable social positions in the structures of the complex. They share certain participations in the prevailing structures; but there is also differential participation by the individuals of different cultural or subcultural groups due to unique cultural orientations and social structures and due to the ways the individuals in the dominant system react to members of the different subordinate groups.

A social system is able to persist, however, because of unifying principles or social values and norms.

Social values are the broad generalized conceptions of desirable social ends toward which social activities are geared in a hierarchy of importance. Norms are the implementive means for putting these values into operation in concrete interactive settings. (Smelser and Smelser 1963: 10). These values and norms, defined, modified, and perpetuated by institutionalized behaviors, provide the basis for a general orientation of social life within the complex.

Such values and norms are very elusive data to deal with methodically, and it is in this area that the most untested or poorly tested assumptions about acculturation are made. Some assumed value profiles of a dominant social system usually stand at one end of most acculturation continua and are, in most acculturation studies, presumed to be the catalysts which act on and react to the values and norms of the component acculturating groups and individuals. While this study does not pretend to contribute in any major sense to the reduction of this conceptual inadequacy, the occupational complex as a smaller systemic unit has potential in making possible a more manageable social framework within which acculturation and value orientation studies might be conducted at more highly controlled levels of operation. Such operations do not fall within the scope of this study but are anticipated in future research.

All social systems have identifiable sources of strain, both among groups and among individuals. Since there are institutionalized statuses with their corresponding roles, there can be expected to be ambiguity in role expectation, role conflicts, discrepancies between role expectations and actual social situations, widespread value conflicts, and ineffective means for implementing norms. Further, if sources of strain can be acknowledged as characteristic of the

system, then a range of different forms of deviation can be expected (Merton 1957: 140). And with this there will be institutionalized procedures to control these various reactions to strain or what Cohen (1959: 471) refers to as a "dependence upon the institutional order," which encourages conformity even under the conditions of strain.

The preceding discussion of the basic features of a social system helps to identify the occupational complex model being developed here as a unit social system, composed of individuals representing many subsystems and cultural systems. The occupational complex is a social system that provides a "set of standardized models" of social relations in which mutually predictable roles are specified and available for individuals with diverse motives to implement in a complementary manner (Wallace 1961a: 41). On the other hand, cultures also presumably provide models for making behavior mutually predictable within a cultural community. These cultural models for behavior may be antithetical to the models provided by the institutions of the occupational system and may not permit easy accommodation of roles and role-expectations.

Individual cases have been chosen to aid in the identification of some of these "models" or social structures in which individuals participate. The occupational complex is developed here as a means of linking the two sets of structures — those structures peculiar to the individual and his culture, and those structures that the individual shares, by his participation in the larger system, with other individuals having diverse cultural heritages. However, due to the limited number of individual cases, this study is necessarily more suggestive than conclusive.

OCCUPATIONAL COMPLEX AS A UNITARY STRUCTURAL MODEL

Mayer (1962: 577) has recognized the need for a unitary structural model that could logically interlock the "tribal" and "urban" or "nontribal" roles of an individual tribesman. He sees in his studies of African labor migrancy that personnel circulate in a "town-plus-hinterland field," at times participating in tribal structures (actively when in tribal residence and when in a town enclave of tribesmen, and sentimentally when detached from tribesmen) and at times in non-tribal structures (when participation in nontribal

behavior leaves no alternative). Mayer (1962: 577-8) suggests that one means of identifying the social structural features of individual role behavior in an occupational field

. . . would be to begin at the study of the migrant persons themselves, by mapping out their networks of relations from the personal or egocentric point of view, as well as noting their parts in the various structural systems. In doing this we would not be postulating any structural unity of the migrancy field. We would merely be noting that it is, in fact, a field habitually traversed by migrating persons. The starting-point would be the observed fact that individuals who play roles in town A also play roles in tribal (or rural) societies B, C, or D; the task would be to observe the networks of social relations which arise when this fact is multiplied into a mass social phenomenon, and to analyze their special characteristics.

This follows very closely Fortes' (1936: 46) suggestion that attempts should be made to trace the nature of the selective processes in the contact situation by turning to individual case studies that offer examples of the many kinds of selective processes going on. While Fortes would include statistical interpretation as a necessary part of overall studies, he states that there is an initial need to get family and individual sentiments through the study of individual cases. In this manner, the number and kinds of influences of the contact milieu on tribal society institutions, social practices, habits and beliefs, and social attitudes can be identified.

There are assumed to be "double roles" (Mayer 1962: 579) for workers who alternate between the tribal and nontribal structures. Some of these roles can be compartmentalized and kept somewhat discrete, thereby causing no sizable individual conflict. Some "double roles" might be complementary and operate to enhance each other. But a good number of them might be expected to be antithetical and lead to a number of alternatives; i.e., role ambiguity in one or the other or both tribal and nontribal contexts; role reinforcement in one at the expense of the other; abandonment of social roles in both structures and the taking on of a private delusional system of one's own, etc.

The Individual Case Study

This study seeks to focus on individual Papago workers involved in networks of social relations embracing both Papago, tribal, or reservation structures, and non-Papago, nontribal, or nonreservation structures as a result of some kind of nonreservation occupational activity.

In the very beginning of the field work, I became acquainted with a small number of individuals who, subjectively, seemed to represent a range of personal variables, social contexts, and occupational activities. From these few, an even smaller number was selected to permit an extension of observation and personal relationship. In a sense, this is working from the individual outward into a compounding network of social relations, assuming from the ensuing discoveries that these individual participations in social structures can be "multiplied into a mass social phenomenon" that would presumably characterize other Papagos in similar situations. While the reality of the latter point would need to be substantiated by empirical and quantifiable proofs, intensively studying a few individual cases should reveal significant social roles and behaviors that in a large sample of individuals might, by nature of the research design, have to be overlooked. Observing individuals operating in a network of social relationships over a period of time should reveal unit behaviors and unit structures that could then provide more and better categories for further efforts at quantification or for dealing with larger samples.

The Individual in an Extended Network of Social Relations

The simplest point of departure is the individual Papago worker participating in a specific occupational role or activity attached to a specific occupational institution. The most immediate extra-work social context is some kind of a kinship or kinship/surrogate unit, the nuclear or extended family, relatives or other kin-substitutes, etc., in which the individual resides and with which he interacts in a primary way. His dependence on a specific occupational role extends into this primary structure in that the latter is likewise dependent on his occupational activity. There may be others in this primary structure who are aligned to the same occupational institution and same or similar roles.

Beyond this primary structure, usually the family in some particular dimension, there is a larger residence unit such as a neighborhood, an encampment, a cluster of dwellings, or a village, that has some relationship, ecologically and socially, to an occupational institution. Individuals, in addition to their interactions in kinship and neighborhood units, extend themselves into other institutions (schools, stores, churches, courts, jails, recreation facilities, etc.) that have become established in the vicinity largely because of the presence of a central occupational institution, or in more complex situations such as an urban area, a series of major occupational institutions. In addition, there are social behaviors and social relationships that are not institutionalized; that is, the individual must be seen as an actor in random bits of behavior as well (Loomis 1965: 501).

The Cultural Dimension

So far, the occupational complex as a social system has been presented as if the individual grew up within it and lived most of his life within it. But the influence of the individual's cultural system on his behavior within the complex has not yet been fully acknowledged. It should be possible to intersect the occupational complex at a number of points to represent the varieties of cultural systems and subsystems that influence the individuals and groups who participate in the complex. For purposes of simplification, since we are dealing with Papago workers, the model will be intersected at one point in order to reveal the influence on the occupational complex of what may be called Papago-reservation structures. It should be noted that these influences are through Papago individuals and the primary social units through which they come to participate in occupational roles within the complex.

The reservation influences are, of course, never uniform but consist of complex features which operate within the occupational social system. The influences may be either institutionalized or random social behaviors. That is, there are Papago institutions consisting of people, social roles, activities, and norms oriented toward particular culturally valued ends, as well as noninstitutionalized or random behaviors. This Papago complex, characterizing a heterogeneous reservation population, presumably has its native Papago, native modified Papago, Anglo modified Papago, and Anglo marginal Papago subcultural dimensions. As is true with the non-Papago social structures of the occupational complex, the Papago-reservation subcultures need to be exposed as individuals participate in them. By focusing on individual case studies, Papago-reservation cultural behaviors and non-Papago occupational and related behaviors can be seen intersecting in individual personalities.

Roles, Statuses, and Institutions

The interest in this study is not primarily in the psychological structure of a scant number of Papago workers, although psychological data are accessible. Rather, the major focus is on the sociocultural aspects of personality or the ways personality systems extend themselves into meaningful social structures, or what Arensberg (1954: 113) refers to as "the topography of interconnections" between institutions and behaviors. As Hallowell (1962: 360) indicates, ". . . examining the factors underlying the psychodynamics of individual adjustment" has pointed toward "the major central tendencies that are characteristic of a series of individuals who belong to a single society, tribal group, or nation." It assumes that "membership in a given sociocultural system, or subsystem, subjects human beings to a common set of conditions that are significant with reference to the personality organization of these individuals." In other words, the structural character of the society can be seen as it manifests itself in the life style of an individual. As Opler (1964: 522) points out, ". . . it is as important to study man in his culture-binding and culture-manipulating roles and in every cultural context as it is to examine the consequences and products of his actions."

This study assumes that similarities in personality type may emerge due to participation in the same sociocultural system, while it acknowledges that genetic constitution and unique individual experiences prompt variation (Bruner 1964: 78). Further, differential participation in stratified social units stimulate patterning of shared experiences; that is, outgroups function as references for crystallizing in-group behavior.

As Opler (1964: 524) notes, cultural behavior is not the result of a conscription to a "rigid cast," but the result of individuals straining against the "plastic borders" of their shared cultural heritage. In this study, individual Papago men are seen "straining" against the "plastic borders" of their shared social and cultural experiences. It is the individual and groups of individuals straining that eliminates the static quality of a sociocultural system. Acculturation becomes a straining process where there are both attempts to revitalize familiar cultural ways and to abandon, sometimes willingly, a set of cultural behaviors for those potentially more rewarding.

Individual life styles are preferred for identifying social structures and cultural processes. Occupational activities and the networks of related role behaviors become the major units of observation and analysis.

There is a relationship between sociocultural systems and the activities and motivations of individuals. As Spiro (1961b: 96) seeks to demonstrate, the human social system is a functional requirement of human life in that it fulfills biological and psychobiological needs of the individual. The social system, in other words, has adaptive functions in that it promotes the physical survival of human societies. Similarly, it has adjustive functions in that it provides models of social interaction that make it possible for individuals to attain some degree of psychological order in their social relationships.

The social system, therefore, also has integrative functions in that it may promote social solidarity by reducing interpersonal and intrapersonal tensions. Spiro (1961b: 100) suggests that

... the concept of personality becomes salient for the understanding of human social systems, for it is in the concept of role that personality and social systems intersect. If personality is viewed as an organized system of motivational tendencies, then it may be said to consist, among other things, of needs and drives. Since modes of drive-reduction and need satisfaction in man must be learned, one of the functions of personality is the promotion of physical survival, interpersonal adjustment, and intrapersonal integration by organizing behavior for the reduction of its drives and the satisfaction of its needs.... But *if* social systems can function only if their constituent roles are performed, then, in motivating the performance of roles, personality not only serves its own functions but it becomes a crucial variable in the functioning of social systems as well.

In the individual Papago worker, then, certain statuses and certain role behaviors comprising both his occupational life and the tribal aspects of his life are seen as crucial variables. How these roles are balanced in the life of a single Papago individual, how he enacts them, how he conceives of them, and how he reconciles them become of major importance. The occupational complex provides the most meaningful social context for the interplay of these manifold roles.

There have been numerous extensions, modifications, and criticisms of the status and role concepts since Linton's (1936, 1945) ambitious attempt to distinguish them. Linton's basic distinction will be observed, but some important extensions will also be utilized. Linton (1936: 113-4) distinguishes the positions or statuses extant in social structures, wherein there are culturally patterned expectations, rights, and duties by nature of the positions themselves, from the roles, or the individual performances of those rights and duties. As Goode (1960: 246) indicates, contemporary role theory continues to recognize the status-role concept as the main structural unit of social institutions. He proceeds to present a

revised definition of role-status as a further attempt at integrating role theory and institutional theory. Goode insists that while all roles enacted by individuals contain elements that are more or less institutionalized, specific role relationships may manifest disagreement as to the appropriate norms among ego, alter, and a whole network of "third parties." He then defines a role as "a set of mutual (but not necessarily harmonious) expectations of behavior between two or more actors, with reference to a particular type of situation," whereas he defines statuses as "the class of roles which is institutionalized." It is this institutionalization of roles into statuses that becomes significant for social change studies; that is, "the mutual expectations between actors are coming to be institutionally sanctioned" (p. 249). In other words, a role relationship is structured by the statuses of those involved in the relationship. Such a relationship becomes institutionalized or "normatively backed by 'third parties' " (p. 250).

Role, then, is an important concept in relating the individual to a social network of relations. The individual has a commitment to carry out certain role duties consistently since there are rewards and punishments in any role relationship. When the latter prevail, under certain kinds of situations the individual may prefer to abandon unpleasant role responsibilities (Goode 1960: 253) or alienate himself from role responsibilities that find little or no normative support in terms of his own value orientations (Zurcher, Meadow, and Zurcher 1965: 548). For these reasons, as Goode (1960: 252) clearly points out, adults also experience socialization or resocialization. That is, an individual's total role network, supported by institutionalized norms, places learning and relearning demands on adult individuals. Institutions not only socialize children and prepare them for successful functioning in particular institutions, they also have effects on the socialization and personality formation of adults (Cohen 1961: 4).

There is a mandatory as well as a personally rewarding side to the performance of social roles, making for an "imperative dimension of human social systems" (Spiro 1961b: 102). This is so because there are extrinsic motivations to cultural behavior. The performance of social roles is stimulated by persons other than the actor. Similarly, personality needs can correspondingly be satisfied through role performance, which makes role behavior "intrinsically motivated" (p. 103). Spiro (p. 112) points out that there are manifest and latent personal and social functions served through role behavior. He states that there is a relationship between unconscious and conscious motivation, and the functioning of the sociocultural system.

Weinstock (1963) introduces the concept of role elements into the framework of role theory in his attempt to demonstrate a dynamic and motivational relationship between occupational status and acculturation. Role elements are the specific behavior patterns expected of the status holder by different members of the role-set. Central role elements are the strict occupational requirements of an occupational status, such as technical know-how and work performance. Peripheral role elements refer to nontechnical but institutionally required aspects of a role, those not counted as part of the official job description (pp. 144-5). Weinstock suggests that the more social involvement attached to a given occupation, the more likelihood there would be of structured peripheral expectations, and vice versa.

When occupations are viewed in terms of the social structure, they may be seen to differ in terms of the total number of role elements they require. Lower occupational statuses will demand a few central role elements related to specific job performance; but as one ascends in the occupational structure to assume higher occupational status, the peripheral role elements become more numerous, and the incumbent must meet these demands or expectations in addition to the central role requirements of the job. In this sense, while lower status jobs have less financial and less prestigious rewards, they demand much less in the way of peripheral commitments; that is, an occupant need not contribute to United Fund, need not be a social entertainer, need not invite the boss home, etc. Hence, if the United States occupational structure prescribes role elements and if there are more role elements demanded of higher occupational status, then acculturation as it pertains to the occupational structure is the process of taking on and performing the role expectations or elements of higher occupational statuses. And individuals will aspire to acculturate or mobilize themselves socially because they begin to feel needs for new kinds of roleship, to become and remain a part of a new reference group or status (p. 148).

This aspect of role theory is of particular import because there are likewise counterexpectations by ethnic or cultural systems and status groups within the social structure or social system. This means that the value orientations of a particular cultural system may demand or prescribe certain role expectations that may not be related to occupational role elements and may even run counter to them. While the occupational structure may be a relatively fluid thing in the United States and thus invite a great deal of anticipatory socialization (Merton 1957: 265) into nonmembership reference statuses, membership groups may act to retard the process of actual achievement by the role expectations which they foster.

Our model of the occupational complex, then, must include a network of status and role-sets (Merton 1957: 369-70) and role elements (Weinstock 1963: 144-5) that characterize every type of institutional participation or social behavior in which the individual Papago is involved. As Merton (1957: 381) indicates,

... status-sets plainly provide one basic form of interdependence between the institutions and the subsystems of a society.... Complex status-sets not only make for some form of liaison between subsystems in a society; they confront the occupants of these statuses with distinctly different degrees of difficulty in organizing their role activities.

Institutions are perceived as "organized enactments of norm complexes and value orientations" (Loomis 1965: 506) that provide a degree of unification of purpose for a group of people (Bohannon 1963: 358). Institutions provide the normative patterns or moral imperatives that guide the motivations and activities of individuals and groups within a social system. Thus, social institutions regulate and pattern social life around shared cultural norms. Each social institution has, in turn, its own social system or network of structured status-role relationships, its own system of material culture, its own idea or sentiment system, and its own range of historic and contemporary events or characteristic activities (Bohannon 1963: 359). A number of these social institutions are integral parts of the occupational complex social system. Where there are individuals representing different cultural traditions participating in the complex, there are a number of additional institutions which directly or indirectly function within the complex. Figure 1 diagrams the occupational complex structural model.

In summary, an occupational complex is conceived as a social system with its own subsystems. It is called an occupational complex because it is the pursuit of

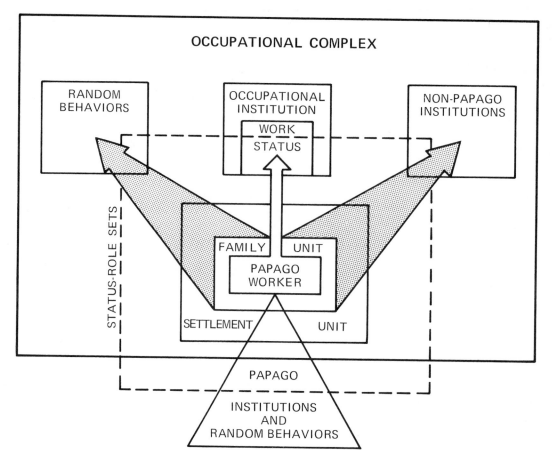

Figure 1. Occupational Complex Model

statuses within a central occupational institution and a reliance on specific occupational activities (roles) within the complex that motivate individuals to become parts of it. In so doing, individuals participate in a number of other subsystems which are of pivotal importance to the enculturative, educative, economic, legal, recreative, and welfare functions of the complex. There are a number of social institutions that perform these pivotal functions and provide normative bases for individual behavior. Through these interlocking institutions, there are interlocking statuses and roles that bring together individual actors.

Since an interplay of Papago institutional roles and non-Papago institutional roles is anticipated, the points where they intersect or confront each other in a single individual are of prime importance in a study of occupational adaptation and acculturation. The occupational complex provides the social context where the major acculturative adaptations are expected to occur.

OCCUPATIONAL COMPLEXES — A PARTIAL TYPOLOGY

The need for conceptualizing a complex of social structures in which a number of Papago workers share a whole network of social experiences and role relationships has been stressed. At the same time, there is the acknowledgment that each individual's experience in such a structure is also an idiosyncratic one. Further, it is expected that there should be a variety of such complexes since there is a variety of occupational activities in which Papagos are known to cluster. Within each discrete occupational complex, a range of variation in occupational statuses should be expected.

In suggesting a partial typology of occupational complexes, partial to the extent that it does not claim complete comprehension of all possible types, certain difficulties arise, as is true for any typological scheme. Wallace points out some of the problems:

Because of the duration and phenomenological complexity of these types of events [referring to processes such as enculturation, acculturation, revitalization, etc., which occur in the life-spans of individuals], continuous first-hand observation is difficult to arrange, and the investigator is forced to rely on historical and autobiographical data whose reliability, completeness, and standardization is low. Sampling is awkward because the universe of events is difficult to define. Typologies are hazardously constructed because of the extreme complexity of the dimensions (Wallace 1961b: 154).

Nevertheless, some kind of a typology seems necessary in order to locate an adequate range of variation in the kinds of role relationships connected with diverse occupational activities. Any selection of individual case studies, by means of which individual Papago workers can be traced through a network of social relations related to their occupational activities, must be done within such a broader framework, that is, with some assurance that the individual's experience represents a type of experience shared by many others who likewise participate in similar social structures.

Enough exposure in the field to the occupational life of individuals has provided a subjective basis for establishing a typology. With the aid of the Papago Employment Survey (1965), conducted by the Bureau of Ethnic Research of the University of Arizona at the same time this field work was in progress, it has been possible to study the kinds of occupational experiences represented in the sample and thereby identify certain features that would permit a categorizing of main occupational types and the ranges of variation within them. This has seemed a helpful way of substantiating the conceptual reality of certain occupational complex types. The survey data provide substantive support for identifying the features of certain discrete occupational types. Individuals can be seen to represent participations in a limited number of certain kinds of social structures because of their attachments to specific kinds of occupations.

Commercial Farm

Padfield (1965: 431) takes a very comprehensive look at the farm harvest system in Arizona, seeing it as a composite institutional system made up of a number of participant institutions. He describes three major harvest systems in his provocative analysis, namely the citrus, lettuce, and cotton technologies. The study reveals that "farm workers consistently revolve around ethnic groupings" since "these groups to a great extent define the limits of social intercourse, and form the natural basis of associational and institutional participation" (p. 260). Hence, Padfield is able to describe four major subcultures, the Mexican-American, the Anglo-isolate, the Negro, and the Indian farm, which tend to attach themselves predominantly to certain kinds of farm harvest systems. His use of the term subculture corresponds to the term cultural system which is preferred in this particular study.

As Padfield's study shows, Papagos predominately attach themselves to the cotton harvest system, although it does not deny that some Papagos who are farm workers do follow other kinds of harvest system patterns. The point to stress here is that Padfield does conceptualize from his data a composite farm harvest system in which a number of participant institutions and subcultures may be isolated. As he notes, the farm plays a key role in Indian occupational life (p. 264). With Padfield's contribution in mind, it is possible to conceptualize a general occupational complex type, which can be referred to as the Commercial Farm Occupational Complex. While the Papagos have largely participated in the cotton harvest system, the general type is inclusive of any central farming institution that may employ Papagos to perform occupational roles, regardless of the particular commercial product. At the same time, different kinds of harvest systems have different structural features, but since the cotton harvest system is a prevailing subtype for Papagos, other harvest systems may be viewed as variations within the general type set forth here. The particular case examples presented in Chapter 6 represent participations in the cotton harvest aspect of commercial farming, although other types of farming activities are noted. The establishment of the Commercial Farm Occupational Complex as a type assumes that the kinds of commercial farming in which Papagos participate do have shared structural features in terms of occupational activities and the related institutional activities which are integral parts of the complex.

Ajo Mine

The typology also includes another unique social system or occupational complex that is nonagricultural in nature but traditionally has involved Papagos for several generations. The Ajo Mine Occupational Complex is the second social system lying adjacent to the reservation systems. While knowledge of Papago Indian involvement at the Ajo copper mine has been generally shared for years, one finds hardly anything relative to studies about this particular complex. With so many Papagos having been involved in this commercial operation, considerable attention will be given to a discussion of some of its structural features, not only as they are revealed in the case material, but as they have been revealed through direct contact with Phelps Dodge officials. While other lesser mining operations involving Papagos might be considered as subtypes, since similar structures likely exist, there is some hesitation for doing so, mainly because most attention has been devoted to the Ajo mine occupational structure, especially important so far as Papago studies are concerned.

Oscillating Farm-Nonfarm

A third complex important to the typology presents a difficulty in that it consists of dual, unrelated occupational institutions, each of which is composed of its own distinct networks of related institutions. Such a type conceptualizes the characteristics of a social situation in which activities within the rural Commercial Farm Occupational Complex interrelate with nonfarm or urban activities in the life pattern of a single individual. This type of occupational situation is given a unitary structure, not because it operates simultaneously as such in the life of an individual but because it distinguishes the commercial farm pattern from an urban, nonfarm pattern, while it at the same time acknowledges the effect that the dual pattern has on the individual's overall occupational pattern. In terms of occupation, the pattern oscillates, wherein the individual and his family use one or the other pattern as a primary basis of activity, with the alternate pattern serving as a supplementary one.

This complex is considered because of its potential importance in studying the rural to urban occupational shift, an important transition in terms of occupational, residential, and social mobility. It is important also from the standpoint that the Papago urban enclave, while trying to tie onto the urban economic base, also retains ties with the rural and reservation hinterlands. Some conceptualization seems necessary to embrace this particular kind of social experience as it is dramatized in the life of a Papago individual. This type will be called the Oscillating Farm/Nonfarm Occupational Complex, using oscillating in the sense of fluctuating between farm and nonfarm as opposed to Padfield's (1965) use of the term, referring to the oscillating from reservation residence to seasonal farm work. The latter type would be a variant under the commercial farm type, since for part of the year an individual would share the same structures as the more permanent participants in the particular occupational complex, although perhaps not as intensively or persistently.

Urban, Nonfarm

It is particularly difficult to conceptualize a type that will embrace a complex range of nonfarm occupations. This fourth type is designated as the Urban, Nonfarm Occupational Complex, but the dimensions are far more complex than can be adequately handled in the scope of this study. The oscillating type introduces us to a certain variation within the nonfarm category, namely, a predominantly rural-oriented activity that weakens and becomes oriented to a nonfarm occupational activity and related structures. The range of actual nonfarm occupational activities is so great in modern technological society that it becomes hazardous to expound a single structural type. Papago participation over this range is not extensive, which makes the present concern less complicated. In this respect, a general nonfarm category can be conceptualized, but some quantitative support becomes absolutely necessary to apprehend the many distinctive occupational and related structures that make up this general type.

All variations within this general type might share certain urban structures; however, depending on the particular occupational status, certain urban structures will be open to some and not to others. That is, people who attach themselves to an urban setting and become somewhat dependent on its structures, whether they do so as transient individuals or by joining an ethnic enclave through kinship or friendship, will come to participate in the class system. This involvement makes people aware of their positions and acquaints them with the accessibility or inaccessibility of certain kinds of participations in the structures of the urban surroundings.

The identification with an urban enclave of one's cultural experience provides the buffer for his participation in the various structures of the urban setting. This is a base line for the ways people will operate and how they will play the roles demanded. In such a setting, stereotype interaction (Padfield 1965: 413) predominates; that is, the cultural enclave as well as the larger society create a number of stereotyped images of each other, and their interactions begin to conform to these projected images. Some members of a cultural system, for instance, may in the course of time attach themselves to a particular kind of occupational activity. Other members then incorporate these stereotyped roles into their own behavior patterns; and as the stereotypes gain strength, the actual participations in the stereotyped occupational patterns increase, becoming the base for a relatively secure network of occupational roles. In other words, certain occupations receive cultural support, not because they are either monetarily or always socially rewarding, but because roles are defined and how to behave in them can at least be predictable, offering some degree of psychological security along with a meager but helpful source of income. Certain occupations that have drawn members from cultural enclaves over a period of time become a source of role identification that can be shared by others and passed on generationally.

By participating in certain unskilled occupations, urban Papagos attach themselves to the class structure. Participation in low occupational statuses grants them access to certain social structures and stands in the way of participation in other social structures. As members of an urban enclave, Papagos likely will have modal characteristics in terms of their relative positions in the urban class structure. This is largely due to the kinds of occupational roles that are open to them or they themselves open. Certain kinds of occupational statuses will prevail; Papagos, as well as the rest of the urban community, will accept these stereotyped statuses and try to conform to them.

Because social mobility is externally encouraged by the dominant structures, the identification with the prevailing modal roles, which is encouraged by cultural support of the stereotypes, is weakened; and individual Papagos begin to anticipate socialization into new occupational statuses and roles. As this shift in reference group proceeds, participations in certain other social structures, once closed, now become possible. With increased involvement in the mobile class system, there is a decreasing identification with the modal behaviors that the cultural enclave continues to support. Hence, there is a progressive depletion of ethnic identification and greater identification with the values of the prevailing society.

It is possible to speak of lower class urban Papagos because stereotypic occupational roles constitute the modal feature of a sizable number. It is less feasible to speak of middle class Papagos and currently impossible to speak of upper class Papagos, for there are not enough individuals in either arbitrary category, however class is defined, to provide a modal representation. That is, Papagos have not distributed themselves throughout our class system, and this is largely because certain occupational statuses have been closed to them. Individuals, however, have moved in the direction of opening up certain statuses as they have made certain shifts in behavior and taken on new roles in the larger society.

It is possible, therefore, to identify one variation or complex within the general nonfarm type. A minimum range of occupations has become stereotyped and, thus, more open to Papagos. These unskilled, often spotty jobs, expose a goodly number of urban Papagos to certain kinds of social structures and restrict their activities in the larger setting. These shared features, promoted largely by a residential or neighborhood enclave, help in conceptualizing a unit complex wherein certain limited occupations are central and social life clusters around them. This common labor-spot job occupational complex becomes a major variant of the nonfarm type.

The number of Papagos who operate in semiskilled and skilled occupational roles do so largely as individuals and stand in the minority. The types of work vary and have not yet become representative of many Papagos. They therefore become difficult to conceptualize in a single occupational-complex category. Yet, because there is some means for identifying some of these occupations, so far as Papagos are concerned, they can be classified into a semiskilled-skilled occupational complex, another variant of the nonfarm type.

Because of these complexities and the lack of detailed data to provide the support for an adequate conceptualization of the Urban, Nonfarm Occupational Complex, its treatment is most rudimentary.

This study suggests, with some quantitative support, a range of variation in nonfarm occupational roles, both skilled and unskilled, and future avenues of research to clarify the complexity. Chapter 6 includes case materials representing the interplay of roles in both skilled and unskilled nonfarm occupations.

2. PAPAGO OFF-RESERVATION OCCUPATIONAL ACTIVITY

PRE-RESERVATION ECONOMIC ACTIVITY

Behavior patterns are linked to some kind of cultural tradition or related to the conventional designs for living that people work out for themselves in the process of coming to terms with their environments. Therefore, some attention must be given to the past in order to evaluate present and possible future environments. Much of what "has been" still "is," and has a significant function in the direction and form in which the future will become manifest.

Papagos traditionally have been semisedentary farmers who supplemented their field crops of corn, beans, and squash with a variety of gathered plants and wild game from their desert and mountain surroundings (Joseph, Spicer, and Chesky 1949: 28-9). More precisely, there were three major kinds of Papago groups, according to variations in subsistence and settlement patterns: (1) the western centrally based nomads called the Sand Papagos whose wanderings in the arid western Papagueria were oriented to scarce water holes and temporary encampments; (2) the central flood farmers between the Ajo and Baboquivari mountains; and (3) the riverine sedentary peoples east of the Baboquivaris (Kelly 1963: 3-4).

To make a living, all members of the family had to perform some kind of labor, whether in the fields, in the preparations at home, by gathering the many kinds of desert plant foods, or by hunting. Thus, subsistence and survival was a family enterprise (Joseph, Spicer, and Chesky 1949: 29).

In addition to these basic subsistence activities, Papagos extended their contacts beyond their kinship villages when bad years made such movements economically necessary. As Fontana (Arizona Commission of Indian Affairs 1957: 6-7) notes, when Papago fields were nonproductive, entire families either went to work for the Gila River Pima or to the Altar-Magdalena river valleys in northern Sonora to work for riverine farmers. In either case, compensation for these services was a portion of the produce. These contacts must have been continuous because the word of the movements of the first Spaniards

traveled rapidly and people "from the interior" came to see Kino at *Nuestra Señora de los Dolores* "from parts so remote, from the north, from the west, etc." (Bolton 1919: 161). The same was true as Kino arrived among the Gila River Pima or among the Sobaipuris along the San Pedro (Underhill 1939: 17). In fact, it could be that contacts largely stimulated by economic necessities are the sources for the many cultural traits that pre-Spanish Papagos shared with other peoples beyond the extremities of their usual habitat (Underhill 1939: 270-3).

With the establishment of Spanish towns and missions or mission stations in some of these more favorable riverine areas, Papagos came from their remote villages to attach themselves to these settlements, at least for portions of the year. The advent of cattle ranching and the introduction of wheat made it possible for Papagos to continue the ancient pattern of moving to these sources of work when their own resources were insufficient. Establishing temporary encampments outside Mexican towns[1] in the Altar Valley where they would work as harvesters or ranch hands (Spicer 1962: 137) followed the earlier patterns of attaching themselves to the missions and the precontact patterns of working for other Indians. The same kinds of patterns were well established in the riverine valleys to the north (Gila River) and east (Santa Cruz and San Pedro rivers).

The movements of entire families or kinship villages to work for other people are of ancient vintage. It is not surprising that similar movements for similar reasons are still prevalent. The patterns have remained essentially the same, although the political changes since the Gadsden Purchase, the economic innovations, and the accelerating settlement of non-Papagos into the area have changed some of the networks. The more prosperous enterprises on the fringes of their homelands are sources of livelihood for an increasing

---

[1]One of my informants told me that he had learned from his grandfather that some of his ancestors had gone as far as the east coast of Mexico to work in the fields.

number of Papagos, as were the wheat fields of the Pimas or Mexicans a century ago.

With the introduction of cattle and horses, another method of livelihood became a fixture in the Papago economy, for ranching had become a major tribal enterprise, and cattle ranches of Anglos or Mexicans provided another source of occupational activity for Papago men.

Another source of work for the Papagos energies were the dozens of mines scattered over the Papago country during the last half of the nineteenth century. However, the majority of Papagos likely were little affected in terms of active involvement in those operations (Spicer 1962: 137). Most of the Papagos involved in these early mining ventures were from the western and northwestern portions of the present reservation, where many Gu Vo and Hickiwan people worked in the mines at Ajo. A significant number of western Papagos from the Sonoita and Quitovac vicinities in Mexico also became involved in these early ventures. These people still work in present mine operations.

With the growth of towns and cities in southern Arizona, sizable settlements of Papagos have emerged in sectors of the larger towns. To these enclaves, individual Papagos have temporarily attached themselves with the hope of picking up a little work to supplement other means of livelihood. The trend, however, has been toward relatively permanent settlements of Papagos through the years although individuals come and go.

In addition to the above movements, largely stimulated by economic necessity as well as traditional patterns of circulation, the well-known movement from winter-well mountain villages to summer-fields plain villages accentuates the prevailing tendency of Papagos to move whenever it is necessary. These patterns were well established long before the reservation system.

MOTIVATIONAL FACTORS AFFECTING OFF-RESERVATION OCCUPATIONAL ACTIVITIES

The implication that Papago movements away from their home villages are in large part economically motivated is an essentially valid position, for Fontana (Arizona Commission of Indian Affairs 1957: 13) notes that "Papagos have been truly migratory only as long as there has been a need for it." Visits or returns to the villages by those who have been settled elsewhere for long periods of time indicate that this desert land is a social base for almost all Papagos, although fewer and fewer can call it a permanent home (p. 13).

But there are motives behind Papago movement other than economic ones. As in any small, cohesive, relatively simple society, the Papago kinship village type of social organization is occasionally a threat unto itself. Tribal and kinship restraints, while deeply rewarding and integrative, are also repressive, and temporary departures from the village and kinship-based society can be extremely functional (Sofer 1956: 604). Seasonal involvement in other types of organized or even disorganized social relations helps to reduce some of the personal discomforts that people in kinship society experience but must repress.

Thus, the seasonal or periodic movement of a nuclear family away from the usual extended family or kinship-based society is functional in that it helps to maintain the mechanical solidarity of the kinship-based local group. Or migration of members of the extended family to a distant source of economic activity — where they live under different social arrangements in a varied context for part of the year — similarly relieves the repressions that accumulate in the noncontrastive kinship village, even though the individuals are still together.

The mountain to field to cactus camp to round-up kind of mobility probably served a similar function. Such movements are not undermining forces of the kinship-based society but actually undergird it by allowing some experience in a contrastive, and thereby more disorganized, social setting. As Sofer (1956: 604) has suggested, it is this very disorganization or periodic freedom from repressive social control that attracts individuals to other areas. It does not necessarily lead to wholesale permanent settlement into disorganizing areas (disorganizing from the kinship village organization perspective) because there is constant turnover and return. This bears witness to the inadequacies of nonnative organization in satisfying social and psychological needs over long periods of time. But as a temporary escape, seasonal movement serves to reinforce the indigenous social system.

It has been suggested that temporary emancipation from intense kinship and village relationships might be functional for families, both nuclear and extended, as well as for the village unit. An additional factor is that individuals, quite apart from family social units, can find reprieve from some of the excessive restraints of kinship by going away for periods of time. Relocation, following the cotton harvest, attraction toward surrounding towns and cities, and going away to the service or to school all provide greater freedom in atmospheres of anonymity; but the articulation with these new forms of social organization is in utter contrast to the familiar and secure, although repressive, features in the kinship village. Thus, people away for varying periods of time return from these settings if there are any kinship and village ties remaining at all.

Another motivation might be prompted by enjoyments or cherished experiences and memories in certain kinds of movement or travel. If other kin are also away, there are additional sources for socializing, for having fiestas, and for moving about. Sentiments can be strong for certain areas of work activity, for the activities themselves, for the people, and for the familiar scenes and experiences. These may not be substitutes for the pleasures and sentiments one might find at home, but they do exist. Some of the experiences away from home are more numerous and varied than those at home.

It also must be conceded that people go places and do what they do because individuals they have known in their kinship circles traditionally have gone these routes. There may be economic reasons for going away, but why go to one place instead of another? In other words, patterns emerge which are more than habits created by economic necessity. They persist because certain experiences stand out, because certain social relations with non-Papagos are rewarding, and because certain places have been found to be less devastating emotionally and psychologically than others. Hence, movement to specific places constitutes a transcultural network as well.

Another factor, although largely economic in nature, also has been instrumental in stimulating movements of tribal or kinship groups for reasons

other than the essentially economic ones — that is, the establishment of the Papago reservations and the increasing involvement of government in the economics of tribal life. Through programs of directed change, such as the extensive wage work programs during the 1930s, the growing public services of the past two decades, and the influence of government-directed programs of relocation since the 1950s, the importance of wage work has increased considerably in the minds of more and more Papagos. This has caused a shift in the subsistence base and has made dependence on wage work a greater necessity. As Kelly (1963: 41) points out,

As recently as thirty or forty years ago community needs were simple, and most Papago villages were self-sufficient. Today this is true only for Sells. Other villages look elsewhere for one or another of the essential community services: shopping, education, health services, religion, government, and the like.

Papagos, as a result of the role of the federal government, have been motivated to become increasingly dependent on a whole host of activities not traditionally characteristic of Papago life. Forde (1956: 12) notes that in Africa, since subsistence economies are inadequate to meet newly stimulated consumptive needs, wage labor must be undertaken, even if only on a temporary basis, to get the necessary monetary returns to support a more than subsistence way of life. The establishment of a tribal reserve in areas of extensive nonindigenous settlements tends to accentuate the increasingly precarious character of the subsistence economy since there is thrown into the labor supply a large number of people with a low level of efficiency at operating in a highly technological economy. As Forde (1956: 12) goes on to say,

For while they [the reserve natives thrown into the wage labor market] have thus been insulated in some measure from the direct effects of Westernization, their growing populations have become less and less able to support themselves and have increasingly depended on the export of unskilled labour . . . . In urban areas, the effect in general has been to produce large floating populations with low and insecure incomes, little differentiation in skills and education, and very limited means for material and social advance.

The significant point, in addition to the purely economic factors behind population movements, is that floating populations provide a form of pattern or tradition since floating becomes a way of life for some who are alienated from their kinship-based villages. They float to pick up whatever work they can find to meet minimum personal needs. Floating becomes a style of life, involving certain other people, Indian and non-Indian, and consists of certain kinds of shared experiences, even if the experiences appear to outsiders to be economically and emotionally unrewarding. Certain bars, congregating places, acquaintances, and shared experiences become parts of the floating culture or subculture. Therefore, floating or transience becomes the only meaningfully articulate style of life for those who have lost all other ties, and the motivations behind this type of movement are not explainable in terms of economic necessity only.

Thus, with the stimulus of government and other directed change programs, certain individuals will learn to play the appropriate roles that will aid them in taking advantage of the newly induced ways of life. These individuals integrate well into the emerging reservation subculture and are able to abandon roles or modify roles to fit into the new social structures. They learn to communicate with the Anglo agents; they perceive certain economic, social structural, and

even value orientations behind the change programs. A new kind of leadership makes an appearance; some are enterprising enough to turn certain features of the programs to economic advantage, and thus the progress desired by Anglo agents of change begins to evolve.

But there are many more who find it more difficult to communicate with Anglo agents or who find it more difficult to grasp the significance of programs and projects, or who are cut off in the struggles for new kinds of role taking. They fail to articulate adequately with the new reservation subculture and have been less successful in appropriating its features to their economic improvement. Thus, they either live off the public services, follow traditional networks of wage work, or become a part of the floating subculture.

What has been suggested in this section is that while there are underlying economic reasons behind Papago patterns of occupational movement, there are many other motivations which lie behind these patterns and which reinforce the economic features. One of the major objects of this study is to explore this compound of factors and motivations that has been and is instrumental in the kinds of adaptations Papago workers make to wage-labor systems and to specific kinds of occupational roles.

NETWORKS OF OCCUPATIONAL ACTIVITY

Off-Reservation Occupational Areas

There are certain areas, particularly those lying in proximity to the three Papago reservations, that have attracted Papago wage workers. With the exception of traditional visits to the Altar Valley, which were terminated as wage opportunities in Arizona increased (Spicer 1962: 139), other traditionally established networks were kept open as railroads were built, irrigation and commercial farming expanded, mining ventures blossomed, and other wage opportunities opened up in the areas where Papagos were accustomed to visit.

By utilizing some of the more recent quantitative data on the Papago population (Hackenberg 1961; Kelly 1963),[2] it is possible to trace the demographic dimensions of occupational activity for a large portion of the Papago tribe. According to Kelly (1963: 64) a total of 5,249 Papagos[3] were known to

reside off the reservation at the time of the enumeration in 1959. By processing an IBM deck for Papago males of employable age (15-65) who were known to be off-reservation in 1959,[4] it has been possible to chart the areas of concentration for off-reservation

----

[2] The Bureau of Ethnic Research at the University of Arizona maintains a set of demographic records. These records are the source from which both Hackenberg and Kelly derived their data.

[3] The reliability of enumeration is admittedly in need of test, particularly for those living for some length of time off the reservations and especially for those Papagos outside of Arizona. Kelly (1963: 48-64) discusses at length the risks involved in interpreting the statistics.

[4] Because of limited funds and time, the list selected only those who were living and working off-reservation in southern Arizona. This would include the vital farming, mining, and industrial areas which have drawn a majority of reservation Papagos. This has been the geographical limit within which the field work and field interviewing have been carried out.

settlement and to relate these concentrations to places or origin.

The establishment of the so-called occupational areas is arbitrary, although the areas seem to conform to rather clear-cut types of occupational activities that prevail in the geographical areas located. The feature of origin also helps in demarcating these relatively discrete areas since, as the data show, certain sectors of the reservation populations are inclined toward some areas more than others. It may be that some other arbitrary division of areas will prove more beneficial, but for our purposes there are six occupational areas bordering the Papago reservations which have drawn a large number of Papago workers.

The IBM deck for tabulating off-reservation Papagos reveals that during 1959, there were 1,106 Papago males of employable age (15-65) living off-reservation in the areas of southern Arizona described here. Of these individuals, 767 had reservation origins, 73 had origins in northern Mexico, and 266 were of off-reservation origin, predominantly southern Arizona. Figure 2 depicts the six occupational areas; and Table 1 indicates the area, reservation (other than Sells), or district (Sells Reservation) of origin for the 1,106 Papago individuals living and/or working in these areas during 1959.

Ajo

In 1959 there were 282 Papago men between ages 15 and 65 residing in the vicinity of Ajo, Arizona. The figure must be considered as including those residing in smaller surrounding hamlets, such as Darby Well, Bates Well, and other rural residence units, as well as the concentration of Papagos in the Ajo Indian community and Ajo proper. There has been a large concentration of Papagos in Ajo for several generations, dating back to the first part of the twentieth century (see Chapter 4). As indicated in Table 2, 90 (32%) of the 282 Papago males were born in Ajo, most of whom are second generation Papagos whose parents claim origin from villages now within the reservation boundaries or along the border in Mexico. Table 2 also shows the districts of origin for the 282 employed or employable Papago males within the Ajo Occupational Area in 1959, indicating also the villages of origin most represented.

The distinctive feature behind the concentration of Papagos in the area of Ajo is the Ajo copper mine. Thus, little more needs to be said to justify the

TABLE 1

Origins of 1,106 Papago Men Living and/or Working Off-Reservation in Southern Arizona, 1959

Origin	Number	Approx. Percent
Reservation		
Sells	672	61
Baboquivari	129	12
Sells	107	10
Chukut Kuk	83	7
Gu Achi	83	7
Hickiwan	69	6
Gu Vo	56	5
Pisinimo	53	5
Sif Oidak	50	5
Schuk Toak	42	4
Gila River Pima	43	4
San Xavier	35	3
Gila Bend	12	1
Salt River Pima	4	-
Ak Chin Maricopa	1	-
	767	
Off-Reservation		
Ajo Area	102	9
Mexico	73	7
Tucson Area	56	5
Coolidge Area	52	5
Gila Bend Area	11	1
Phoenix Area	9	1
Marana Area	5	-
Marginal Southern Arizona	3	-
Other Rural	14	1
Unknown	13	1
Non-Arizona U.S.	1	-
	339	
	1,106	

distinctiveness of this area as an occupational area. This is the most concentrated of the six occupational areas in terms of Papagos off-reservation.

Coolidge

The largest area spatially and numerically for off-reservation Papagos is the area described here as the Coolidge Occupational Area. Its dimensions include

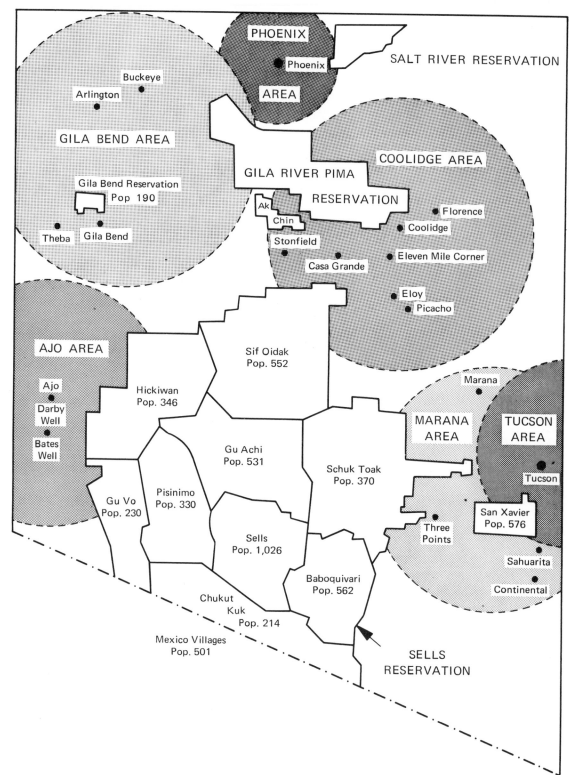

Figure 2. Off-Reservation Occupational Areas Adjacent to Papago and Pima Reservations in Southern Arizona, 1959

TABLE 2

Origins of Papago Men Residing in the Ajo Area, 1959

Origin	Number	Percent	Villages of Origin Most Represented
Ajo Area	90	32	Ajo Indian village
Sells	33	12	Sells, Cowlic
Baboquivari	28	10	Topawa
Chukut Kuk	25	9	San Miguel, Stan Shuatuk
Gu Vo	23	8	Gu Vo
Mexico	20	7	Sonoita, Quitobac, Jack Rabbit Falls Down
Pisinimo	17	6	Pisinimo, San Simon
Hickiwan	13	5	Hickiwan
Gu Achi	12	4	Covered Wells, Ko Vaya
Schuk Toak	8	3	Chiawuli Tak
Other	13	4	Scattered
	282	100	

the belt of commercial farming activities that spreads from west of Stanfield through an area encompassing the communities of Casa Grande, Eleven Mile Corner, Coolidge, Florence, Eloy, and Picacho. Within this geographical area Papagos depend largely on wage labor from commercial cotton farms. A total of 285 Papago men, 201 of whom are of reservation origin, are found in this extensive area. Three subareas are: Stanfield-Casa Grande (100), Coolidge-Florence (115) and Eloy-Picacho (70). The circulation of workers within the total area and the accessibility of one subarea to another make it possible to treat them under one large area for our purposes. Table 3 represents the districts of origin and the villages of origin most represented by the 285 Papago males in the area.

Tucson

Third in the number of resident Papago adult males is the urban area of Tucson. It is significant that 51 of the 56 Papagos with origins in Tucson still lived there in 1959. The occupations of these Papagos cover a wider range of both skilled and unskilled jobs, which are primarily urban in character. There is likely a significant number of unemployed or spasmodically employed as well as a number who vacillate from spot jobs, to periodic unemployment, to seasonal farm work in the adjacent farming area (the Marana Occupational Area). Table 4 contains the places of origin and the villages of origin most represented for the 240 Papago men residing in Tucson in 1959.

Gila Bend

The fourth major concentration of Papago workers consists of the commercial farming area surrounding the communities of Theba, Gila Bend, Arlington, Buckeye, and Laveen, including the Gila Bend Papago Reservation. The justification for this area as a composite whole lies not only in the geographical contiguity of the farms enveloping these communities but in the very networks that tie the Papagos in the area to reservation origins. The pattern of movement to this area from certain points on the reservations gives the area its identity, although, except for the distinction in the central occupational activity, it shares this characteristic with the Ajo area. Table 5 reveals the network.

The Gila Bend Papagos are connected historically to Hickiwan (Hackenberg 1964: IV-57), and the farms in the area still draw largely on seasonal workers from the Gila Bend Reservation and the two westernmost districts of the Sells Reservation.

Marana

The last major farming area in southern Arizona, in which there is a sizable, relatively permanent concentration of Papagos, is the commercial farming area extending from the vicinity of Marana through the Avra Valley west of Tucson, to the Santa Cruz Valley as far south as Continental. The Avra Valley and Continental-Sahuarita sectors can be treated as distinct areas, but there seems to be no reason why they cannot be grouped together as a single farming

TABLE 3

Origins of Papago Men Residing in the Coolidge Area, 1959

Origin	Number	Percent	Villages of Origin Most Represented
Coolidge Area	51	18	Coolidge, Eloy, Stanfield
Gu Achi	45	16	Gu Achi, Ak Chin
Sif Oidak	42	15	Chui Chuichu, Anegam, Gu Komelik
Gila River	24	8	Blackwater, Sacaton
Mexico	24	7	Pozo Verde
Pisinimo	22	7	Pisinimo
Sells	15	5	Big Field, Cowlic
Hickiwan	14	4	Ventana, Kaka
Baboquivari	11	4	Komalik, Topawa, Ali Chukson
Gu Vo	10	3	Ak Chin, Ali Chuk
Chukut Kuk	8	3	San Miguel, Vamori
Other	19	7	Scattered
	285	100	

TABLE 4

Origins of Papago Men Residing in the Tucson Area, 1959

Origin	Number	Percent	Villages of Origin Most Represented
Baboquivari	57	24	Topawa, Choulic, Ali Chukson
Tucson Area	51	21	South Tucson
Chukut Kuk	35	15	San Miguel, Vamori
Sells	33	14	Sells, Cowlic
San Xavier	22	9	Bac, Oidak, Opposite
Schuk Toak	16	6	Chiawuli Tak, Kom Vo, Hoi Oidak
Mexico	9	4	Pozo Verde
Gu Achi	8	3	Ak Chin, Covered Wells
Other	9	4	Scattered
	240	100	

area adjacent to the Tucson area. Many Tucson as well as reservation Papagos have access to both sub-areas with equal facility. Table 6 portrays the districts of origin and the main villages represented by the individuals living in this area.

Phoenix

The Phoenix urban area is the smallest of the six occupational areas in terms of the number of Papagos living and working within. Phoenix was outside the limits of direct field work and field interviewing, but it is included in this discussion of occupational networks because of the sizable number of Papagos concentrated in Phoenix and because the Phoenix area provides additional dimensions to the Urban, Nonfarm Occupational Complex, discussed in Chapter 5. Table 7 contains the districts or origin and villages of origin most represented in the Phoenix Occupational Area.

The remaining 90 of the 1,106 individuals cannot be precisely placed in terms of patterned networks to occupational areas. The population register has an "other rural" category of 66 Papagos that defies

TABLE 5

Origins of Papago Men Residing in the Gila Bend Area, 1959

Origin	Number	Percent	Villages of Origin Most Represented
Hickiwan	24	31	Hickiwan, Kaka, Stoapitk
Gu Vo	13	17	Gu Vo, Ali Chuk
Gila Bend Area	11	14	Arlington, Theba
Ajo	7	9	Ajo, Darby Well
Gu Achi	7	9	Gu Achi
Gila Bend Reservation	5	6	Gila Bend (town), Daik
Mexico	3	4	Jack Rabbit Falls Down
Other	8	10	Scattered
	78	100	

TABLE 6

Origins of Papago Men Residing in the Marana Area, 1959

Origin	Number	Percent	Villages of Origin Most Represented
Baboquivari	18	27	Ali Chukson
Sells	9	14	Big Field, Lincon
Schuk Toak	8	12	Kom Vaya, Pan Tak
Pisinimo	6	9	Pisinimo, Nestor's
Marana area	5	8	Marana
Chukut Kuk	4	6	Vamori
Gu Achi	4	6	Gu Achi
Mexico	3	4	Pozo Verde
Other	9	14	Scattered
	66	100	

TABLE 7

Origins of Papago Men Residing in the Phoenix Area, 1959

Origin	Number	Percent	Villages of Origin Most Represented
Gila River	13	20	Sacaton, Casa Blanca, Blackwater
Baboquivari	8	12	Choulic
San Xavier	8	12	Bac, Opposite
Phoenix	8	12	Phoenix
Sells	7	11	Big Field
Chukut Kuk	5	7	Scattered
Salt River	3	5	Scattered
Gu Achi	3	5	Gu Achi
Sif Oidak	3	5	Chui Chuichu
Other	7	11	Scattered
	65	100	

description as an area. A total of 24 Papagos is classified as living and working in marginal areas, that is, at the eastern and western extremities of the areas of greatest concentration. This latter category is too scattered to lead to any network or pattern of occupational movement. The individuals appear to be of individual families operating largely in commercial farming wage systems.

In summary, there appear to be networks of movement which characterize each district or reservation of origin. The districts closest to each other appear to share similar postures toward off-reservation occupational areas. Figure 3 represents the variety of patterns, by district or reservation of origin, to off-reservation areas. The fact that each off-reservation area has a sizable number of adult male Papagos born within it (Table 1) indicates the extent to which these networks are built on the movements of past generations.

Plotting the profiles of off-reservation movements to specific occupational areas for each district (Sells Reservation) or reservation (San Xavier, Gila Bend, and Gila River Pima) provides a basis for comparison as well as a means for pinpointing the character of the several occupational networks (Figure 3). The entire region, consisting of reservations and off-reservation occupational areas, can be abstracted in the form of a circle (Figure 3) with points A, GB, Ph, C, M, and T representing the Ajo, Gila Bend, Phoenix, Coolidge, Marana, and Tucson areas, respectively. Districts or other points of origin are located in terms of their approximate positions in the entire region. Lines or networks from these points of origin are extended to the occupational area points at the arc of the circle. These networks are drawn in proportion to the numbers of Papagos emanating from certain points of origin.

The southeastern and central districts of Baboquivari, Sells, Chukut Kuk, and Gu Achi — the districts of greatest population density — had the largest number of individuals in off-reservation occupational areas in 1959. The first three share very similar profiles, with sizable representations in the Ajo and Tucson areas. The Gu Achi district, however, reveals a quite different orientation with a sizable representation in the Coolidge area. In this respect, it shares the features of the Sif Oidak district profile so that Gu Achi could be grouped, in terms of occupational network, with Sif Oidak.

Comparing the profiles further, Gu Vo and Hickiwan can be grouped together with respect to their strong orientations to the Ajo and Gila Bend areas. Both fade out south and east of Casa Grande, with no representation in the Tucson area.

Papagos of Mexican origin reveal the widest range of representation in all six occupational areas, with a considerable number of Sonoita, Quitobac, and Jack Rabbit Falls Down Papagos oriented toward the Ajo area, and a fair number of Pozo Verde Papagos oriented toward the Coolidge area.

Pisinimo also has some of the features that characterize the Mexico profile in that its main networks appear to be toward Ajo and Coolidge. In many respects it is closer to the pattern which characterizes Gu Achi; hence, it can be grouped with the Gu Achi and Sif Oidak profiles.

The Gila River Pima Reservation Papagos have a unique profile oriented predominantly either to the Phoenix urban area or the Coolidge rural area. The Schuk Toak and San Xavier networks approximate each other except for the latter's almost exclusive orientations to either Phoenix or Tucson, as compared to the former's stronger orientations to the rural Coolidge and Marana areas. The Gila Bend Reservation Papagos have another aberrant profile that defies grouping with any other profile, although Gila Bend and Hickiwan people are of known historic relationship. This may be the reason behind the similarities in the profiles of these two groups.

Fringe Settlements

As noted by Arensberg (1954: 110), a method is needed for studying the nature and dynamics of behavior and attitudes of individuals and their interactions in the surroundings of an identifiable social unit or particular community. When Papagos leave their reservation villages, they establish some kind of settlement unit within which the dynamics of behavior and attitudes transpire. The historical dimension of Papago economic patterns as they relate to movement to more distant areas for temporary periods of work activity has been discussed. Similarly, the resulting network (1959) of these historic patterns has been presented. Some attention will be given to a better description of the kinds of communities, settlements, or residences Papagos assume as they attach themselves to the areas fringing their reservations.

27

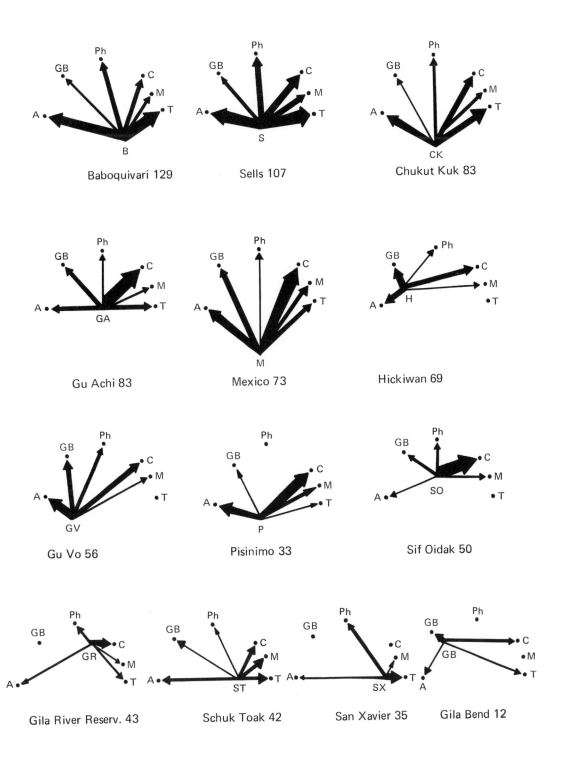

Figure 3. Comparative Profiles of Off-Reservation Movement in Terms of Origin, 1959

The field experience, while not revealing the complete range of possibilities, has permitted a basis for an impressionistic formulation of settlement patterns as they occur in the off-reservation occupational areas already discussed. The dimensions are observational rather than experimental or statistical (Arensberg 1954: 111). These types of social units are deemed to be extremely important to the manner in which Papago families relate to an occupational complex. In fact, specific occupational complexes seem to support certain kinds of settlement or residence arrangements, which in turn are functional for Papagos participating in the complex. Some of these types of settlement patterns will be presented. Impressionistically, there appear to be six major categorical types of fringe settlement: (1) Rural Family Cluster, (2) Rural Family Isolate, (3) Planned Settlement, (4) Off-Reservation Indian Village, (5) Urban Family Cluster, and (6) Urban Isolate.

Rural Family Cluster

This particular type — by far the most prevalent — is so named because of the number of occupiable dwellings that make up an encampment attached to a particular commercial farming enterprise. The cluster consists of a permanent nucleus of one or more nuclear or extended families attached to the encampment the year around. The small nucleus persists although individual members of the permanent families, as well as other more temporary families, come and go. There is a seasonal enlargement of the encampment during the height of the season when reservation families and other ethnic group families or individuals move into the unoccupied dwellings on a temporary basis. Dwellings are rent-free.

One or several members of the permanent households may have steady work, while other members of the family may supplement the household income by part-time or seasonal work. Sometimes several members of the family spread temporary work throughout the year, although not one is a steady hand. Even the few permanent families expand during the season of greatest agricultural activity to temporarily incorporate relatives from the reservation.

The encampment may have a makeshift family chapel, usually kept up by the permanent families but used by temporary residents. There are periodic visits by Roman Catholic priests to these religious centers.

Contractors pay regular visits to the encampments. These contractors may work for the farm on which the camp settlement lies, or they may pick up workers and take them to any number of locales in the area to chop or pick cotton. The permanent families avail themselves of these services, but at least one member of the family performs most of his services for the farm on which the camp is located.

The camps also become centers of regular visits by public health nurses, public school buses, salesmen and peddlers, and ministers. The permanent family members usually function as spokesmen in official visits, while seasonal families are more isolated and utilize the permanent individuals as mediaries to these outside contacts.

The features described above characterize settlement clusters in all of the occupational areas. Figure 4 represents a few examples of variations in this type although by no means are the variations exhausted. The camp settlement seems to be an environment which places different kinds of modifying demands on the Papago family structure, and detailed ethnographic studies would certainly reveal more of these processes. Only one farming occupational area has been studied with any intensity in terms of rural Papago family structures. The case studies in a subsequent chapter will expose this type of settlement in more detail.

Rural Family Isolate

Seldom in the field work has a rural isolated Papago family actually been encountered. However, either by the occupancy of a single dwelling relatively isolated from a larger encampment or by the failure of some camp dwellings to be filled by seasonal occupants from the reservation, it is possible to identify a discrete type which consists of a nuclear family occupying a single household and detached from a collectivity of other dwellings. On occasion there may be an accommodation of individual members of one's extended family or network of relatives, but the spatial arrangements are not sufficient for taking in other nuclear families as wholes.

In this isolated type, the nuclear unit depends on the occupational activity of the male head, while other adult members may supplement the income. The activity of the male head takes on the nature of a permanent farm hand. The house is provided by the farm so long as at least one member of the family is

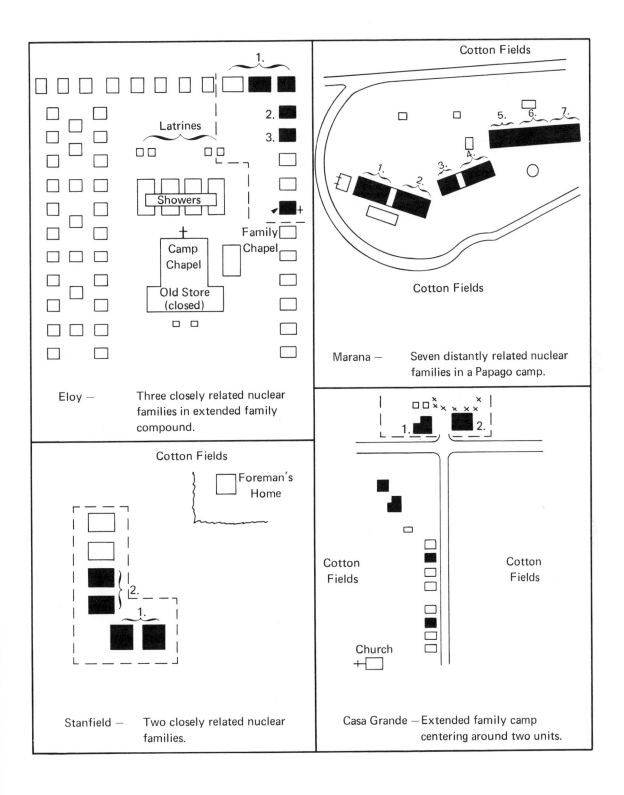

Figure 4. Examples of Rural Family Clusters

employed or available to be beckoned in the case of work to be done. The household may be a part of a larger camp complex but set apart from it. Termination of one's status as a permanent hand in the isolated type necessitates a move, since there is not a body of extended kin or relatives at least temporarily employed to keep the unit going.

Some of the variations of the first type may be tending in the direction of the rural family isolate type, although it is not to be perceived as a second stage in a processual sequence.

Planned Settlement

While most of the former settlement variations are attributed largely to more haphazard, unplanned, and undirected growth and utilization, and are available for those interested in "squatting", there are a few settlements which are distinct in that they are planned and operated by some form of housing authority or agency. The authority may be either independent of any occupational enterprise or it may be a part of that enterprise. In any case, there is a settlement pattern laid out to some specific plan where streets have some pattern and individual residence units are arranged in some organized fashion along these thoroughfares. The dwellings are of low-rental variety but in a price range commensurate with a family's ability and desire to pay. In some variations of this type there may be rent-free access, but there is opportunity for low-price rentals if desired.

Ideally, the houses are open to any who desire to meet the specifications; but in the case of the Ajo Indian community, a segregated Indian settlement has emerged into which only Indians desire to settle. In the other variations, ethnic neighborhoods or enclaves may informally emerge as vacant dwellings are occupied by incoming people.

There is usually ready access to stores, churches, schools, and other services. Examples of this type are such settlements as the Pinal County Housing Authority Farm Labor Camp in the Coolidge Occupational Area, the Theba settlement planned by the Gillespie Ranch in the Gila Bend Occupational Area, and the Ajo Indian community in the Ajo Occupational Area. The Theba settlement is more difficult to identify as representative of the planned settlement, and it shares features with the Rural Family Cluster type, although its history is that of a planned community to accommodate agricultural workers.

The nuclear family is the most common unit, as the houses are designed to accommodate the family in terms of the Anglo American conception as to the importance of the nuclear family. In this respect, the planning and building of dwellings fail to acknowledge the importance of larger kinship units such as the extended family. Therefore, those peoples, including Papagos, who participate extensively in extranuclear family relationships, must accommodate their family patterns to this planned incapacity. Thus there are informal alignments, apart from formal policy, of kin and relatives whenever vacancies permit. As in the case of the Ajo village, there is informal "swapping" of houses rented by the company in order that the extended family can be accommodated in a contiguous cluster of dwellings, although this is contrary to the housing authority's policy.

As a type, it does represent some unique features that have an effect on the way families align themselves. It is conceivable to classify urban projects in this category by virtue of their planned nature and the direction by low-rent housing authorities. This particular variation has not been observed, however.

Off-Reservation Indian Village

In at least three of the occupational areas presented in this study, there is a type of settlement that takes on the character of a Papago village similar to those that are familiar on the reservation. The settlement is exclusively or predominantly Papago and has many clearly identifiable features that distinguish it from the other types of residence. While the Ajo Indian village is predominantly Papago, it is in no sense a typical Papago village and therefore is typed as a planned settlement by a non-Papago authority, although it has sociopolitical organization similar to that found on the Papago reservation.

There is a history of long-time Papago settlement in the area before there was any sizable number of Anglos. As the Anglos moved in to inhabit the area, the Papago settlement had to shift itself in response to changing Anglo settlement and expansion patterns. As the land came under the control of Anglos, Papagos in these village settlements continued to lease land or to "squat" as the Anglo community grew up around it. The Papagos in these settlements have continued to build their own adobe houses, ramadas, corrals, feast houses, dance pavilions, chapels, and

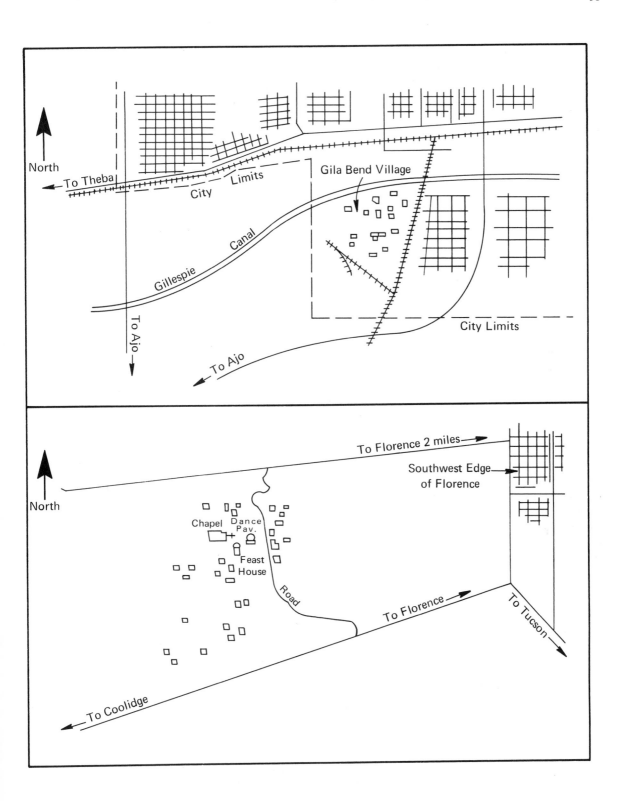

Figure 5. Gila Bend and Florence Indian Villages

other structures. They have maintained some of the traditional features of the village organization and have also incorporated organizational features that characterize the political influence of the Bureau of Indian Affairs on the reservation. Politically a chief, as well as village councilmen, are elected, and formal and informal spokesmen or speakers are acknowledged. There are kinship and sociopolitical ties with certain reservation villages and districts.

Contractors visit these villages regularly because of their location in the heart of farming occupational areas. Many of the adult males are either relatively permanent hands on neighboring farms or they circulate in employment for several different farms for differing lengths of time. There is permanent access to the surrounding farms; and since the individuals are well known for the kind of work they can or do perform, foremen and recruiters make frequent personal contacts to get the men when their services are desired or needed. The Florence Indian village in the Coolidge Occupational Area and the Gila Bend village in the Gila Bend Occupational Area are examples of settlements which rely predominantly on rural occupational opportunities (Figure 5), although the villages are adjacent to towns, and individuals have access to nonfarm jobs as well. The settlements of Darby Well and Bates Well in the Ajo Occupational Area are similarly Indian villages and some of the inhabitants are involved in the mining operations at Ajo. In times past, Theba may have been classified as an Indian village; but there are several ethnic groups now attached to that settlement and, like Ajo, it has the characteristics of a planned community.

Urban Family Cluster

This type of residence pattern consists of permanent enclaves or clusters where Papagos have established somewhat permanent relationships with a larger urban community and have maintained households in recognizable Papago neighborhoods. These patterns have an extended history and have permitted the modification and maintenance of Papago family relationships in an urban setting. The clusters are not totally discrete; and Papago neighborhoods are dispersed, being mixed with peoples of other ethnic backgrounds. The nuclear family clusters function as permanent nuclei through which mobile reservation Papago kinsmen may come and go in the process of testing the credibility of the urban area as a source of

wage work. Adult males of the nuclear households may be involved in part-time wage work, indeterminable spot jobs, or relatively steady urban jobs; or they may have prolonged periods of idleness as long as other members of the family, such as a wife who may be a domestic worker, have some adequate means of income. Some may do cotton chopping and picking in the adjacent farming area as a last resort kind of wage work. Some may begin to prefer the urban style of life and may find farm work less desirable than urban occupations.

Houses are of low-rent variety but may also be owned and have higher evaluations as a result of longer personal care. Residence types therefore must be viewed as representing a considerable range. There is a predominance of second- and third-generation Papagos born within the urban enclave whereby there have been continuous relationships with urban institutions such as stores, schools, churches, and urban agencies. Although Tucson has a much larger Papago enclave, Phoenix Papagos could also be classified within this type.

Urban Isolate

Papagos who do not reside in an urban cluster of Papago families are included in this settlement type. The stable isolate is a nuclear family, or a single individual, living largely in a non-Papago neighborhood and maintaining stable residential and occupational patterns in that neighborhood over an extended period of time. While not all reservation or Papago ties are completely broken, men and women work in occupations that have not employed a large number of Papagos; and children attend schools where there may be no other Papago children. The motivational factors that have stimulated Papago movements into non-Papago neighborhoods also operate to ensure that Papago individuals reflect the socioeconomic status indicators of non-Papagos immediately around them, characteristics not traditionally shared by Papagos. There may or may not be frequent interaction with Papago friends, relatives, or kinsmen, either on the reservation or in the urban enclave; but in any case there is not a complete break with Papago identification.

Those individuals and families classifiable under this settlement type demonstrate features of behavior that do not characterize the behaviors shared by all of the preceding types; there is a greater identification with things non-Papago. Papagos on relocation in various urban areas likely fall within any of the urban variations discussed.

There is also a transient variation under the urban isolate type wherein individuals may be permanently connected to an urban setting but make their residences in jails, hotels, and flop houses, or sleep on the streets. They may rely on very infrequent spot jobs but are on the verge of economic deprivation and personality disorganization. However, there are extensive interactions with other ethnic transients as well as with other Papago transients. Chronic alcohol consumption, the frequenting of downtown bars, and begging or other forms of soliciting may be features of this type of isolation. The individual may have established a pattern or style of life that detaches or alienates him from any extensive kinship involvements. It is too dangerous, however, to preclude all kinship connections; hence it is possible to too quickly label such individuals as lacking orientation to a normative system. Regardless of how atypical the patterns are to either Papago or non-Papago cultural expectations, the urban isolate transient type does operate within a style of life. Behavior is still oriented to reference groups even though it is not typically Papago or middle class Anglo behavior. The family may be disintegrated in the traditional sense, although individual family members may be interdependent on each other some of the time.

In identifying types of settlement in which off-reservation Papagos are found, an effort has been made to account for a range of residential or settlement environments within which off-reservation Papago males of employable age interact. Occupational activities within any of the occupational areas discussed use as their bases one or several of these fringe settlement variations. Care must be exercised in trying to place individuals or families in any of these settlement types. The types and variations are not exhaustive, and likewise it is never a case of either one or the other; in any one case any of the types may be manifest, depending on the time and circumstances. The typology should provide a better framework for understanding the chapters to follow, particularly for putting the case studies presented in their proper ecological perspective.

3. COMMERCIAL FARM OCCUPATIONAL COMPLEX

As Chapter 2 has shown, there are networks of a traditional and historical nature by which Papagos move to certain fringe areas and attach themselves to the primary occupational institutions of these areas. As residence is established, whether for a temporary period or a prolonged period, Papago workers and their families become participants in the complex of institutions that is integral to the functioning of the particular occupational system. The complex of institutions to which Papagos are exposed as they attach themselves to certain kinds of wage work provides a social field that is shared by individual Papago men and that confronts them with situations demanding the performance of both familiar, well-established roles and uncertain, ambiguous, and conflicting roles.

This is not to say that all adult Papago males participate in the wage system or assume occupational roles in the central occupational activity of an area simply by virtue of their off-reservation residence. However, the merit in utilizing the occupational area and occupational complex conceptualizations is that they take into account the fact that there are spatial and institutional environments through which individuals circulate and within which they interact. In this way, the problem of what constitutes a permanent or a temporary off-reservation status is not a major concern. Instead, environments of adaptation are identified, and all Papago individuals who attach themselves to an occupational complex, regardless of their overall residence and occupational patterns, are subject to similar experiences in accommodating their role behaviors to the demands of living within the complex. Thus, whether a seasonal worker, a temporary worker, or a permanent employee,[1] or whether a more permanent resident or a seasonal resident of the area, the individual Papago is exposed to a range of non-Papago institutions in addition to the occupational institution which draws him to the area in the first place.

There are certainly differences in the ways temporary and seasonal workers experience this occupational environment. The seasonal pattern that relies wholly on crew leaders does provide some insulation from non-Papago institutions, such as avoiding the pay check-social security-income tax complex; reducing the need for learning English; keeping the extended family and village patterns intact; or maintaining control over when, how, or whether to participate in the system (Padfield 1961: 23). This may hold true particularly for some individuals who are predominantly reservation residents but who "hire out" to contractors only during the period of greatest demand. The temporary and permanent off-reservation workers certainly confront non-Papago institutions to a much greater degree. Some people who have been off-reservation for years similarly may depend on contractors exclusively or in part, but in any case it is questionable whether they are able to totally insulate themselves from involvement in non-Papago institutions.

Certainly, if the trend from seasonal to temporary to permanent farm work is actually the case (Kelly 1963: 117-8), there must be some explanation for it. One possibility is that the occupational complex does present a contact situation wherein Papago individuals are slowly learning to adapt their behaviors to the demands of the sociocultural system, and the non-Papago employers are slowly becoming more aware that Papagos are capable of a wider range of occupational roles and can be counted on for certain kinds of important services hitherto unacknowledged. In other words, occupational stereotypes, as supported by both Papagos and non-Papagos, give some indication of weakening.

Papagos traditionally have been a rurally oriented people, living in rancherias, depending on the soil, combating the elements, and exploiting the offerings of the natural surroundings. As semisedentary subsistence peoples, traditionally they are to be equated with the peasantry since their subsistence obligations were, in part, as agricultural producers who retained a degree of effective control over the desert land, producing or obtaining for themselves and not for

---

[1] The seasonal worker is one who is hired by labor contractors or crew leaders during the height of the seasonal demand, while the temporary worker is one who is hired by the farmer himself to perform the needed tasks as they arise (Kelly 1963: 113).

reinvestment (Wolf 1955: 454). When markets became available, production for a market occurred only as a way of supplementing their own subsistence needs. As they became a part of a larger social field when their lands were surrounded by Mexican and Anglo settlers, they had to adapt their internal organizations to this larger field although most of their daily activities remained local in nature.

This kind of background has always proven to be exploitable by market and industrial economies. Large-scale commercial farming and ranching enterprises have been able to take advantage of this kind of background as the subsistence economy has become increasingly inadequate to meet emerging needs and the people have become dependent on cash earned through wage labor. There has been an alteration in attitudes about what constitutes needs and how to meet them. Social relations have come to be projected outside of the kinship group to include employers from whom they can earn some needed cash in order to meet a range of accumulating derived needs. The center of attention and the interests of members of a kinship community are now focused outside it, toward economic ventures in wage systems (Mair 1957: 30-1). But their rural subsistence backgrounds make the commercial farming enterprises the most attractive wage-system environments toward which to turn their attention. The physical landscape remains similar, the tasks are comparable and demand little in the way of reorientation, their homes are accessible, their kin can remain close to them, the farmers find their services useful, and they have access to that little bit of needed wage.

It is not surprising, then, that the commercial farm occupational complex as a type involves a large number of adult Papago males. Chapter 2 described three major agricultural areas that provide a fringe around the Sells Reservation. Each area comprises a number of commercial farm complexes; and each area has a different history of settlement, agricultural and commercial development, and political alignments.[2] There are major town centers around which the social life of those attached to various commercial farm enterprises is oriented. Therefore all commercial farm complexes, regardless of the area, are expected to share certain basic structural features. This should permit generalization about the Commercial Farm Occupational Complex as an ideal type. Specific farm complexes become the empirical referents from which the general type is derived. What is said about one specific commercial farming complex within an area should contribute to an understanding of other complexes, because we are dealing with a type of institutional complex which spans the three areas.

As Padfield (1961: 33) points out, the Papago reservations are surrounded by 370,000 acres of farm land, which calls for a labor force in excess of 10,000. This is a fairly large area to adequately treat as a unit, although there are features shared by the entire area that might justify doing so. It seems more desirable and more meaningful, however, to restrict our attention to concrete examples of a commercial farm complex, in order to make the discussion comparable to the other occupational complexes, particularly that of the geographically compact Ajo occupational complex. Some of the general features shared by the specific farm complexes will be projected into generalizations that characterize the ideal Commercial Farm Occupational Complex type. The same procedure will be followed in arriving at generalizations concerning the range of variation in occupational statuses and roles characteristic of this type of complex.

The Marana occupational area is used as the particular spatial entity for the discussion of specific occupational complexes within it.

TEMPORAL, SPATIAL, AND DEMOGRAPHIC FEATURES OF THE MARANA AREA

The floodplain of the Santa Cruz River and its tributaries spreads through Pima and Pinal counties in southern Arizona, comprising an extensive commercial farming region where most commercial cotton for the two counties is cultivated (Dobyns 1950: 15). While the Santa Cruz Valley is a major fringe area which draws Papago wage workers into commercial farm work, Dobyns draws some rather

---

[2] The Gila Bend Occupational Area embraces Maricopa County, while the Coolidge and Marana occupational areas lie within Pinal and Pima counties, respectively.

clear distinctions between Pinal and Pima county farms with regard to Papago patterns. First, the Pinal County Papagos are oriented to one of three trading centers or more recent smaller centers, while Pima County Papagos are oriented toward the Tucson urban area as well as the smaller centers (Dobyns 1950: 17, 27). There are more town-dwelling Papagos who are hauled to the farms in Pima County, whereas in Pinal County the large majority live near the fields in farm camps (p. 28).[3] In addition, Pima County farms have a smaller proportion of Anglo American farm laborers and a higher proportion of non-Anglos (Negroes, Mexican-Americans, Orientals, and Indians) than in the case with Pinal County (p. 66). While Pinal County contains more Papagos working on the cotton farms, there are more Anglos involved as well. Hence Papagos in Pinal County are less numerous in terms of proportional ethnic representation than they are in Pima County. Only one-tenth of the Pinal County labor force is Papago, while close to one-fifth of the Pima County labor force is Papago (p. 134).[4] Further, the Papagos are concentrated in larger groups in Pinal County whereas in Pima County they are more dispersed among other ethnic peoples (Dobyns 1950: 66).

Considering these distinctions, it seems justifiable and practical to treat Pima and Pinal counties within discrete occupational areas, although the same kinds of commercial farming activities are found in each. The Marana occupational area comprises the Pima County commercial farming lands, primarily devoted to cotton as a major crop. Within the area (Figure 6) it is possible to identify two major commercial farming complexes, the Avra Valley complex, oriented to the farming community of Marana, and the Sahuarita-Continental complex, oriented to these farming communities. Perhaps the Three Points complex could represent a third farming complex, oriented toward Three Points and Tucson. Although it is at the southern extremity of the Avra Valley, it is somewhat by itself and may be treated as a separate complex within the area.

Within each of these major complexes there are a number of commercial farms of varying sizes and organizational structure. It is through their occupational roles on these farms that Papagos are linked to the institutions of the respective farm complexes. The proximity to Tucson may also link them to institutions characteristic of an urban setting, and Papagos may oscillate in an urban-rural social field, as discussed more fully in Chapter 5.

Non-Indian settlement along the Santa Cruz River Valley dates back to the seventeenth century when Spanish interests for settlement, and economic and spiritual exploitation were being thrust northward by hardy adventurers. Missions, presidios, ranches, and other forms of settlement grew up along the river valleys and their tributaries since the greatest possibility for sustaining these interests was to be found there in the riverine valleys. Wherever Indians were located, there was always an attempt to settle them on some river where there were more fertile lands (Manje 1954: 31). After a settled nucleus was established, it was Jesuit policy to extend attention to surrounding rancherias (Bancroft 1886: 439-41) and occasional visits were paid to them.

Kino, in the course of his journeys throughout the *Pimería Alta,* noted rich fertile lands and good rivers, an area which could support many ranches of cattle, sheep, goats, and horses, as well as farming and mining interests (Bolton 1919: 93). In his visits to the villages along the Santa Cruz and San Pedro rivers, he took livestock and introduced wheat and other vegetables (Kino 1954: 99, 119). A greater portion of the Papagos, however, could never be induced to live in the pueblos or villages established by the Jesuits. They chose to live in their rancherias, inhabiting their winter sierra homes where water and grazing lands were available and moving into the broad valleys in the summers to cultivate their crops (Lumholtz 1912: 25-6). The Spanish innovations were appropriated to native settlement patterns.

The settlements along the Santa Cruz and San Pedro rivers were predominantly Sobaipuri and were already fortified at the time of Spanish contact (Underhill 1939: 16). The area was on the Apache frontier; and during Kino's time (1687-1711) in the *Pimería Alta,* the Sobaipuri were leaving the Apache

---

[3]In a more recent study by the Arizona State Employment Service (1960: 41), a sample of 1,850 interviews in Maricopa, Pinal, Yuma, and Cochise counties presents data to contradict Dobyns' position. Of 72 Indians included in the survey, 54 of them were in Pinal County. Only one had farm housing, 28 lived in farm labor camps, and 26, or almost 50 percent, went to the fields from urban residences. This either indicates a change in ten years or the fact that the ASES survey included Pima and other Indians beside Papagos. Dobyns' data concern only the Papagos. Only a new study could clarify this point. The ASES study reveals that in the four counties, 53 percent lived in urban housing.

[4]The ASES survey of 1959-60 reveals that of 540 cotton laborers interviewed in Pinal County, 196 were Spanish American, 159 were Negro, 75 were Anglo, 54 were Indian, 54 were Mexican Nationals, and 2 were "other". Indians constituted about 10 percent of the sample.

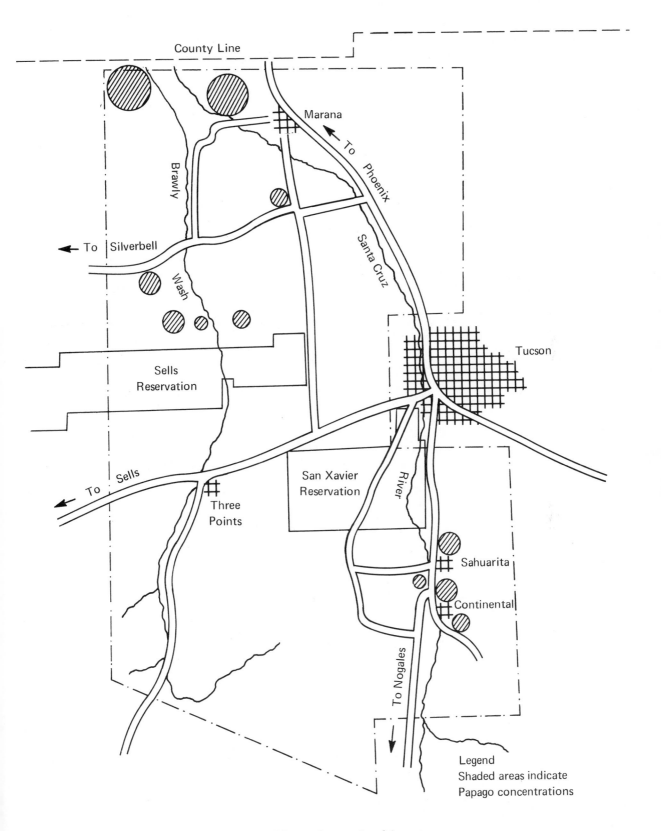

County Line

Marana

To Phoenix

Brawly

To Silverbell

Santa Cruz

Wash

Tucson

Sells
Reservation

San Xavier
Reservation

River

To Sells

Three
Points

Sahuarita

Continental

To Nogales

Legend
Shaded areas indicate
Papago concentrations

Figure 6. Marana Occupational Area

border and scattering among the Pimas, with only San Xavier del Bac remaining as a sizable settlement (Underhill 1939: 17). The Apache attacks caused a general abandonment of the eastern riverine villages and made the whole area very inhospitable to Spanish settlement. Nonetheless, the rich lands prompted the importation of cattle from further south in Sonora, and as early as 1720 there were great cattle increases (McClintock 1916: 446). But the herds were constantly killed or driven off. Ranches such as those at Calabasas, Revanton, Sopori, and Arivaca did last for some time, however. As McClintock (1916: 446) mentions,

. . . around 1820 a number of great ranchos had been established, mainly in the upper San Pedro and Santa Cruz valleys, where yet are to be seen the ruins of large haciendas. By 1843 the Indians had become so bold that the last of these haciendas had been abandoned and the population of the region had been concentrated in the walled presidios of Tucson and Santa Cruz.

During this period of Spanish settlement in the latter part of the eighteenth century and the first part of the nineteenth century, the majority of interests in the area centered in ranching and mining ventures. As Wyllys (1950: 256) observes:

. . . The Spanish-American settlers raised little more than enough for themselves and their animals. The owners of such great haciendas as Arivaca, Revanton and Sopori seem to have been much more interested in cattle raising than in the cultivation of the soil. Nevertheless, there are traces, along the Santa Cruz, of Spanish-made "acequias" or irrigation ditches leading out from the river to small enclosed vegetable gardens and to larger grain fields.

Some of the same haciendas also served as centers for mining operations, so farming as a commercial enterprise was largely nonexistent.

The presidios at Tubac and Tucson date from 1753 and 1776, respectively. These served as Spanish presidios to protect settlers from hostile Apaches. When Browne and Poston made their journey southward along the Santa Cruz, the land between the Gila River and Tucson was described as ". . . a hard, gravelly desert, partially covered with a scrubby growth of mesquite and cactus, and . . . destitute of water except at two or three points, where wells dug by the Overland Mail Company still remain" (Browne 1950: 129-30). Browne noted (p. 135) that the threat of the Apaches prevented grazing or much cultivation

beyond three miles of Tucson, although the Papagos could be counted on to follow up and kill menacing Apaches. He spoke of

. . . abundant tracts of rich arable lands lying within a few miles, upon which it would be mere pastime for the men to raise fifty or sixty bushels of wheat or corn to the acre at the extra compensation of fifty-cents per day — convenient places where the Papagoes would be willing to protect them from the Apaches for the trifling consideration of a few strings of beads or yards of manta (Browne 1950: 136).

The two or three hundred Papagos who had settled around the mission were described as peaceable, industrious, and friendly. They cultivated the low grounds in the vicinity by a system of irrigation (pp. 140-1). Both Browne and Poston (pp. 144, 252) describe the Santa Cruz Valley as one of the richest grazing and agricultural regions they had seen, but both were equally depressed with the thought that such a promising country could be so desolate because of the depredations of the Apaches. The only relatively secure places to carry on such activities were at Tucson and at San Xavier, although the area along the Santa Cruz had been extensively cultivated prior to 1854 (Bartlett 1854: 295).

To what extent Papagos in the Santa Cruz Valley area worked for the Anglo or Mexican ranchers and farmers is difficult to document. The historical sources consulted in this brief overview seem to speak of the majority of Papagos as subsisting on their own efforts. The most frequent references having to do with their use by Anglo settlers speak of Papagos as useful trackers and killers of Apaches; as protectors from the Apaches; or as scouts, guides, and interpreters (Browne 1950: 135, 257, 288). In the Commissioner of Indian Affairs Annual Report (1865: 31), the agent serving the Papagos reports that they ". . . have from time to time furnished soldiers to aid the whites against the inroads of the Apaches, and have been very efficient." The deputy agent, C. H. Lord describes Papago activity in his report (Commissioner of Indian Affairs 1866: 113): "At present they are a source of much assistance to the whites struggling to open the country; as laborers they are excellent help."

Hinton (1878: 187) mentions a temporary camp of 100 Papagos in the vicinity of Tubac prior to 1861, but there is no mention of any activities related to the interests of the mixed settlement of Anglos and Mexicans. Around Tucson there was little demand for labor:

Mexican field hands are not so much above the Chinese level as to habits and compensation. They get fifteen dollars per month and sixty pounds of flour, eight pounds of beans and four pounds of salt, or one dollar a day and board themselves (Hinton 1878: 268).

There is no mention of Papagos working as farm hands for Anglos or Mexicans. Instead, Papagos are referred to as having always been self-supporting, depending on cultivated wheat, corn, pumpkins, and melons but principally on stock (Hinton 1878: 286, 365). Individuals or small associations of Anglo or Mexican cultivators had, at the same time, several thousand acres under some kind of cultivation in the Santa Cruz and its lateral valleys (pp. 286, 305-6), so there would seem to be some opportunities to utilize the services of the Papagos. The Commissioner of Indian Affairs (1876: 8) reported that the Papagos found considerable employment among the settlers and that they were a valuable aid in harvesting fields as well as good workers in towns and mines. The Indian agents were probably more familiar with the activities of Papagos under their eyes than were travelers and townsmen, and in the light of known Papago patterns of periodic work-exchange for Mexicans and Pimas, the agents' statements are probably more accurate.

The Indian agents, in a series of annual reports to the Commissioner of Indian Affairs, present a little different picture of the activities of Papagos in the vicinity of their jurisdiction. There is the continued acknowledgment of their valuable services as soldiers (1865: 13; 1866: 113; 1867: 65). They are still described as being nomadic agricultural people, cultivating lands in the valleys but also dependent on the hunting of game and desert plants or, finally, being "compelled to seek employment and food in more favored localities" (1867: 164). R. A. Wilbur, agent for the Papagos, reported:

. . . they have been orderly, industrious and anxious in every way to show their appreciation of the efforts being made in their behalf. . . . The tribe is still broken up and scattered over a large stretch of country. . . . As has long been their custom in the harvest season, they came in this year from various villages, to engage as laborers in the grain-fields, and their assistance is valuable to the farmers. . . . They have again commenced to scatter through the southern

part of the Territory and northern portion of Sonora, engaging as laborers where they can, or gathering such of the natural products of the country as they can find for their winter wants (Commissioner of Indian Affairs 1872: 320-1).

At any rate, Papago involvement on farms in the area now comprising Pima County in the latter part of the nineteenth century could not have been extensive because the operations were on a very small scale, and there was no great demand for hired farm laborers. As Peplow (1958: 329) suggests,

. . . the interest of the early white man in Arizona was centered mainly upon mining and secondarily upon livestock. What farming had been undertaken prior to the Civil War was, like most other white men's ventures in Arizona, completely wiped out by the Apaches as soon as the Federal troops were removed during the early Civil War days.

But it was not long after the Civil War that a variety of agricultural practices began in earnest. These developments, mainly in the Santa Cruz and its lateral valleys, are of major interest.

While cotton was grown in the vicinity as early as 1874 (Martin 1963) and near Phoenix a year earlier (Wyllys 1950: 265), it was not until a whole series of congressional land acts was approved that irrigation on a large scale became possible: the Homestead Act of 1862 made lands accessible; in 1866 and 1870, territories were granted some degree of control over the construction of canals and the development of irrigation; the Desert Land Act of 1877 permitted settlers to get title to 640 acres of desert land provided they irrigate the land within three years and pay a small sum per acre; the Carey Act of 1894 allowed states to make contacts with promoters who would sell to persons interested in settling it, irrigating it, and cultivating it (Wyllys 1950: 259-60).

During the period of these land acts, a number of communities (Phoenix, Tempe, Mesa, Buckeye, Peoria, and Glendale) emerged as a result of settlement from different parts of the United States (Wyllys 1950: 227). In conjunction with the appearance of the farming towns was the start of irrigating in the Salt and middle Gila valleys with the building of canals and the location of several hundred immigrant families. The earliest irrigation of the Casa Grande Valley, stretching over the same area dotted by ancient irrigation canals, dates back to 1870 when there were six small ditches. In 1884 the Florence canal was begun, consolidating the smaller ditches (McClintock 1916: 442). By 1884 several canals fed 45,000 acres of land, and 35,000 acres were under cultivation. Canals were owned by incorporated companies of farmers who held shares of water-rights entitling each holder to enough water to irrigate 160 acres of land (Wyllys 1950: 257).

During these developments, some of the first considerations were being given to the growth of commercial cotton in the Salt River Valley (Martin 1963). By 1900, both Federal government sponsored and aided programs, such as the Salt River Valley Project, and the many little irrigated districts along the Santa Cruz under private group enterprise were the beginnings of large-scale commercial farming in Arizona (Wyllys 1950: 261).

The first experimental plantings of Egyptian cotton took place in the Salt River and Yuma River valleys in 1902, but the first commercial crops from the same areas were not produced until 1912, the first in Arizona (McGowan 1961: 60).[5] The first large-scale production of cotton occurred south of Tempe in 1916 with 275 acres of scientifically cultivated cotton. By 1918, the Southwest Cotton Company, a subsidiary of the Goodyear Tire and Rubber Company, was the largest cotton grower. It built two towns, Goodyear and Litchfield, and employed 2,500 men. South of present-day Chandler, under the direction of Dr. A. J. Chandler, 8,000 acres were developed with the construction of irrigation systems (Peplow 1958: 333-4). Such farming centers as Coldwater, Chandler, Tolleson, Gilbert, Scottsdale, Laveen, and Alhambra all came into being during these commercial farming developments after statehood in 1912 (Wyllys 1950: 227).

For the Santa Cruz Valley and the area under consideration in this chapter, most irrigation projects up to the end of the nineteenth century were those carried on by private initiative (Peplow 1958: 337). Most of the small farming communities now dotting the floodplain of the Santa Cruz in Pima County were either nonexistent or were just forming at the beginning of the twentieth century. Sahuarita settlement had sprung up around the James Brown ranch about 1879 with a school house and stage station, but with the selling of the Sahuarita ranch in 1886, the settlement fell into decline until 1911 when a railroad station and a post office were established (Barnes 1960: 278). Continental, a few miles further south, came into being in 1914 when the Continental Rubber Company purchased part of the Canoa Land Grant (Canoa Ranch). In 1917, a railroad terminal and a post office existed, as well as headquarters for a *guayule* rubber operation, which was discontinued in 1929 (p. 263).

Land around Marana was first cleared in 1909 by a man named Post, and in 1910 the small community of Postvale grew up along the Santa Cruz. A post office was established in 1920. The railroad name for the point was Marana, meaning a "tangle of brush" or "brambles", which characterized the surrounding landscape. A post office was established in 1924, and by 1925 Postvale and Marana had consolidated under the name of Marana (Barnes 1960: 271-2). In 1920 a post office was established in Cortaro, the center of location for Cortaro Farms lying along the Santa Cruz between Marana and Tucson; Avra, lying on a tributary of the Santa Cruz, had a post office by 1932 (pp. 259, 264).

In 1909 there were 6,000 acres being irrigated and cropped along the Santa Cruz and its tributaries (Forbes 1911: 80-1). Forbes (p. 77) describes the area:

The San Pedro and Santa Cruz Valleys resemble the Upper Gila agriculturally. . . . The Santa Cruz Valley is less developed than the San Pedro, partly because railroad connections have not been so good until recently. Summer flood waters are utilized on both these streams for a quick-growing crop of corn planted in July and harvested in October, while in similar manner the winter rains afford water for crops of wheat and barley harvested in May.

Forbes (1911: 77) further notes that there were 45 small canals from the San Pedro and 60 small canals from the Santa Cruz to channel the water to the fields. This suggests a network of small, individual cultivators along these rivers around 1910. McClintock (1916: 444) mentions further agricultural development in the same area shortly thereafter:

During the past few years [after 1910 and before 1916 when McClintock's work was published] a Chicago corporation has spent over $1,000,000 in the purchase of lands along the Santa Cruz and in the installation of an irrigation system that has served to add a considerable farming community within a short distance of Tucson [Cortaro Farms?].

---

[5] McGowan (1961: 62) credits Herbert Atha, whose farm was seven miles north of Phoenix, with the first commercial crop in 1911. The crop was sold for $100. The 1912 effort involved 75 farmers in the Salt River Valley plus 44 farmers from Yuma and Imperial Valley, California.

In an undated brochure put out by the Agriculture Bureau of the Tucson Chamber of Commerce, Brown (n.d.: 1) mentions that the Santa Cruz and Rillito valleys, the principal sections in Pima County under cultivation, had been farmed on an extensive scale only a few years. The main crops produced on the 18,000 acres of irrigated land were alfalfa, barley, beans, corn, wheat, peanuts, and cotton. According to Brown (p. 4), it was the first season for commercially produced cotton in Pima County and there was a plentiful supply of laborers, who were paid $2.50 to $3.00 per day without board. McGowan (1961: 83-4) mentions that in 1918, 69,000 of the 72,000 acres growing American-Egyptian cotton were in the Salt River Valley; but the practice was spreading to the Casa Grande and Florence area as well as to the Santa Cruz Valley near Tucson.

In the light of the dates and other information presented above, the time of Brown's brochure might be dated around 1918 or 1919. McGowan (1961: 86-7) seems to date the pamphlet when he mentions that in 1918 only 150 acres were planted in cotton, and in 1919 it had jumped to 1,100. By 1920, 4,000 acres of cotton were planted, with the Tucson Farms Company having some success; and one company claimed 250 men had purchased cotton land in its irrigation project.

A pamphlet printed in 1925 concerning the Pima Farms at Cortaro 12 miles northwest of Tucson (Pima Farms 1925: 6) mentions a strip of 14,500 acres along the Santa Cruz, 10,000 of which were cultivated by "practical farmers." The same brochure (p. 6) states that 12,500 acres of cotton were under cultivation for all of Pima County. The planting season began in April and picking began in September, for which there was reported to be an adequate supply of labor. The wage rate at the time was 1.5 cents per pound of cotton picked. The report mentions the large number of Yaquis (p. 9), but nothing is said of Papagos. The Cortaro operation had over 75 miles of main canals and laterals, 18 miles of the main canals being concrete lined (p. 8).

In 1920, many cotton growers were wiped out, and the big companies even suffered. By 1924, and certainly by 1926, the setback of the early 1920s had been reversed, largely due to the fact that farmers became less obsessed with exclusive planting of cotton and returned to diversified farming (Brown and Cassmore 1939: 50; McGowan 1961: 89-90). The depression of the early thirties brought another

collapse, with some recovery by 1934, and commercial production reached a peak in 1937 with the largest cotton crop in Arizona's cotton-growing history to that time (Brown and Cassmore 1939: 49-50).

Papagos were involved in hand labor as cotton pickers as early as 1913 when they, along with Pimas, earned about $20,000 for cotton picking in the Salt River Valley. Large crops were produced in 1913-14 near Mesa and Tempe, for which Indians were trained as pickers at Sacaton. They earned the reputation of being slow but good pickers (McGowan 1961: 68). Before 1925, Papagos were involved to some extent in the Salt River Valley in the Phoenix area,[6] but cotton farming on a large scale was not under way in Pima County until about 1925 (12,500 acres). This is not to say that Papagos were not working as farm hands for the other crops being cultivated; but whatever their involvement in farm wage labor, there are no figures that indicate to what extent.

By 1937, the demand for workers in the cotton harvest was so great that it could not be met by available local or domestic workers. Thus there was extensive recruiting of migrant workers outside of Arizona and about 30,000 of the 37,000 cotton labor force were from Texas, Oklahoma, Missouri, and Arkansas (Brown and Cassmore 1939: xix, 61). The resident Spanish Americans and Negroes, unemployed miners, stay-over, out-of-state migrants from prior years, and Indians could supply only a small proportion of the demand (p. 63). Due to extensive road building and other government programs on the reservation during the thirties, Papagos were able to stay home and work for wages. This is an important factor behind the inability of Papagos to meet the growing demand for cotton laborers during the period. This was certainly true in Pima County, where the sizable Spanish-American and Indian populations, combined with other local workers, amounted to only one-third of the actual Pima County pickers. The rest were out-of-state migrants (p. 62).

It appears, as Dobyns (1950: 63) observes, that a few of the cotton farms' camps have been in use for several decades, but most are quite new since expanded cotton production is of a recent date, much of it after World War II. However, Brown and Cassmore (1939: 6) noted in 1937-38 several good camps, such as the "two spacious tent cities" on Cortaro

---

[6]See the occupational history of the extended family of informant Raymond Victor in Chapter 6.

Farms property, which were built on wooden platforms, provided with showers, laundry facilities, electric street lights, and under the care of superintendents and nursing services. This suggests no small operation, but once again we are in the dark about how many Papagos were involved. While Papagos have been known to participate in the cotton harvest for many years, the number that have moved to the farms and taken more or less permanent jobs as farm hands has increased steadily since 1945 (Dobyns 1950: 23). Dobyns (p. 22) estimated about 800 "permanently" off-reservation in 1950, including 200 workers, their wives, and their families. His estimate is based on the fact that one-fifth of all his interviews were of this type.

Certainly the overpopulation of lands plus other inducements have been behind this trend. Padfield (1961: 24-5) provides further support for this trend. His data suggest that there must be 400 adult male Papagos in Pima County, with Papagos accounting for one-third of all farm work in the county; two-thirds of those in farm work are not just seasonal workers, although they are not all permanent. In 1961, there were 66,875 acres of Pima County cropland under irrigation (p. 8). Thus, commercial farming in the Marana occupational area has grown significantly since its beginnings, with an increasing use of Papagos as steady, year-round hands.

Figure 6 portrays the entire Marana area and Figure 7 depicts the ecological domain of one of the major commercial farming complexes within the area. The whole area consists of many commercial farming operations of various sizes. The activities of each complex are oriented largely either to the farming towns of Marana or Sahuarita or, for some purposes,

to Tucson. Each farming center has market, educational, religious, political, and, to some extent, recreational facilities, although residents are dependent upon Tucson for additional services such as additional educational opportunities, health services, better market facilities, and more diversified recreational privileges. Despite these orientations to the urban center, most of the day-by-day activities are within the areas where people live and work. These are the contexts or socioecological environments in which Papagos are functioning and adapting their roles.

The Papago Population Register (1959) enumerates 66 Papago men of employable age (15-65) residing within the area in 1959, 38 in the Marana vicinity, 24 in the Shauarita-Continental vicinity, and 4 in the vicinity of Three Points (Table 8).

The register data provide a general picture of Papagos in the area for one specific year and include a general summary of each individual's employment history. Fifty-one (77%) are coded as being oriented off-reservation in relatively permanent reliance on farm labor of some sort, while six (9%) are coded as being in school. Of the remainder (14% of the total) five have no employment information provided and four have some other pattern than regular off-reservation farm labor.

The employment data for the 1959 study are rather incomplete, however. Padfield (1961) helps to fill in some of the details regarding the nature and range of variation of Papago employment in the Marana occupational area through his pilot study of the Papago farm worker in Pima County. His sample included 20 percent of all Pima County farm owner/-operators (21 of 119 operators) and 44.5 percent of all

TABLE 8

Papago Men (ages 15-65) in Marana Occupational Area According to Age and Locality, 1959

	Age				
	15-19	20-29	30-49	Over 50	Total
Marana-Avra Valley	3	12	20	3	38
Sahuarita-Continental	6	4	8	6	24
Three Points	1	1	2	0	4
	10	17	30	9	66

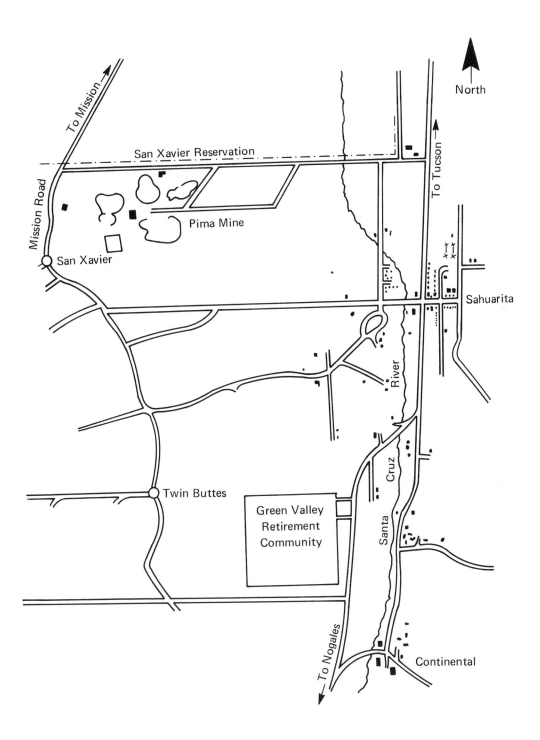

Figure 7. Ecological Domain of the Sahuarita-Continental Occupational Complex

TABLE 9

Number of Employees Reported by 20 Farms in Pima County, 1961

	Total	Percent	Full-time	Percent	Part-time	Percent
Non-Indian	207	43	160	81	47	16
All Indians	271	57	37	19	234	84
Papagos	253	53	29	15	224	79
Total	478*	100	197	100	281†	100

*Does not include 21 non-Indians and 15 Papago Indians from the sample who were working at a farm located in Pinal County.

†In most instances part-time employees were distinguished from those employed by contractors for seasonal work, but a few of the operators reported contracted workers along with temporary or part-time hands. This confuses the "part-time" category somewhat, although in reporting Papagos they named only those who were hired directly by the farm. Papago workers named as part-time hands numbered 22 individuals, in contrast to the 193 unnamed Papagos who were contracted.

land under irrigation (29,767 of 66,875 acres). Table 9 represents a breakdown of the number of employees that 20 operators in the sample reported to Padfield.[7]

Of the 253 Papagos reported as employed in some manner, the 29 full-time and the 22 part-time Papagos are the most significant for this discussion. While Papagos made up 53 percent (253) of the entire Pima County farm labor sample, or one-half of the work force on 20 farms, the 51 full-time or part-time Papagos together make up about 10 percent, or about one-tenth of the entire farm worker sample. A number of unemployed or spottily employed adult males attached to households of these more permanent off-reservation workers would be expected; hence, there would be more off-reservation Papago men residentially oriented than the counting of employed Papagos would imply. This is especially so in the case of so many seasonally contracted workers.

The 1959 enumeration of 66 employable Papago males living in the Marana occupational area (Table 8) is not too incompatible with the 51 Papago males involved in full-time or part-time work in the same area in 1961 (Table 9). While not too much should be made of the comparability of these two sets of figures, they do suggest a general picture of the number of Papagos participating more or less permanently in this particular off-reservation farming

area. A number of them are rather steady farm hands with long periods of residence in the area, perhaps being in the employ of one or two farms for many years. Others have only part-time involvement as farm hands but maintain residence in the area most or all of the year. A larger number maintain very brief residence during the seasonal height and work through contractors. Table 10 depicts the amount of tenure that each Papago in Padfield's study had at the particular farm reporting him as a part-time or full-time employee.

The data thus far have shown a considerable number of Papagos whose lives have been somewhat oriented to specific complexes of institutions associated with the particular farming institutions in which they enact their occupational roles. An even larger number come to participate to some extent as they make temporary residences at farm camps or as they commute daily from the nearby reservations. In either case, they rely heavily on contractors, although there are some who make their own contacts at farms which have long entertained these direct contacts.

The Sahuarita community is depicted in Fig. 8. There are a number of institutions in which social activities for the surrounding farming area take place. Papagos, as residents within the farming complex, orient their behaviors toward some of these institutions. Prolonged participation would be expected to bear signs of assimilation of the dominant values which lie behind these institutions. The nature of the participation and the specific ways behaviors are accommodated to the forces of assimilative change need to be exposed through observing behavioral

[7]The data have been derived by the study of Padfield's field schedules on file in the Bureau of Ethnic Research, Department of Anthropology, University of Arizona, Tucson.

roles of individuals involved in the activities of the complex. This is the central intention of this study.

Continental is the other small community within the larger Sahuarita-Continental complex and consists of a shop and office for the same large company that has offices in Sahuarita and Tucson. In addition, there are smaller, independent farms surrounding Continental with their own labor camps. The main company has a labor camp in the town as well as near the large stock yard. There is also a general store run by a Chinese family and an elementary school to serve residents of the immediate vicinity.

The procedure of breaking down each unit-complex into still smaller units as has been done by way of example for the Marana occupational area, could be done for the other areas in a similar manner. First, there is a general geographical area (the Marana occupational area) within which there is a prevailing type of economic activity involving a number of occupational activities. The general occupational area can then be divided into still smaller complexes of activities which center in specific towns (the Sahuarita-Continental Commercial Farm Occupational Complex). A still smaller unit-complex is a specific town and its local institutions and activities (the Sahuarita community). A last unit-complex would be a particular farm, its organization, its settlement arrangements, and its complement of family groups and individuals performing a range of occupational roles (Barnes Farm, Figure 9).

TABLE 10

Tenure of Full-Time or Part-Time Papago Farm Workers at 20 Farms in Pima County, 1961

Tenure	Full-time	Part-time	Total
15 to 20 years	3	1	4
10 to 14 years	7	2	9
5 to 9 years	6	1	7
1 to 4 years	10	13	23
First year	1	4	5
	27*	21†	48

*In two cases, tenure not reported.

†In one case, tenure not reported.

In this kind of approach to the social fields in which individuals operate, it is possible to link individual behavior to the environments — physical, social, and mental — in which they are found to be living much of their daily lives. By extending the analysis to an additional unit-field, it is possible to construct a larger environment of culture contact in which Papagos interact and to which they react. Once the complex-units are demonstrated empirically, they can be compared with other similar units for ascertaining their shared features. This leads, finally, to a statement of general propositions about the Farm Occupational Complex type.

STRUCTURAL CHARACTERISTICS OF THE COMMERCIAL FARM OCCUPATIONAL COMPLEX

If the Coolidge and Gila Bend occupational areas are similarly broken down into commercial farming complexes oriented to certain town centers and made up of specific farms, certain shared features should be noticeable. Using the above discussion of the Marana area and the impressions gained from field work in the other two areas, the general characteristics for all farm occupational complexes can be established.

First, the Commercial Farm Occupational Complex revolves around the production of a marketable crop, a sufficiently large operation demanding some cooperative utilization of the resources (ginning facilities, water, labor supply, etc.) of an area by a number of independent farm complexes. The complex also consists of institutions (schools, stores,

churches, public health facilities, etc.) that serve the people in the area.

Second, the type of operation and the tradition of the commercial operation demands a large supply of unskilled and a smaller group of semiskilled or skilled agricultural laborers. In the case of southern Arizona, the proximity of Papago, Pima, and Yaqui Indians as well as the availability of Mexican-Americans, Negroes, and members of other ethnic groups as laborers, makes the occupational complex an arena of sociocultural contact. That is, the institutions of the dominant society act as agents for inducing behaviors which are compatible with the values and norms of the dominant system. Further, cultural behaviors that characterize particular cultural or ethnic group values

46

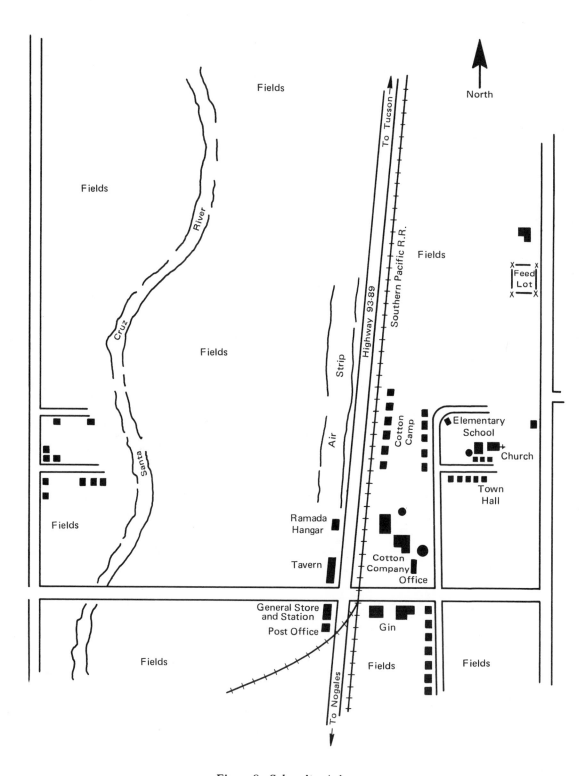

Figure 8. Sahuarita, Arizona

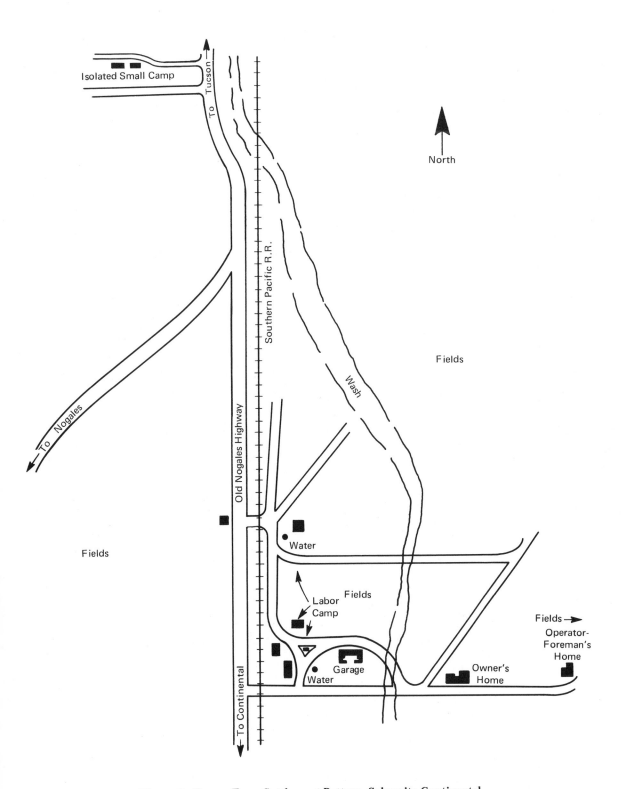

Figure 9. Barnes Farm Settlement Pattern, Sahuarita-Continental

and norms must in some manner confront the prevailing Anglo values and norms. Commercial farm organization and management in southern Arizona is in itself an agent of cultural contact and provides an environment where these contact situations occur. Commercial farms provide familiar occupational roles and offer opportunities for earning minimal but essential wages in familiar physical and social surroundings. But in so doing, the work situations they make available to Papagos demand certain kinds of work and extra-work participations which differ from those demanded by life on the reservation.

Third, to more readily utilize the unskilled members of ethnic groups, the commercial farm complexes attempt to reduce the factors which threaten a dependable labor force. The farms provide some means of settling families or individual workers in residences that are accessible to the sources of work and that are available with little or no cost to low income groups. They also deal with the high turnover rates and absenteeism that characterize the occupational behavior of low income transient peoples. In other words, commercial farms institutionalize certain hiring, firing, or "laying off" practices and must accommodate their operations to the values and behaviors which are characteristic of the specific cultural or ethnic groups on which they rely. Farm operators come to know the channels whereby they can refill a constantly depleting pool of workers to do specific jobs-at-hand, whether it be through independent labor contractors or through the informal channel of "someone knows someone else." A cheap but exploitable labor supply is a vital element in the risks of market-farming, and commercial farms seek to stabilize or institutionalize their access to their supply as well as the performances they expect. For instance, workers must have access to grocery markets in town without the danger of employees lingering to get drunk; hence, one of a farm's trucks may make regular trips to the store on weekends with a load of employees and try to get them back to their houses at the camp.

Finally, a certain number of full-time or more permanent type of jobs are essential to the successful operation of farms within a complex. Therefore, certain workers of demonstrated worth do have access to a select number of steadier jobs, such as a regular farm hand, an equipment operator, or an irrigator. The farm complex thereby encourages a stabilization of some work roles by providing longer term jobs for those who can accommodate their personal behaviors to certain central-role elements, and perhaps a minimum number of peripheral-role elements, demanded by specific jobs. This is certainly a crucial type of contact situation, where the demands of employer confront the cultural behavior or the style of life of an individual. Regardless of the particular occupational area or the specific farm complex, these features appear to characterize the commercial farm type.

RANGE OF VARIATION IN OCCUPATIONAL STATUSES AND ROLES

Thus far, studies of Papago farm labor (Dobyns 1950; Padfield 1961) have revealed a somewhat limited range of occupational statuses and roles. The nature of the commercial enterprise is in itself restrictive in this sense, although the range of skills is greater than Papagos have succeeded in actually filling. Padfield's sample provides data on 51 full-time and part-time Papago laborers on Pima County farms. Table 11 summarizes his data on the range of skills and the accompanying wages for 49 of the 51 Papagos.

A crucial question in dealing with Papago off-reservation farm work concerns whether or not there is any detectable pattern in terms of stabilizing work roles into some degree of permanency. It is, of course, very difficult to ascertain any "stabilized" pattern in young Papago men under thirty; although some may indicate, in their early twenties, a tendency to stick it out in a particular job. In most cases, however, the earlier periods of manhood appear to be times of shifting about, or trying relocation, or going away to make a trial at a vocational school or military service. For this reason, there are certain features that have been sought in an individual Papago's work history which indicate the stabilization of an off-reservation occupational and residence pattern.

First, the major attention has been focused, for the most part, on Papago individuals 35 years of age and older; although in some field contacts younger men were occasionally interviewed. The individual

TABLE 11

Papago Work Statuses on 20 Pima County Farms, 1961

Statuses	Full-time	Part-time	Total	Hourly Wage Rate Range
Equipment operator	17	6	23	$0.85 - $1.25
General hand (including equipment)	5	6	11	$0.70 - $1.00
Irrigator	6	9	15	$0.65 - $1.00
	28	21	49	

must, therefore, exhibit in his overall work history at least ten years of commercial farm work with a predominant year-round residence in a geographically limited area, although occasional contacts with his reservation kinship villages may have been maintained. In most cases, the availability of farm work and the services of the farm complex tend to restrict reservation residence to infrequent and spasmodic visits.

Next, the individual need not necessarily restrict his work activity to one farm or locale, but his entire pattern reveals a tendency to be restricted to a major occupational area over at least a ten-year period, with at least eight months of each year attached to some type of wage work on a commercial farm.

Third, the prolonged residential and occupational pattern emerges after the individual has spent a period of several years as a seasonal farm laborer, and more than likely he becomes established at a farm or in a locale where wage work was established by a preceding generation.

Further, although the period of employment may limit full participation in reservation activities, the reservation village may remain as a source of emotional sustenance or a place to which to return if the farm complex no longer provides an adequate source of economic and emotional satisfaction.

Finally, the occupational roles in a stabilized pattern consist of other roles besides a total reliance on contractors for chopping and picking; that is, the occupational roles characterize steady farm hands, although work may not be available for the whole year. Even during slack periods, residence is maintained off-reservation except for periodic reservation visits.

Individuals who have thus stabilized a pattern of work are apt to be those Papagos whose interactions within the occupational complex contact environment have been more prolonged and intense. At the same time, the stable pattern may be nothing more than a satisfactory accommodation to the new behaviors confronted in the complex of institutions, and assimilation may not be necessary in achieving certain expectations that individuals may map out for themselves. In other words, permanent farm-worker Papagos may have proven more adaptable to certain situations to which their activities have exposed them, but they may not necessarily be the most assimilated of Papago farm workers in terms of assimilating Anglo values and norms.

Participants in the Commercial Farm Occupational Complex are of several kinds. They may be drifters or those who shift from complex to complex without any lasting commitments to a single farm complex or farming area. These have prolonged periods of idleness or incarceration, picking up only spotty work. Then there are the workers from either off-reservation or from reservation villages who follow seasonal harvests, either by relying on contractors or going directly to farms where they and their kinsmen before them have cultivated attachments to specific farms and areas. Once the season is over, they return to their usual residences and activities. Another kind consists of those Papagos who become seasonal farm hands and take on a more permanent off-reservation residence status, although much of the year may find them idle. Last there are the steady hands, or those who are usually available on either a full-time or part-time basis because they have proven to be dependable employees. They are usually equipment operators, general hands, irrigators, or cowboys. The steady hand category has been discussed in the preceding paragraphs and constitutes the category of Papagos with the most stabilized patterns.

TABLE 12

Lifetime Work Patterns of 25 Papago Commercial Farm Workers, 1964-65

	Age Category			
	35-49	50-65	Over 65	Totals
Predominant farm pattern for over 10 years	15	9	1	25
Life-time off-reservation pattern	8	4	0	12
Predominant farm pattern for last 10 years	15	4	0	19
Predominant farm pattern but not in 1964	1	4	1	6
Other-than-farm work experience	3	3	0	6

An inspection of the Papago work schedules obtained by the Bureau of Ethnic Research in its 1964-65 Papago Employment Survey reveals that of the 300 interviews conducted, 25 Papago men over 35 years of age had work histories which could be classified as predominantly off-reservation with stabilized patterns in commercial farm occupational complexes. Table 12 sums up the lifetime work histories of these 25 Papagos. It further provides a body of data about the kinds of work patterns that characterize Papago farm workers who have achieved relatively stable attachments to some type of farm complex.

These 25 individuals are the only ones in the entire sample of 300 Papagos who reported relatively steady employment patterns on commercial farms for a period of ten years or longer. Of the 25, six had terminated their patterns and returned to reservation homes after long periods of residence on Arizona farms. Only six individuals had had any other-than-farm experience — four at the Ajo mine in their earlier years, one on construction, and one with a railroad gang. Many others of the sample, of course, reported some kind of seasonal or intermittent involvement in some off-reservation farm complex; but the data provided in the schedules did not reveal any immediately apparent patterns.

4. AJO MINE OCCUPATIONAL COMPLEX

The Ajo open pit copper mine is an operation of the Phelps Dodge Corporation, New Cornelia Branch, located in western Pima County at the mining town of Ajo, Arizona. The operation of this mining enterprise, in both the historical and contemporary sense, has played a significant role in the changing life of a considerable number of Papago Indians. Ajo, as a one-industry town, or as a "company town," provides a unique complex of institutions which Papagos encounter through their participation in the mining operation.

Leonard (1954: 48) notes that in 1950 the community of 6,588 people drew $5,953,000 in wages and salaries, amounting to $904 per capita, the latter being almost $200 more than the per capita figure for the whole of Arizona and comparable to the national per capita figure. These wages and salaries, springing largely from the one industry source, accounted for 65 percent of total income payments. The activities related to the actual mining operation (the pit, the concentrator, the smelter, and the railroads) are basic activities, and the small proportion of the employment that is marginal to the mining operation itself, such as businesses, is not at all proportional to the number dependent on the mine. In 1950, for example, basic employment or direct employment in some phase of the mining operation amounted to 1,126 individuals, as compared with 383 individuals employed in business activities not directly a part of the mining operation but dependent, obviously, on it (Leonard 1954: 38). Hence, the Ajo complex of institutions clusters around and is dependent on the operations of Phelps Dodge.

It is within this social system or complex that many Papagos have come to confront certain aspects of the dominant system of Anglo institutions and values. In other words, the Ajo mining operation, which has relied heavily for years on Indian labor, provides an identifiable social context where Papagos straddle Papago and non-Papago environments and are thus enmeshed in acculturative processes, some of which we hope to identify in the course of this research.

TEMPORAL, SPATIAL, AND DEMOGRAPHIC FEATURES

In our utilization of the concept of occupational complex as an environment of adaptation for Papagos, it is important to identify the "environment" in its total dimensions, both temporally and spatially, as well as to point out the particular structural features as they impinge on Papago individuals. Delineating the time perspective is a sizable undertaking, and for this particular area, the past, not only as it pertains to the Papagos but also as it concerns mining operations utilizing them, is shrouded in either mystery, myth, or speculation. It is possible to reconstruct, with some degree of accuracy, a little of the historical background pertaining to the emergence of this particular occupational complex as it has involved Papagos.

The Ajo complex lies in the eastern portion of the Sonoran Desert region occupied by the so-called Sand Papagos (Clotts 1915: 76, 77; Bryan 1925: 417; Joseph, Spicer, and Chesky 1949: 69; Dobyns 1954: 27ff; Hackenberg 1964: IV-2). In this Arizona Upland, there are water sources and flora and fauna that could well have supported Papago subsistence patterns. Occupancy depended on the conjunction of food and water sources within the extensive Sonoran Desert region. While the most favorable area was the Sierra Pinacate vicinity 40 miles southwest of Sonoita, the Growler Pass area, just south of present-day Ajo in the Organ Pipe National Monument, was rich enough in resources to support roving bands with hunting and camping sites, although the lack of a surface water supply would not support permanent settlement (Hackenberg 1964: IV-17).

In historic times, Quitovac, in the same vicinity, has been known as an old head village for other settlements of Papagos in the Sonoita Valley (Hackenberg 1964: IV-21). Hackenberg (p. IV-26) further notes that during Anza's time, around 1774, there were usually wintertime encampments of Papagos in Spanish settlements, when they would abandon their own desert country farther west. The conflicts with the

Mexicans in the 1840s saw a reduction of Papagos in the whole area, but a few survivors remained in the vicinity of Ajo and Sonoita as well as in other Papago rancherias to the east of the Growler and Ajo mountains.

A. B. Gray, while making a survey for the proposed Southern Pacific Railroad in 1854, made reference to Papago Indians who were mining the surface deposits of red oxide and green carbonate of copper, so abundant in the area of the Ajo Mountains (Hackenberg 1964: IV-35). These deposits were used as a source for deriving body paints as well as to trade with the Mexicans (Dobyns 1955: 158).[1] The last two references provide some of the documentation that Rose (1936: 2) fails to provide when he mentions that the Papagos made many expeditions to the water shrine (*moivavi*) to work the native coppers at the site of the shrine. Rose (1936: 3-5) also claims, again without citing a reference source, that Papago tradition says that villages were established near the mines and that expeditions were made to the region of Caborca in Mexico to barter copper and placer gold to the Mexicans. In the early 1800s the Mexicans soon discovered the source and began sending expeditions to exploit the same mines, driving the Papagos from the water shrine. The Mexicans were soon set to flight by the pestering Apaches, and the mines were soon back in the hands of the Papagos.

According to Dobyns (1955: 158), "Living Papagos still retain traditions of their forebears having made use of the spring at the site of the Ajo mine before mining operations began there. Their place name for the spring bears no relation to *ajo*. This term was derived entirely from their custom of mining the brightly-colored copper ores for mineral paints."

These "living Papagos" may be the source for the tradition of the water shrine or *moivavi*[2] of which both Rose and Dobyns speak. In another reference, Dobyns (1954: 31) cites Thomas Childs, Jr., as saying that his party came across some Sand Papagos while it was digging Ten Mile Well near Ajo in 1884, and that in 1886 a number of Papagos fled the Sonoita area and came to live either at or near the Childs's place, part of which is now where the mining operation is conducted. Rose (1936: 14) mentions that Thomas Childs, Sr., and 19 men in his party first came into the Ajo area in 1847 and stopped at *Moivavi* "west" of the mine.

The spring site was not, however, a permanent settlement for Papagos.[3] An 1858 map locates known Sand Papago settlements all to the east of Ajo or south of the Mexican border, and many of the people of these "villages" spent much of the harvest season in Sonora. The occupation of the Quitobaquito, Growler or Bates Well, and other places near Ajo was largely due to intermarriage with non-Indian residents of the area. In 1910 there were about 50 people in all, including some Mexicans, some Papagos, and a few Anglos, the main business being that of cattle grazing (Barnes 1960: 257). Hackenberg (1964: IV- 41) states that ". . . the Indian settlement at Ajo, dated by Childs as no earlier than 1884, is described by Clotts under the name of Ajo Indian Village, or *Moivajea*. At the time of his visit in 1914 it contained five houses, with a population of 29."

A 1915 memorandum by Clotts also states that Ajo employed a few transient Indians in the mines as there were very few Papago families in the vicinity of Ajo. Thus, the actual Ajo Indian settlement and surrounding Papago settlements are very recent, although the general area can lay claim to Papago occupancy for a much longer period (Hackenberg 1964: IV-45).

----

[1] For an interesting discussion of the origin of the name Ajo, see Dobyns (1955), wherein he presents evidence that the term Ajo is not, as popular tradition has made it, the Spanish word for wild garlic but a hispanization of a Papago term *au'auho* for paint. The Quitobaquito band (*Ali Waipa Au'autam*) moved within the territory in which the Ajo Mountains, the valley, the mine, and the town lie. The Indians exploited the surface metals for making body paints, or *au'auho*.

[2] Lumholtz (1912: 383) makes reference to the Papago rancheria Pozos Muchos or, in Papago, *Moivaxia*, meaning "Many Wells," which lies south-southeast of Gila Bend or eight miles east of Sauceda and which had from eight to ten families. These are the site names of Moi Vaya (*Moivaxia*) and Chiulikan (Sauceda), which are in the Hickiwan District. This *Moivaxia* and the *moivavi* (Rose 1936) or *Moivajea* (Hackenberg 1964) springs at the mine site are obviously not the same.

[3] One of my Papago informants, who lays water pipes throughout the extent of the huge pit, mentioned that when they lay some of the pipelines, the crew members run into springs sometimes a half foot to a foot wide, which run down the sides of the pit. He has heard of camps of Papagos that would settle close to the springs, but he has heard this from other Papagos who know more about it. Other townspeople have mentioned to me that there used to be encampments on the south rim of the present pit, but the enlargement of the pit has made any settlement impossible for a long time. I have not pursued this with any other knowledgeable Indians, although I am sure they can be found.

The history of mining operations in the Ajo vicinity is a little clearer and, since there is ample documentation of this (New Cornelia Copper Company n.d.; Mathewson 1933; Rose 1936), only a brief recapitulation as it pertains to Papago employment is necessary.

The finding of primitive mining implements and signs of working the earth indicate that the Ajo mining area may have been worked by Spaniards and Mexicans at least as early as 1750, although the area was abandoned when Childs and his party stopped there in 1847 (Mathewson 1933: 1). With the coming of the Arizona Mining and Trading Company in 1854, intermittent working of the mine continued through to the twentieth century. These operations were shallow surface workings of high grade native copper ore and cuprite ore. The ores were hauled by mule team 400 miles across the desert to San Diego or to Yuma where they were floated down the Colorado River to the Gulf of California to be shipped to Swansea, Wales (New Cornelia Copper Company n.d.: 1-2). Rose (1936: 23) mentions that Peter Brady, one of the leaders of the Arizona Mining and Trading Company, used an Indian friend from *Petato* (Papago word for the vegetable green, lamb's quarter — the Gila Bend of today) to urge Papagos to come to the camp at Ajo where the huskiest and most willing were used to clear the surface ground. He further mentions that they were at first frightened by the blasting and fled to their rancherias, being very reluctant to return to work. There is also reference to some "renegade" Papagos who lived outside the camp and made a nuisance of themselves stealing horses (Rose 1936: 28).

This gives some hint that the Papago settlement at the mine is, as Childs believed, a rather late occurrence. They attached themselves to the mining camp temporarily but maintained their homes in surrounding rancherias and returned there whenever the mining operations came to a halt. Those that did settle in the area of the mine were attached in some way, usually by marriage, to Anglos at the camp. Lumholtz (1912: 336), in his journey through the area in May, 1910, says, "On my return to civilization from Sonoita, I crossed the boundary into Arizona, stopping first at Ajo, the name of an apparently great copper mine, on which work had been temporarily abandoned."

Lumholtz' observation likely was made following the 1907 panic and the boom of 1909-10 after which operations were forced to close, and the life of the Ajo district temporarily ended (New Cornelia Copper Company n.d.: 5). It was after Lumholtz' visit that John Greenway came in 1911 to aid in the consolidation of mine options. Greenway's coming led to the eventual formation of the New Cornelia Copper Company in 1917. Only four Anglos were residing in old Ajo in 1911 when Greenway made his appearance (Barnes 1960: 257). With the exploitation of an underground water supply seven miles to the north and the completion of the plant, the process of mining, transporting, crushing, leaching, and chemically preparing the ores was insured and the venture was on solid ground (New Cornelia Copper Company n.d.: 26; Rose 1936: 52, 54).

With the security of the operation insured, the planned townsite of Ajo emerged, being laid out in mission architecture. In the early years of Ajo, the old-time residents of Ajo and the new mining officialdom had many battles, one of which was a dispute about the location of the townsite. The old town close to the huge deposits objected to the company townsite a mile farther north (where the town now stands). The old Clarkston town, renamed Rowood in 1918, was the more popular site of the two in 1916 but in 1917 went into decline and was largely destroyed by fire in 1931 (Barnes 1960: 263). An early description of the new townsite, presumably recorded sometime between 1917 and 1920, reveals something of the community's planned segregation: "Over the hill toward the mine is the Mexican townsite with its one, two and six family hollow tile houses, all harmonizing with the general architectural plan. The Mexicans take pride in their clean and attractive homes" (New Cornelia Copper Company n.d.: 36).

This reveals that the planners of the townsite actually conceived of segregated communities for Anglos and Mexicans, but nothing is mentioned of a third, or Indian village, townsite; yet, as noted earlier, Clotts mentions that there was a small Indian settlement of five houses and 29 people in 1914. So we can account for three distinct settlements of Anglos, Mexicans, and Indians, each in a well defined location, as early as 1914 and certainly by 1920. This feature [as will be noted] is of significance, although little is said in the literature of Ajo's origins about the Indian community.

In 1917 the New Cornelia Cooperative and Mercantile Company was organized to sell merchandise to

employees. Employees of at least four months' standing with the company could share the annual distribution of profits. The four months' rule was invoked to
promote the stability of the working force. The distribution of profits for the years 1917, 1918, and
1919 is of interest because it reveals that there were
472, 777, and 618 employees in the respective years
(New Cornelia Copper Company n.d.: 57). These
figures give no indication as to how many Indians
shared the employee access to the distribution of
profits.

Although the evidence is sparse, it seems that the
Ajo Indian village noted by Clotts probably was the
one that now exists to the west of the open pit, flank-
ing the eastern slope of the Little Ajo Mountains, just
to the south of Ajo town proper. Other than Clotts's
observation, there is no other demographic description of the Ajo Indian settlement except references
dating back to January 1936 showing the number of
Indians employed in the mine. From these figures, it
may be presumed that the large majority of Indians
and their families attached themselves to the Indian
settlement, thus reinforcing the segregation feature of
the entire Ajo community, a feature which currently
exists.

The company started building the present houses
in the Indian community in 1936 when the first
block of 10 or 15 houses was laid out. Before that
time Indians were leasing small parcels of company
land for one dollar a year and building their own
dwellings out of anything they could manage — tin,
railroad ties, scraps of lumber, or adobe.[4] Two
Papago informants have indicated that when they
began working at the mine in 1941 and 1942, the
company must have just started building the houses
because they were still new; while before that time
Indians either built their own dwellings, rented
houses in Mexican town, or lived in what remained of
the now defunct Rowood or Clarkston community,
where there was a sizable temporary settlement of
Indians.

One Papago employee of long standing at the mine
remembers an interesting bit of historical information.[5] When the mine operation closed down from
1932 through the first few months of 1934, the
Indian community must have been abandoned; for
when the operation resumed, the company sent
trucks out to the reservation villages to round up the
Papagos and bring them in to work in the mine. This
particular individual recalls that they were brought in

and dumped out where the present Indian community now stands. At that time there were some old
abandoned adobe houses, some makeshift houses of
different materials, and a few scattered health service
latrines that must have been used by Papagos prior to
the shutdown. They had to make their own fires and
repair what was there until the company began building low-rent houses for them in 1936. This innovation
by the company has proceeded gradually up to the
present time. Some Indians continued to lease land
and build their own houses up to less than ten years
ago, but the better condition of the low-rent company houses and provision of utilities have enticed all
Indians to select in favor of the company houses.
Some have purchased houses from the company and
moved them to leased lands in the northern section of
the Indian community.

In his discussion of Franciscan missions in the
Papagueria, Geiger (1939: 41) refers to Ajo as being
"... without chapel or school but whose Indian
population at times mounts to 900 souls, making it
the third largest Indian town in the country." He
does not indicate the source of his enumeration; but
the company records, dating back to January of
1936, are of interest in terms of the number of
Indians on the payroll (Table 13). Using the 1960
figure of 4.2 individuals per Ajo Indian family
(Table 14) for the 1940 number of Indian employees
(193, Table 13), an approximate Indian population of
810 is derived, which certainly approaches the 900
figure given by Father Geiger for the year before.

In Table 13, the 4 percent increase in 1945 in the
number of Indian employees is due to the fact that
Indians were least affected by the war, and they had
to fill the vacancies created by the departure of members of the other ethnic communities to the war
effort. The drop in Indian representation after the
war is due largely to the introduction of a company
literacy requirement for employment. In 1950 the
Mexican proportion increased at the opening of the
new smelter plant, which has since consisted almost
entirely of Mexicans. In 1957 the company began a
battery of tests which has to be passed before an
applicant can be considered. Exceptions were made
for Indians at first, with a gradual stiffening of the
expectations in test performance in order to achieve

---

[4] Obtained in a personal interview with John W. McLean,
Phelps Dodge Employment Agent, November 6, 1965.

[5] *Ibid.*

the equality of treatment ideal. The Indian mine population reached its lowest ebb in 1965 but has hovered around the 10 percent level since 1960.

The more recent efforts of the company have been directed toward stabilizing the ethnic composition of the labor force at a controlled 65 percent Anglo, 25 percent Mexican, and 10 percent Indian proportion. The 1965 ratio is 64 percent Anglo, 27 percent Mexican, and 9 percent Indian. The company at present is discouraging the keeping of records on ethnic identification and officially holds to the current emphasis on equal opportunity for all. Such a policy actually appears rather incongruous with the tradition of segregation which has been a historical characteristic of the mining operation and the community settlement patterns along segregated ethnic community lines. This incongruity is due to a rather sudden departure from a well established history of ethnic segregation. There has been a tendency for the segregated ethnic communities to selectively maintain their ethnic identifications (Figure 10).

There are marginal areas which accommodate the flow of individuals seeking, for some reason or another, to break from one ethnic community and identify with another, but the de-identification with ethnic community seems to move in the direction of marginal status rather than a completely new identification or assimilation into a new ethnic community (see Table 14 and Figure 10).

TABLE 13

Number and Percent of Indians on Mine Payroll by Year, 1936-65*

Year	Number of Indians	Percent of Indians on Labor Force
1936	232	18.8
1940	193	15.9
1945	168	19.3
1950	172	14.5
1955	161	10.8
1960	174	12.2
1964	136	10.0
1965	125	9.0

*Figures provided by John W. McLean, Employment Agent, in interviews on June 5, 1964, and November 6, 1965. The year 1936 is the earliest available statistical record showing this ethnic breakdown.

TABLE 14

Identified Indian Households According to Residence Patterns Within the Community of Ajo, 1960*

Ethnic Community	Households	Indians	Average per Household	Home Owners	Working at Mine
Indian village	143	703	4.9	22	122
Mexican town	6	26	4.3	3	5
Projects (mixed)	3	11	3.6	0	2
Gibson (mixed)	3	19	6.3	2	3
Anglo town	4	21	5.2	1	4
Totals	159	780	4.2	28	136

*These figures have been deduced from the Ajo-Gila Bend City Directory (1960), wherein all household heads, children under 18, and those over 18 are presumed to have been enumerated. Names were further checked against the Ajo segment found in the Bureau of Ethnic Research, University of Arizona, Papago Population Register (1959) in order to identify Papagos living outside the Indian community. Some error is expected, especially in identifying Indians outside of the Indian community.

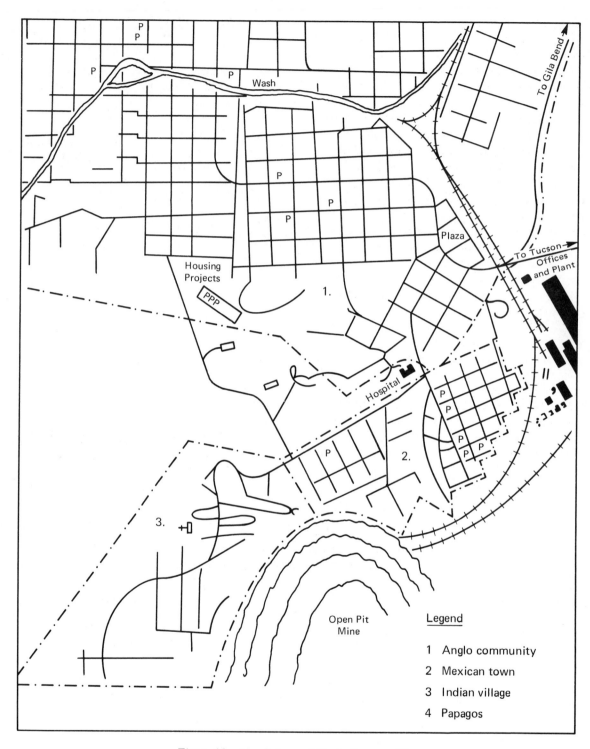

Figure 10. Ajo, Arizona, Ethnic Communities

The figures in Table 14 probably do not include Papagos living in rural households and rancherias around the vicinity of Ajo, such as Darby Well. Nonetheless, when the total number of Indians in 1960 is compared with the 812 "others" besides Anglos, Mexicans, and Negroes listed in the 1950 census, the figures seem fairly reliable considering the comparability of the number of Indian employees in 1950 (172) with the number listed for 1960 (174). The total of 136 Indians employed at the mine in 1960 as listed above probably does not include the few in Ajo that I failed to identify, those from the hinterland who commute to their jobs, or the difference that may be a result of the turnover factor, since the 1960 figures from the mine and the census probably were not taken at the same time of the year.

The Anglo community is stratified in terms of occupational statuses with the company and has almost all the highest statuses, so that movement from one of the other ethnic groups should be expected to be toward the lowest social status of the Anglo community. In reality this does not seem to occur. Rather, there appear to be discrete ethnic communities, each with their hierarchies of occupational statuses. Some of the occupational statuses in the separate communities are identical, but this does not lead to the assimilation of Papagos or Mexicans into the Anglo community. Individuals who seek to de-identify with the Indian ethnic community altogether must move into a marginal status as isolates in marginal areas of one of the other ethnic communities without making a complete de-identification with his ethnic group. Forms of economic integration in terms of occupational status do occur, but the ethnic identities largely remain.

The extent of ethnic de-identification or assimilation of Mexicans into the Anglo community has not been explored except that townspeople have mentioned that it does occur. There is also a small amount of identification of Anglos with certain segments of the Mexican community. As far as the Indian community is concerned,[6] some trends have become more apparent, largely due to a preoccupation in this study with the Indian community to the almost total disregard of the dynamics of the other groupings. Some of these trends will be considered later when an effort will be made to draw some conclusions about Papago mobility, acculturation, and de-identification or assimilation.

It is of interest to note from Table 13 the gradual decrease over time in the number of Indians employed in the mine. Part of this is due to efforts of the company to bring the ethnic compositions of the employment force into a comparable proportion in terms of the populations of each ethnic community, which is approximately 65 percent Anglo, 25 percent Mexican, and 10 percent Indian. The decline of the Indian segment should not be construed as an index of assimilation into one of the other ethnic communities. Rather, the raising of requirements to qualify for employment,[7] company controls to stabilize the proportions, and automation and job specialization demanding higher skills probably are the chief contributing factors.[8] The Indian community remains a discrete ethnic settlement segregated from the larger community.

---

[6] The majority are Papagos but there are a few Pimas, some Pima-Papagos mixed, and a small number of Apaches and Yavapais.

[7] According to John W. McLean, in a personal interview June 5, 1964, only 10 percent of the Indians who take the battery of tests pass, although an exception is made for them, and they are given a second chance to pass it. The Anglo and Mexican groups fare somewhat equally, each group having about 40 percent who pass the tests.

[8] Although 10 percent of the payroll in 1964 was Indian, that ethnic group accounted for 25 percent of all turnover. Sixty-five percent of the turnover is Anglo, largely because Anglos are more mobile, upgrade themselves more quickly, and do not have as many compelling reasons to remain in Ajo. The Mexican group from the standpoint of turnover is the most stable group with a 10 percent figure.

STRUCTURAL CHARACTERISTICS

The definitive features that set the Ajo Mine Occupational Complex apart as a social system are essentially structural in character. First, the mining operation has, for a good part of the present century, provided year-round work for Indians desiring to conform to the menial demands that such labor imposes. More recently, this has been increasingly true only for those who can qualify according to company literacy and testing requirements and who can maintain some kind of consistent effort to meet the requirements of the available work roles. The setting of selective minimum standards for qualifying for a whole range of work roles, from unskilled to highly skilled and supervisory statuses, creates a somewhat select group of Indians, even though the seniority system still operates in the case of older employees who came before the imposition of such requirements.

Second, the three-shift operation around the clock and scheduled shutdown periods permit the Papagos to maintain dual residence patterns. While the operation is in full swing, the Ajo Indian community is a network of activity, both in terms of itself as well as with regard to its interaction, through its individual residents, with the Ajo community as a whole. When the mine shuts down, the Indian community is virtually vacated by the majority of its Papago residents who have reservation ties; Papago employees and their families return to their reservation communities and have access to reservation activities and institutions. In other words, the mining operation has structural features that foster and maintain a situation, making a straddle adjustment to two distinct ways of life necessary — one centering in Ajo and one centering in the reservation communities. This is one of the reinforcing situations that controls the extent of acculturation and operates against any tendencies toward rapid assimilation. Father Oblasser[9] points out that an important feature of the Phelps Dodge Indian town is that it is modeled after the old mission system; that is, provision has been made for a community which could retain its ties to its many reservation "clan-villages."

The Ajo Indian community is a unique community arrangement for the majority of Indian employees, since it has its own ecological unity separate from the rest of the Ajo community. There is an Indian village

mission church of St. Catherine, operated by the Franciscan Fathers, which ministers to the Indians' needs for both worship and festive celebration. Also, since 1961 the Indian village has been constitutionally organized with its own chief and councilmen and has had a recognized representative on the Sells Tribal Council.

The ecological unity of the village is in a sense misleading, however, in that it is a kind of company-managed village unit, made possible by special low-rent provisions. In terms of sentiment and cooperation, the Indian village is not a single unit but a series of smaller, neighborhood groupings within the larger village complex (Figure 11). The full implications of these structural features are yet to be discovered in some possible forthcoming study. But in any case, the Indian community does depend on linkages with the economic, political, recreative, educational, and welfare structures that operate in the larger Ajo community and beyond. Some of these structures are the cooperative store, the paycheck and social security complexes, other retail stores, banking facilities, optional insurance benefits, law enforcement facilities, local union activities, public parks, recreational establishments and programs, taverns, public schools, company hospital, and churches, to name only a few of many community-wide social institutions ideally open to all members of the larger Ajo community. The case material in Chapter 6 traces the life of an individual Papago miner as he operates in or straddles the dual structures of reservation and Ajo institutions in the course of fulfilling occupational necessities.

---

[9] Letter from Father Bonaventure Oblasser, O.F.M., to Senator Carl Hayden in reaction to House Resolution 2680 having to do with promoting extensive off-reservation relocation employment (Bureau of Ethnic Research files, University of Arizona, Tucson, 1955).

RANGE OF VARIATION IN OCCUPATIONAL STATUSES AND ROLES

The Ajo mine operation has a wide range of occupational statuses, with each status being positioned at some level in a hierarchy of levels according to the extent of the skill required to perform the corresponding roles. These positions are supposedly open to any who can qualify and who have the necessary seniority when a given status is open for filling. Table 15 provides a general breakdown of the major occupational skill categories and the number and

percentage of Papagos occupying pay levels within each skill category. There are many gradations within each pay level, but the data presented should give some idea of how Papagos distribute themselves in a hierarchy running from unskilled to highly skilled and supervisory positions.

The figures in Table 15 reveal the impact of job specialization and the elevation of technical demands on Papago workers and would seem to indicate that

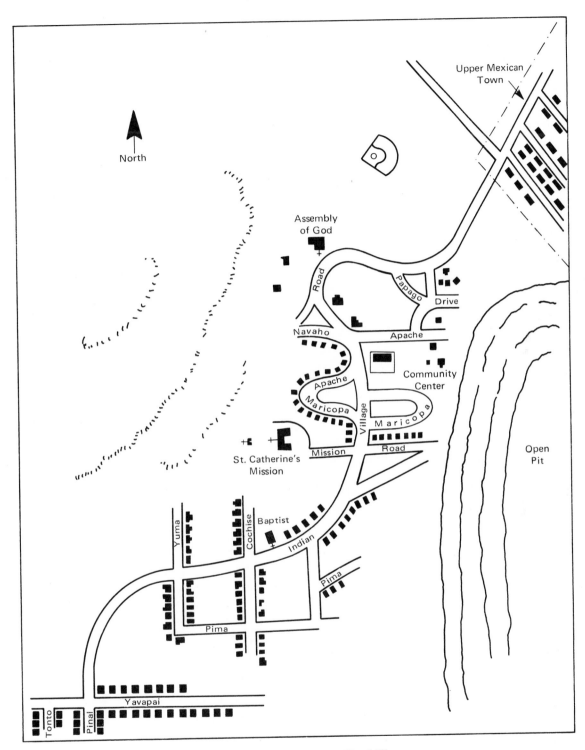

Figure 11. Ajo, Arizona, Indian Village

TABLE 15

Papago Indian Employees by Pay Level Category*

Skill Category	Pay Level	1965	Number of Employees		
			Percent	1940	Percent
Unskilled laborers	B	43	42	105	74
Semiskilled helpers, oilers, etc.	C	11	11	26	18
	D	27	27	1	1
Machine operators stationary and light equipment operators	E	4	4	3	2
	F	10	10	0	0
Equipment operators and repairmen heavy equipment operators and skilled repairmen	G	1	1	1	1
	H	3	3	5	3
Highest mechanical skills journeymen, etc.	J	2	2	1	1
Papagos on payroll		101	100%	142	100%
Other Indians on payroll		26		51	
Total Indians on payroll		127		193	
Total employees		1318		1207	

*Provided by John W. McLean, Employment Agent, New Cornelia Branch, Phelps Dodge Corporation, Ajo, Arizona, November 10, 1965.

the greatest number of Papagos affected over the years since 1940 are those who have not met these increasing demands. There are fewer Papagos at the unskilled level and an increase in the number occupying the semiskilled levels, particularly the D skill category and the machine operators skilled level. This increase in the number of Papagos in the middle-range semiskilled and skilled categories undoubtedly absorbs some who were originally classified as unskilled back in 1940, but no turnover statistics have been consulted to establish the number. It is expected that a goodly number of the unskilled laborers have been among those eliminated in the process of upgrading and that the unskilled category has continued to comprise the highest turnover rate.

In 1940, Papagos accounted for almost 12 percent of the labor force, whereas in 1965, the proportion was just under 8 percent. During the same period, the overall increase in the number of employees reveals that Papagos have come to play a less significant role in terms of the total labor force, but that role has been one of upgrading in terms of skilled performance on the part of a smaller number of Papagos. This raises significant questions. First, does the occupational structure in which resident Papagos are upgrading themselves from lesser to greater skill categories have any correlation to acculturation and eventual assimilation? Second, to what extent are Papagos modifying certain cultural values of the dominant Anglo community and thereby inhibiting complete

TABLE 16

Selfindicators for Job Titles of Ajo Indians According to Official Occupational Levels, 1960

Level B (unskilled)

Laborer	25
Trackman	18
Pitman	10
Cableman	1
Cleanup man	1
Mill laborer	1
Sampleman	1
Sampler	1
	58

Levels C and D (semiskilled)

Supplyman	1
Truck helper	1
Converter oiler	1
Track oiler	1
Panel trackman	7
Helper	1
Jackhammer man	5
Churn driller helper	4
Auto repair helper	1
Pipe man	11*
Dump man	1
Truck driver	2†
Puncher	1
	37

Levels E through H (increasingly skilled)

Powderman	2
Bit sharpener	1
Electric shovel oiler	1
Sharpener	1
Gun guardman	1‡
Oiler	2
Shovel oiler	1
Transport operator	1
Mill operator	4
Air driller	1
Converterman	1
Churn driller	4
Motor car operator	1
Converter operator	1
Driller	1
Furnace operator	1
Bulldozer operator	1
Track foreman	1
Foreman	1
	27

Level J (specialists and supervisors)

Welder	2
Machinist	1∮
Electrician	1
	4

Unable to Classify

Employee	8
Crusher	1
	9

No Such Classification

Fire department captain	1
	1

*Four indicated they were pipe fitters, but the employment agent thinks they are probably pipe men.

†Extends into the E, F, and H levels but here assigned to level D.

‡Gar gun operator.

∮The employment agent reports there has never been an Indian machinist.

assimilation? Finally, to what extent is acculturation controlled by ethnic segregation and the strong influence of reservation structures on Ajo Papagos?

Acculturative processes, as they affect Papago individuals and social units, appear to fall short of assimilation or total integration. The Papago community in Ajo most likely has a number of acculturation categories (Hallowell 1945; Voget 1952; Louise Spindler 1962). These categories typify the psychological adjustments or readjustments that are occurring and the partial economic integration now in process. But the detached Ajo Indian community continues to function in preserving and reintegrating Papago cultural behaviors and thus functions as a resistive control to integration or assimilation. This is the Papago contribution to a persisting plural society, aided by the existent non-Papago cultural traditions and conditions that stimulate resistance to assimilation. This point will be explored in detail in the concluding chapter.

There are two additional ways for establishing the extent of the occupational variation in the Ajo complex. The first is the 1960 Ajo directory, which contains all Papago men over 18 who could be accounted for at specific residences both within the Indian community and in one of the other ethnic communities. It is of interest because occupation is specified for all over the age of 18. While these occupational titles most likely are self-indicators rather than the precise status indicators as officially defined by the company, they do appear to merge with the latter (see Tables 15 and 16). They are further significant in respect to the way Papago workers, at the time the census was taken, conceived of their occupational roles. It is very likely that there are ideal roles in which some individuals conceive of themselves, but which do not always coincide with the company's official status levels at which they are actually found. On the other hand, it is a personal impression gained through contacts with Papago miners that they have a rather clear picture of the various job levels, particularly their own specific roles, and report quite accurately their particular job titles.[10] So the self-indicators are at least somewhat reliable in helping to establish this range of variation. These informal job titles or selfindicators and their corresponding levels in the official occupational status hierarchy are represented in Table 16. It is interesting to see how this distribution, based on selfindicators, compares with that provided by the official records. The former is based on 1960 data, whereas the latter is based on 1965 data, but it is doubtful that overall proportions have changed although individuals have come and gone.

A second means of establishing occupational variation at Ajo makes use of the Papago Employment Survey (1965) conducted by the Bureau of Ethnic Research. While the final report has not been completed at the time of this writing, a perusal of the field schedules has provided the data included in Table 17.

---

[10] Underevaluation as well as overevaluation of one's actual position have both been found in informal contacts, although the point has not been systematically followed up with a very large number of Papago miners.

TABLE 17

Individuals with History of Employment
at Ajo Mine, 1964-65

| | Age Categories | | | | |
	Under 35	35-49	50-65	Over 65	Total
Origin					
Reservation	7	8	6	1	22
Ajo	1	1	1	0	3
Mexico	1	1	6	3	11
	9	10	13	4	36
Residence (1964)					
Reservation*	0	1	8	1	10
Off-reservation, other than Ajo	5	5	1	1	12
Ajo (idle)	0	0	2	2	4
Ajo (mine)	4	4	2	0	10
	9	10	13	4	36

Table 17 - continued

		Age Categories				Total
		Under 35	35-49	50-65	Over 65	
Tenure at Mine						
Ten or more years	Current‡	0	3	2	0	5
	Past	0	0	4	1	5
Less than 10 years	Current	4	1	0	0	5
	Past	5	6	7	3	21
		9	10	13	4	36
Skill Category						
Level B	Current	1	2	1	0	4
	Past	2	3	6	0	11
Levels C and D	Current	2	1	1	0	4
	Past	0	1	2	1	4
Levels E-H	Current	1	1	0	0	2
	Past	0	1	2	0	3
Levels J-N	Current	0	0	0	0	0
	Past	0	1	0	0	1
		6	10	12	1	29‡
Work History						
Commercial farm	Unskilled	4	5	7	3	19
	Skilled	1	0	0	0	1
						20
Urban labor	Unskilled	1	3	0	0	4
	Skilled	0	0	0	0	0
						4
Construction labor	Unskilled	0	3	2	1	6
	Skilled	0	0	0	0	0
						6
Railroad	Unskilled	1	2	3	0	6
	Skilled	0	0	0	0	0
						6
Relocation	Unskilled	3	2	0	0	5
	Skilled	2	1	0	0	3
						8
Ajo mine only	Unskilled	1	0	2	1	4
	Skilled	0	1	0	0	1
						5

*Includes Mexican villages of origin.

†Current indicates those who are presently employed, and past indicates those who are no longer employed by the mine.

‡Seven Papagos in the survey did not indicate the kind of work they did.

The interview schedules of all Papagos in the survey who reported any past or present experience at
the Ajo mine have been studied. There were 36 of
these Papago men,[11] of whom only five with over ten
years' tenure have current seniority, while 21 with
less than ten years' employment at the mine have
terminated their work there. Thus the survey seems
to reflect that turnover in the past has been high. The
employment and residence data also reflect the tendency for Papago men beyond 50 to return to the
reservation or to remain idle in Ajo, the latter living
with younger kinsmen who are employed at the mine.
Ten in the survey were employed at the mine at the
time the interviewing was done, and all but two of
these are men under 50.

The skill category data are the most subject to
question since reporting of job titles was not complete, and for those that did indicate the type of
work they did, there can be no certainty as to the
conformity of the indicated titles to official ones.
The work history data provide the range of reported
work experience indicated by those who have also
specified work experience at the Ajo mine. One can
see from this the combination of a few distinct types
of work experience which this group of the survey
shares. Considering that there are 101 Papagos employed in 1965 at the mine, and ten Papagos currently employed at the mine were drawn in the 1964
sample, it seems that the 10 percent random sample
applied to the whole Papago work force is also
represented in the Ajo data. All skill categories seem
to be represented in such a way as to approach the
distribution provided by Table 15.

---

[11] Thirteen of the sample who were under 35 years of age had
fathers who had past employment at Phelps Dodge, although the 13 did not. Four more had fathers who were
employees of the mine at the time of the survey, although
the four were not. This suggests an even wider influence of
the Ajo complex than Table 17 indicates.

5. OSCILLATING FARM-NONFARM AND URBAN-NONURBAN OCCUPATIONAL COMPLEXES

OSCILLATING FARM-NONFARM OCCUPATIONAL COMPLEX

As noted in Chapter 1, the social field for tribal peoples circulating in industrial society is a "town-plus-hinterland" environment. This is to say that both urban and rural surroundings are part of the social and psychological experience-fields of individuals. These are contrastive cognitive, affective, and normative social fields in which human experiences and behaviors are structured, modified, and restructured. In some cases, there are solid commitments to one or the other type of experience, where either a town or a hinterland way of life prevails. The social field of an individual may never be exclusively one or the other, and individuals may circulate in both, but in such cases the social roles and daily activities are enacted and performed largely in one setting or the other.

For transitional peoples, however, solid commitments to either a rural or an urban setting as a way of life are not always clear. Instead of an avowal to either a rural residence and rural occupations or an urban residence and urban occupations, individuals oscillate between the two kinds of experiences. An individual may choose to do farm work but reside in the city; he may choose to do some type of urban work activity but reside in a rural setting. He may choose to work and live in the city when work on the farm is not available and vice versa. There may be certain advantages or necessities in either kind of pattern.

This chapter seeks to conceptualize a complex wherein occupational and residential patterns are established within both kinds of social fields. Individuals are thereby less committed to either a rural or an urban style of life but are actually committed to both. They may be indecisive in their commitments and may embody a host of motivations which prompt this ambivalence. Or it may not be so much a matter of motivational ambivalence as it is a well-established pattern or style of living. The occupational roles

oscillate; at certain periods of the year, occupational roles prevail that conform to those discussed in Chapter 3, and at other times during the year, prevailing occupational roles conform to those discussed in this Chapter. Since there are distinctive role activities within the commercial farm complex of institutions and the urban, nonfarm complexes of institutions, individuals who establish patterns of committing themselves to both kinds of complexes would be expected to share a unique kind of social field. They thereby share a field of structured experience that differs somewhat from the experiences of those whose commitments are clearly one or the other. The Tucson urban area, surrounded by a hinterland of fertile farming lands under commercial irrigation, provides one such social field.

Temporal, Spatial, and Demographic Features

Figure 6 reveals the spatial features of the complex being described here. Tucson, an industrialized urban center, lies along the Santa Cruz River and its tributaries. The Sahuarita-Continental and Marana-Avra Valley commercial farming complexes lie adjacent to this metropolitan community. In terms of spatial mobility, it is clearly seen why urban and/or rural activities may become either alternative or complementary styles of life. Those who wish, whatever their reasons, to live predominantly in either a rural or an urban complex of institutions may do so. Others may not be able, whatever their reasons, to commit themselves so firmly to one complex exclusively. Some Papagos have made clear commitments to some style of urban life and have thereby become almost totally dependent upon this kind of social field. Others have remained essentially rural and have never become dependent on the urban complex, although they may periodically resort to some of its services and engage in some of its activities. Still others seem to be more or less dependent on both styles of life and actually become attached to and participate intermittently in both kinds of social fields. The spatial arrangements are extremely important to the maintenance of such a pattern.

As long as Tucson has been a town of any size — in the respect that there are other kinds of commercial pursuits and activities than those which characterize rural life — Papagos have had alternatives in commitment to styles of life that most suited them. There have been some Papagos who have preferred and been able to subsist, by-and-large, on their own crops and stock, with some occasional reliance on other forms of activity, either work-exchange or selling wood or hay to settlers. The Commissioner of Indian Affairs (1875: 212) estimated that the greater number of Papagos (6,000) lived in villages to the west, while 2,000 more lived either on the newly established reservation at San Xavier or in the vicinity of Tucson. The former were largely "self-supporting," as classed by the government, and the latter more frequently sought employment in and around Tucson. The occupational activities still were largely undiversified and largely rural in nature, even though they were not exclusively agricultural activities. The point is that some, from the very beginning of contacts with non-Indians, were selectively becoming more dependent on relationships to the growing town while others remained largely independent from the more sizable settlements.

The rural-urban contrasts are still characteristic of the Tucson-Marana-Sahuarita region. Similar settings are found elsewhere in southern Arizona. The Phoenix metropolitan area provides this same kind of town-plus-hinterland environment providing alternatives for role commitments. The smaller urban communities, such as Gila Bend, Casa Grande, Coolidge, Florence, and Eloy, are also town environments surrounded by rural-hinterland environments; and, to a lesser extent, they also provide nonfarm complexes of institutions in which some Papagos choose to make either a partial or a full commitment to urban or town living.

Since most Papago studies have concentrated on either rurally oriented off-reservation Papagos (Dobyns 1950; Padfield 1961) or urban-oriented off-reservation Papagos (Tooker 1952), there is little or no demographic data to account for the number of Papagos who are oriented to both kinds of social systems, that is, a commercial farm occupational complex and an urban, nonfarm occupational complex. There are no figures to indicate the number who might be so committed, nor is there any certainty as to how significant this kind of social field is. Yet it is suspected to be an important social field for a considerable number of Papago individuals since there is still a great deal of town-to-hinterland-to-town circulation of individuals. This circulation would be expected in any situation where tribal life as well as rural life are confronted with the many enticements and complexities of the urban scene (Thurnwald 1950; Forde 1956; Mair 1957; Tumin 1957; Lewis 1959). Familiar roles are contrasted with new roles, yet no clear commitments to either are manifest. This is an important characteristic of the poorly educated, unskilled, and inadequately prepared tribal and rural peoples who are circulating within the urban-rural environment.

The importance of this kind of social field will have to be assumed until further studies are made of individuals who characterize this pattern. That such individuals are identifiable has been confirmed through the empirical experience associated with the field methods employed. The quantitative significance has yet to be determined. Yet it is possible to venture some of the characteristics of this kind of social field experience as they relate to the problem at hand.

Structural Characteristics

An individual who oscillates between dual occupational complexes shares similarly structured social experiences with other such individuals. First, for such an individual there is usually either a predominant urban (nonfarm) occupational-residential pattern or a predominant rural (farm) occupational-residential pattern, but never exclusively one or the other. Fluctuation between urban and rural jobs, where the individual participates in both types, becomes more than a result of fortuitous circumstances but actually becomes a style of life with a prevailing pattern.

Next, the individual's overall occupational and residential history reveals participation in both kinds of complexes but with one or the other standing out, during specific segments of time, as a prevailing pattern. That is, the occupational-residential history depicts a general orientation or culminating direction toward one or the other but never reaches a gestalt. Hence, while one type crystallizes into a dominant tendency, the other remains as a subsidiary or supplemental pattern to fall back on in the event that the prevailing pattern is not, for whatever the reason, immediately accessible.

In addition, the individual has usually had extensive off-reservation experience including some other-than-farm labor. This pattern, although showing no complete commitment to either an urban or a rural occupational complex, is one of accommodating traditional but largely unskilled occupational roles to each other. In other words, the compartmentalized participation by Papagos in both urban nonfarm work roles and rural farm labor roles involves roles that are closely allied to customary and well-established stereotyped Papago patterns of employment, thus ensuring a partial commitment to both since neither one nor the other is a completely fulfilling pattern in and of itself. There may be attractions to the urban surroundings which urban occupations make possible, but there are also emotional or perhaps practical compensations for maintaining identification with a rural complex.

There is some kind of well-established kinship or familial base in either or both the urban nonfarm and the rural farm complexes to which an individual may resort, but the extended family base is somewhat disrupted or realigned as there has also been a history of ambivalent role commitment for other members of the extended family as well. Kinship nonetheless may perform a vital function in the formation of this dual pattern of work and residence.

Finally, the personal history of an individual participating extensively in both complexes reveals signs of acculturative stress; that is, there are periods of transience, inwardly experienced malcontent, and feelings of inadequacy or unfulfillment due to low status in both types of occupational complexes. There is a sense of culture loss in terms of traditional statuses and roles and institutionalized values without the proper cues that would permit a sufficient identification with the dominant sociocultural system. The individual may anticipate socialization into new reference groups but his culturally induced mazeway does not allow an adequate synthesis with the cultural content that characterizes the social field in which he finds himself. The functional explanation for the oscillating pattern is that a subsidiary occupational pattern tends to buttress the failings experienced in the other occupational complex. Neither is totally or lastingly satisfactory, but one provides a temporary reprieve when the other fails to endure. At least one set of roles is available when the other is not, permitting access to some needed cash and other associated services. The roles are accommodations to the dominant system, but the lack of commitment to one complex or the other prevents any occupational or social mobility; hence the individual occupies mundane statuses in both complexes.

Range of Variation in Occupational Statuses and Roles

Studies of Papago occupations have not provided data that might permit a study of the range of possible rural and urban occupations. It is not so much that the oscillating pattern is insignificant as that the research on Papago occupations thus far has not been structured with the intent to elicit these kinds of data. Only repeated and prolonged contact with individuals will permit an advance into discovering the significant features of this type of occupational pattern.

Nevertheless, the Papago employment data available suggest the reality of the pattern. The Papago Employment Survey (1965) provides a number of general employment histories that suggest this pattern. In a review of the field schedules, only eight cases reveal rather clear oscillating patterns, not only for 1964 but over a period of years. This is not a very large number (3 per cent of the sample); but, it is thought that with persistent observation to accompany this kind of field interviewing, the pattern would characterize many more individuals than the survey actually reveals. The work histories are reconstructed through interview technique only and thus would tend to miss features of the individuals' patterns that are not reported to the interviewer. Nonetheless, some individuals did reveal enough of their work habits to suggest that they do oscillate between urban and rural occupational complexes. Table 18 summarizes their work patterns.

Several other individuals have reservation residences but regularly do both farm labor and urban jobs; these manifest similar patterns. If necessity demanded the establishment of off-reservation residence, these individuals would likely continue to maintain the oscillating work pattern, establishing

TABLE 18

Papago Men with Evident Oscillating Work Patterns, 1964-65

Age	Occupation, End of 1964	Single Residence	Dual Residence	Dual Work	Past Work
50	Yard work	Tucson		Yard work, farm labor	Yard work, farm labor
49	Picking fruit		Phoenix rural camp	Spot jobs, fruit harvest	Mine, hospital work, farm labor, spot jobs
45	Unemployed	Tucson		Yard work, farm labor	Railroad construction, yard work, farm labor
45	Unemployed		Gila Bend Buckeye	Lumber yard, farm labor	Farm labor, railroad, lumber yard
40	Yard work		Tucson Sahuarita	Yard work, farm labor	Railroad, farm labor, yard work
36	Unemployed		Tucson Marana Eloy Sahuarita	Yard work, farm labor	Railroad, farm labor, yard work
33	Picking cotton	Tucson		Yard work, farm labor	Cement work, yard work, farm labor
28	Picking cotton,	Tucson		Yard work, farm labor	Yard work, landscaping, farm labor

either a single residence or a dual residence pattern. This is a general characteristic of San Xavier Papagos. Papagos who have recently brought their unskilled occupational abilities off-reservation are highly apt to commit themselves to rural farm complexes. Those unskilled workers who have many years of off-reservation and on-reservation experience and who have had some exposure to the unskilled urban tasks are likely to engage in this dual or oscillating pattern. Those with urban or rural skills or semiskills of value to the labor market are in better positions to make commitments to either an urban or rural pattern, although the possession of skills and training do not automatically present individuals as marketable.

It is conceivable that individuals trained in certain skilled or semiskilled statuses may still lack commitment to a single pattern and thereby oscillate in the unskilled jobs of the urban and rural complexes.

In summary, although the Oscillating Farm-Nonfarm Complex is difficult to verify at this stage of Papago work studies, it is considered a basic complex of transition between rural and urban occupational commitments. Therefore, much attention will be given to a Papago case in which this oscillating pattern is manifest. It provides a framework wherein urban and rural jobs and residences are intermittently assumed, thus committing the individual to a dual participation in two different kinds of institutional complexes.

URBAN-NONFARM OCCUPATIONAL COMPLEX

Town residence is not an altogether new feature of Papago settlement. Attachment to a town or city does not necessarily greatly alter the styles of life to which people are accustomed (Lewis 1965). Indeed, town life provides additional and perhaps different kinds of institutional life than the traditional rural dweller usually experiences. Certain demands, adjustments, and accommodations are necessary when rurally based people assume town residences and engage in activities of the town setting. But if there is a neighborhood comprised of people with similar cultural backgrounds within the town, and if there is an available rural hinterland which can provide a source for unskilled labor, or if there are rather well-defined occupational roles within the town, the contrasts in daily activities between town and country do not have to be very pronounced.

When a town becomes an urban area, with an expanding population, an extensive shifting about of peoples, a rapid rearrangement of land values and land use, an increasing interplay of different values and ideologies, a growing and expanding economic and industrial base, and the multitude of other features which characterize urbanization, contrasts in the two styles of life are much greater. In such a case, urban residence may, although it is assumed within a well-established ethnic enclave of kin and kind, confront individuals with new kinds of anticipatory roles due to the number of new reference groups that the urban surroundings afford.

Long-established stereotyped roles, occupational and otherwise, are abandoned by some individuals of the ethnic enclave as new statuses are achieved. There are, therefore, members of an individual's own ethnic group who come to represent a kind of reference point for new kinds of role behavior. Hence, the ethnic group also takes on a hierarchy of statuses largely related to the different occupational statuses represented. Stereotypic work roles, while they continue to be performed because the statuses they represent have been institutionalized, are no longer satisfactory or totally compensatory due to the fact that there are new references for occupational behavior, reinforced by the successful achievement of new statuses by members of one's own ethnic group. Often these reference groups are comprised of an individual's own relatives. Yet the anticipated new statuses are unachievable for many who lack the combination of factors which are conducive to successful vertical mobility.

Individuals who resort to urban or town living face the inevitable uncertainties that accompany being thrown into new kinds of social settings. A newcomer who has little skill to offer may seek out kin or friends in the urban enclave to serve as buttresses against the complexity and heterogeneity of the new urban experience. Stereotypic roles that are more easily obtained and enacted because of kinship ties and because of the institutionalization of certain well defined statuses provide some readymade situations that may reduce the anxieties associated with adapting to other new kinds of roles. However, because there are others, even in an individual's own network of kin or in his own household, whose occupations may likewise be unpredictable and undependable, the urban experience may be short-lived and necessitate an occasional return to the hinterland. Such low-income neighborhoods therefore have a great deal of circulation in and out; while a core, built around more or less stabilized occupational roles, builds up to give an ethnic community a durability that fosters a second and third generation. And as individuals rise in social status and successfully perceive and behave in terms of middle class Anglo values, the ethnic community proves to be an inadequate arrangement to support the aspiring individuals in the new cultural behaviors which will be demanded of them in order to maintain or to enhance their newly achieved statuses.

As Curtis (1959: 296) notes, there are individual consequences of social mobility; and individuals may become marginal to the extent that there is a "relative lack of intimate social contacts in either stratum of origin or stratum of destination." Vertical mobility seems to involve the necessity of abandoning, discontinuing, or modifying the relationships with people who belong to the stratum in which an individual has originated. Correspondingly, new social ties must be developed with people occupying the stratum toward which the individual is directing his behavior. Vertically mobile people, therefore, must confront periods of relative isolation where solid social relationships with either group of origin or group of destination are at a minimum (Curtis 1959: 267). This probably is the reason why residence may also be marginal since it is difficult to cultivate social relationships in a residence unit where taking on the behaviors of a higher status is "out of character." Vertical mobility therefore suggests patterns of residential mobility — that is, moving "out" of a neighborhood representing a stratum of origin in order to identify more fully with the cultural behaviors of the anticipated stratum or the newly achieved stratum.

There are, then, any number of urban occupational complex variants. The characteristics of any specific variant are dependent first of all upon location within the city, that is, the kind of neighborhood and the kinds of accessible institutions related thereto. The kind of neighborhood will largely depend on both the occupational status occupied and the extent of an individual's identification with cultural values other than those of his ethnic community. Later in this chapter an attempt is made to spell out some of these occupational complex variants and their descriptive features, using the Tucson urban area as a specific example. But first, we shall use the Tucson case to establish the time and space dimensions of Papago urban settlement.

Temporal, Spatial, and Demographic Features

The Spanish settlement at Tucson grew from a series of Pima Indian rancherias scattered about the west bank of the Santa Cruz River near Sentinel Peak or "A" Mountain. The Piman name for this vicinity, Schookson or Chuckson ("at the foot of black mountain"), was first used by Father Eusebio Francisco Kino on one of his journies through the area in 1699 (Greenleaf and Wallace 1962: 18). The name Tucson, then, came to refer generally to this fertile flood-plain area on the west bank of the Santa Cruz, where the Pueblo of Tucson, or San Cosme del Tucson, grew from its Pima base to include, over time, a series of Sobaipuri relocatees, Papago farmers, peaceful Apaches, Spanish soldiers, and, finally, Mexican settlers. The whole Santa Cruz Valley, extending some 12 to 15 miles from the Sobaipuri village of Bac to Rillito Creek, was a chain of ranches and irrigated fields with Bac, San Cosme del Tucson, and San Agustín del Oyaur the largest of the settlements. After 1706, the place names San Cosme and San Agustín del Oyaur were no longer used, and only San Agustín or San Agustín del Tucson are used as place names (pp. 18-9).

After Kino's death in 1711, Spanish activities among the natives of the Santa Cruz Valley were extremely limited due to the seasonal mobility of the Indians, the menace of the Apaches, and the general discontent of some Pimas over the presence of Spanish residents, which culminated in the Pima Revolt of 1751.

In 1753, a presidio was established at Tubac about 40 miles south of the Pueblo of Tucson, in order to stabilize the northern frontier of the Pimería Alta. In 1762, a group of 250 Sobaipuri Indians were relocated in the vicinity of the San Agustín visita and the new settlement or rancheria was named San José del Tucson (p. 19). When the Jesuits were expelled from New Spain in 1767, the Franciscans inherited the main mission at Bac, eight miles south of the Pueblo of Tucson, and its visita at San Agustín del Tucson. The Pueblo of Tucson, from 1770 on, came to be considered a rather stable settlement on the northern frontier and, in 1776, the Spanish military garrison was moved from Tubac to the Pueblo of Tucson. Sometime before 1781 the visita of San Agustín and the San José rancheria were incorporated into the Pueblo of Tucson (p. 20). With the completion of the walled presidio in 1781 and the beginning of the new mission at San Xavier in 1783, both religious and military efforts at Tucson were intensified. With the new presidio offering protection, settlements of Sobaipuri, Papago, and peaceful Apaches were attracted to this agricultural area along the Santa Cruz. Between 1797 and 1810, a large mission organization supported an industrial school at San Agustín visita and Indians were taught European skills (p. 21).

After the Mexican War of Independence, the Spanish soldiers and residents sought refuge within the walled presidio. The Indians abandoned the pueblo, and the mission property slowly fell into ruin (p. 21).

Early Tucson, then, was largely a military community where ranchers, farmers, and friendly Indians to the south and to the west could hope for some protection. Prior to 1843 Tucson and vicinity was besieged on numerous occasions by the Apaches, but Papagos helped to prevent total destruction. After

1856, following the Gadsden Purchase, the town's complexion began to change considerably. A diverse population from many places began to push south and west of the walled town. In 1858 there were about 800 people in Tucson, mostly of Spanish descent and custom. By the end of the Civil War there were about 1,200 or 1,300 people including the military, but only one-quarter were Anglos. Thus, at the time Tucson was incorporated in 1864, and through the 1870s, it was still very much a Spanish-American town. The Papago village just outside the town maintained itself, and Papago vendors were a frequent sight on the streets of Tucson. Papagos had long been involved as cultivators and field laborers under the direction of Mexican ranchmen (Buehman 1911: 35-6; Lockwood and Page 1930: 35).

Between 1875 and 1900, various and numerous franchises were granted for artesian water, plain water, gas, gas lighting, electric lights, street railways, street grades, improved sidewalks and streets, telephone service, etc. Cowboys, miners, transients, businessmen, Mexicans, Indians, Negroes, Chinese, and Anglos from many points provided a growing and constantly changing population (Buehman 1911: 58).

The farm agent at the San Xavier Reservation, J. M. Berger (Commissioner of Indian Affairs 1894: 108-09), categorizes two classes of Papago Indians — those whose ancestors have always lived in the vicinity of San Xavier del Bac and those who come from other Papago villages to the west of San Xavier in southern Arizona. The former had better houses, were better dressed, and better educated; while the latter had traits which were just the opposite. The way that Berger categorizes the Papagos under his observation may be questioned as showing a strong bias for his own Indians at Bac. Undoubtedly the allotments granted to San Xavier Papagos in 1890, the rather continuous attention given them, and the more settled relationship to land and to the nearby town of Tucson have some bearing on Berger's observations. In his report of 1902 (pp. 189-90), Berger states:

For many years a few Papago families have been living south of Tucson, just outside the city limits, maintaining themselves honestly by doing odd jobs in the city, the men chopping wood, etc., and the women washing and doing housework. These Indians behaved themselves well, and consequently were liked by the people with whom they came in contact. Today not less than 200 of the nomadic Indians have made their homes near Tucson, to the great annoyance of everybody, city and county authorities included. A great number of these Papago do not care for work to make an honest living, but, on the other hand, their main occupation is gambling and drinking. They are regular sharps at cards and other devices and by any dishonest means, even by stealing, try to get from their more industrious brother his honest earnings. They can always obtain liquor easily, being well acquainted with localities and persons where they can buy some. They have, of course, no trouble to induce the better Indians to drinking and gambling in order to get hold of his money, as all Papago are inclined to gambling. . . . They are a great detriment to the San Xavier allottees.

In the Tucson City Directory of 1881, *El Barrio Libre* is described as a "slum district" at the end of Main and Meyer Streets, and as not being a suitable place for "cultivated Mexicans." In this region, "lower class" Mexicans and Papago Indians from San Xavier and western villages were described as living in little shacks.[1] The Papagos brought loads of cut wood into town, stayed overnight in the shacks to the south of Tucson, and the next day drove their wagons through the streets selling wood, making stops at the stores for supplies, and enjoying the town (Cosulich 1953:267).

Around 1900 the population and wealth of Tucson were growing rapidly. New businesses, neighboring towns, and railroad systems were all being built up. In 1901, Berger (Commissioner of Indian Affairs 1901: 189) reported that he had many calls from railroad contractors for Papago laborers because they were considered by the contractors to be steadier and less troublesome. In 1900 Berger sent 50 Papagos to the Los Angeles area; 75 were sent to work on the Bisbee-Naco Railroad in southeastern Arizona; and 54 were sent to El Paso. Most of these Papagos worked for a few months, saved money, and returned to Tucson.

In his 1902 report, Berger (Commissioner of Indian Affairs 1902: 167) offers an enumeration of Papagos which is of particular interest in terms of Papagos in the vicinity of Tucson (Table 19). In this same report, Berger (Commissioner of Indian Affairs 1902: 168) has something further to say about Tucson Papagos:

---

[1] William King, in an address before the Arizona Commission of Indian Affairs (1957: 40) suggests that the Mexicans, Yaquis, and Negroes moved into the predominantly Papago community during the 1920s, leaving the Papagos as a small fraction of the total population. Tooker (1952: 18) also mentions the gradual influx of Mexican and Yaquis into the area after 1910.

TABLE 19

J. M. Berger Enumeration of Papagos, 1902

Location	Adult Males	Adult Females	Males Ages 6-18	Females Ages 6-18	Total
San Xavier	270	263	80*	74	687
Tucson Indian village	176	168	52	49	445
Other villages (estimate)†					1,639

*The number of young Papagos enumerated by Berger seems rather small in comparison to the number of adults. I have no explanation as to why this might be.

†Those estimated to be living in the southwestern part of Pima County. He does not give the basis for this estimate.

During the past few years the population of this village [south of Tucson] has increased from about 40 to 344, according to a census taken a short time ago. Most of these Papago are from the Indian villages scattered over Pima County. They support themselves, some by doing odd jobs in the city of Tucson, the women washing and doing housework and the men chopping wood, etc., and others working occasionally on new railroads, or other distant work, for a short time. The inhabitants of this village are of a cosmopolitan character, as from the best to the worst Indians may be found among them, while the greater part of them are earnestly trying to make an honest living, and, in fact, are doing so. . . .

As the village is so near the city of Tucson, the Indians without much trouble, find a low Mexican or a Yaqui Indian willing, for a small consideration, to buy liquor for them.

It seems to be an ancient pattern for Papagos to leave their villages during difficult times, hence the practice of camping on the borders of settlements such as Tucson. With the foundation of the pattern so well laid, it would be expected to continue regardless of the many motives behind contemporary settlement in Tucson.

Tooker (1952: 17) indicates that the first adobe house built by a Papago in Tucson was about 1904 and that after World War I, there were two types of Papago houses — those made of adobe and those made of ocotillo ribs. The earliest settlement through the first decade of the twentieth century was dis-

tributed in two main sections, one along West 22nd Street between South 9th and South 11th avenues and the other a couple of blocks west of the government buildings on West 26th Street. The former is referred to as the Native American Addition and the latter is the section known as Papagoville. The Papagoville section had some Papagos residing there prior to 1910, but the majority were settled in the northern section. Eventually, as the city pushed south, most Papagos gradually moved southward into the Papagoville area, and it became the principal area of Papago settlement (Tooker 1952: 18, 27). South Tucson, or *El Barrio Libre,* has remained the central area of Papago settlement to this date (Figure 12), although those Papagos who have achieved higher occupational statuses have tended to move southward into more middle-class neighborhoods where there are fewer and fewer Papagos (Figures 12-14, and 16).

In 1957 (Arizona Commission of Indian Affairs 1957: 41-2) a preliminary enumeration of Tucson Papagos, short of a complete count, accounted for 865 Papagos from 256 separate households and predicted a total Papago population in Tucson exceeding 1,000.[2] Eight percent of those enumerated had been

[2] The 1,000-plus figure is supported by the Papago Population Register (1959), where 1,098 Tucson Papagos have been enumerated.

in Tucson more than three years. The particular "universe" of Papagos that has been important to the objectives of this study consists of Papago males between the ages of 15 and 65 who were, according to the Papago Population Register (1959), oriented occupationally and residentially off-reservation. Those of this age group enumerated as residing and/or working in Tucson in 1959 totaled 240 males.

This list of Papago names has been checked against an alphabetical listing of Tucson residents, 18 years of age and above, as found in the Tucson City Directory (1958, 1959). In this way, it has been possible to identify with some degree of precision the residences and the elicited occupational statuses for 120 Papago men (50 percent of the total adult male universe). It has been a sufficiently helpful means for the purposes of this discussion in that it does suggest a relationship between occupational status and Papago urban residence patterns. Plotting the residences (Figure 12) of these 120 individuals on a map of Tucson south of Broadway provides a rather distinct pattern of distribution, with a high concentration in the South Tucson and East 22nd Street areas, and a thinning out toward both the north and the south. Proceeding a step further, plotting individuals' residences and their indicated occupations reveals three rather discrete ecological areas of Papago residence and occupational statuses (Figures 13, 14, and 16).

The following symbols represent the occupational roles which characterize the adult male residents within each of the three Tucson neighborhood variants, as they appear on Figures 13, 14, and 16:

A	service station attendant
B	block, brick, cement worker
BO	bowling alley employee
C	construction worker
CK	cook
E	electrician
F	farm laborer
G	ground maintenance man, gardener
H	hotel employee
I	iron and steel worker
L	laundry laborer
l	laborer
M	miner
Mc	mechanic
N	nursery employee
O	no occupation listed
P	plasterer

Po	poultry house employee
R	railroad employee
r	retired
Rh	ranch hand
S	stock or store clerk
SM	service manager
T	truck driver
Y	yard worker

While few of the occupational roles are performed within these three spatial areas, residence seems to be somewhat related to occupational statuses. We therefore can use residence and occupation as the criteria for establishing three general variants of an urban, nonfarm occupational complex. While these residential areas are not totally discrete in terms of the kinds of occupational roles represented in their component households, general patterns seem to characterize each of the three areas to the point of suggesting different kinds of residence-occupational complexes or at least variants of the urban type. These areas, for purposes of description and discussion, are referred to as (1) the Old Pueblo Variant, (2) the Native American-Papagoville Variant, and (3) the Suburban Variant.

Old Pueblo Variant

On the basis of Figure 13 and a certain amount of field study, it is possible to hypothesize some of the distinctive characteristics of this variant of the Tucson occupational complex.

The further away from the area of highest concentration of Papagos, the more scattered are the individual households. The Papago families are more isolated from other Papago residence units and, instead, are located in a highly mixed area of many ethnic groups. Hence this area, which borders the downtown and Old Pueblo areas, contains the "urban isolate" arrangement (Chapter 2) in which both relatively isolated nuclear families or individuals detached from a nuclear family are predominant.

In the case of the isolate Papago families, the working members of the families appear to be attached either to occupations that lie close to the downtown area (i.e., Southern Pacific Railroad, ground maintenance for public schools, laundries, and hotels) or to semiskilled occupations in other locations. There is a difficult-to-establish number of transient or floating Papago individuals who live in downtown cheap hotels, flop houses, bus terminals,

74

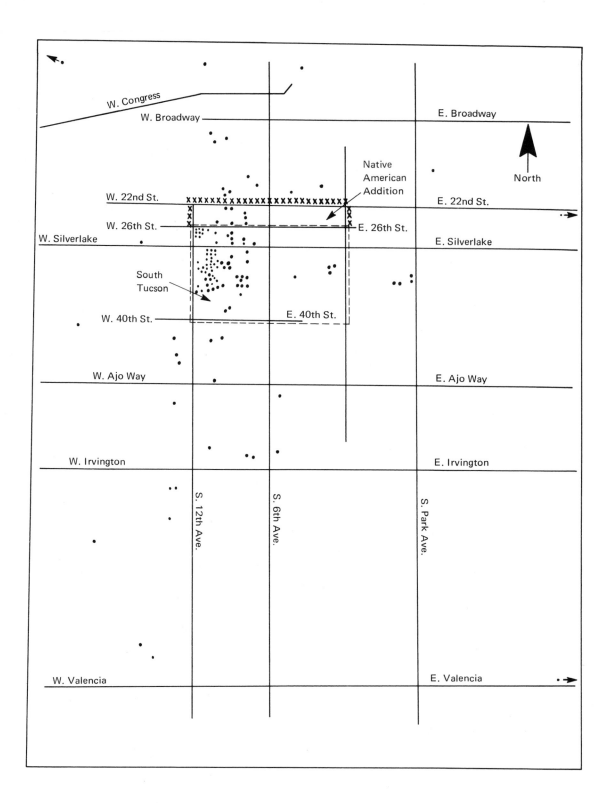

Figure 12. Papago Males (ages 15-65) According to Residence, 1958-59
(Tucson City Directory 1958, 1959; Papago Population Register 1959)

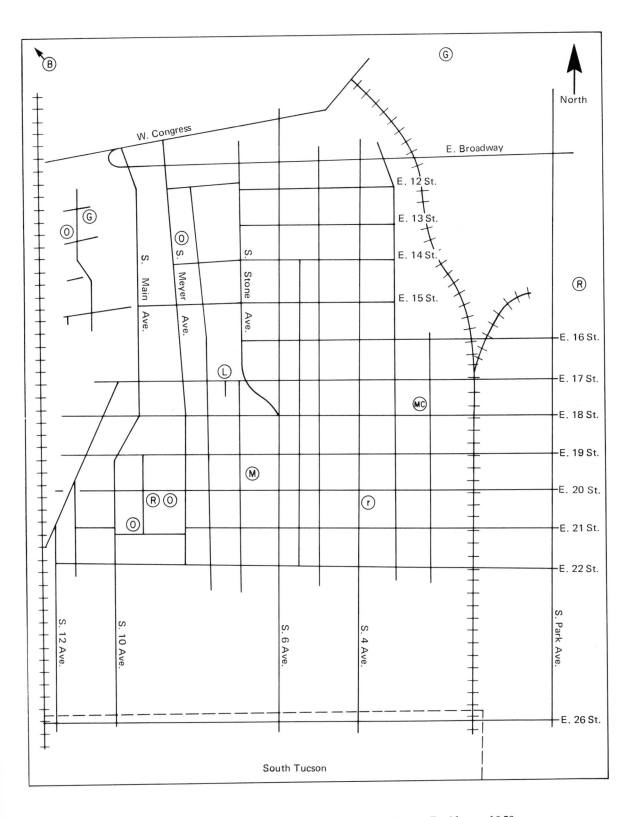

Figure 13. Old Pueblo Variant, Occupations According to Residence, 1959

or abandoned buildings. These individuals are frequently on the move, although their activities are largely confined to this downtown area. Their work habits are irregular and mundane but sufficient to maintain access to certain urban services, such as bars, hotels, cafes, movie houses, pool halls, and correctional facilities.

This area has a smaller percentage of people who actually own their own homes (17 percent). For the 13 Papago men identified as living in this particular area, there are 12 households with a total of 38 individuals attached to them. The number is somewhat smaller than is probably the case, largely due to the greater incidence of transience and the difficulties for census takers in trying to locate individuals who are circulating in a highly anonymous downtown area. The more permanent households, which have been more easily identified, probably are the remnants of a population which has pushed further south as Tucson has grown. Hence these urban isolate Papago households are a significant contrast to the urban isolate transient individuals who float about in the vicinity of downtown Tucson.

The acculturative types, which appear to be most representative of this area complex of institutions, are what have been referred to earlier as Anglo Modified and Anglo Marginal types. The individuals retain their cultural identification, but their activities are largely oriented to the values of Anglo culture. The urban isolate family has been able to modify those aspects of urban Anglo culture to such an extent that its participation is active and unstymied, although its full participation may not have been achieved due to the absence of certain traits such as adequate education or vocational training. Thus while the statuses of individual members of the family are to this extent marginal, their marginality is quite distinct from the urban isolate individuals who can neither fully participate in Anglo culture nor sufficiently modify native or Anglo values in order to fully participate in the Anglo tradition. The transient or floating "subculture" is the social field in which these individuals are able to modify or reconcile their social roles and accommodate their Papago values with those Anglo values affecting the "subculture" of transience.

Native American-Papagoville Variant

In contrast to the previous variant, Papagos in the Native American-Papagoville (Figure 14) area are highly concentrated; and while there are some families and individuals which may be further removed from the neighborhoods of greatest concentration, and to this extent are "more isolated," the enclave of Papagos provides a social field where many of the activities occur in the context of kinship and extended family relationships. While the social setting demands an intermingling with members of other ethnic groups and reliance on a number of urban institutions, the preponderance of Papago kin and the constant circulation of individuals to and from reservation villages helps to maintain a strong Papago identification. Papagos within this area rely largely on the stores, schools, recreational facilities, and other services on the main thoroughfares such as South 4th and South 6th avenues and 22d and 29th streets. However, while much of their activity takes place within the South Tucson vicinity, downtown and suburban institutions are accessible.

A very familiar settlement arrangement for Papagos in this area, which can be descriptively referred to as a residence compound, is similar to that depicted in Figure 15. The residence compound is made up of a number of individual dwelling units, very frequently lying off the alleys at the rear of other houses and facing toward a common "patio" or compound. The dwelling units are usually occupied by nuclear families or individual occupants, who may be related to each other in some way. The larger and better houses facing the main streets may be houses owned or occupied by Mexicans or other Papagos, while the houses to the rear and facing the alley are rented. Life in these alley compounds is oriented to the compound or patio; and all doors may face each other, making a congenial arrangement for face-to-face dealings with other residents in the compound. There is actually a great deal of cooperative activity such as sharing the resources earned by the employable males or females, common cooking and eating arrangements, and other forms of social life which have similarity to Papago patterns in reservation villages. Reservation relatives find it rather easy to attach themselves temporarily to this kind of an arrangement. The residence compound becomes the center for the enlargement and depletion of the Papago enclave. This type of residence makes the problems of enumeration doubly difficult and likely explains why the Tucson City Directory fails to account for a sizable number.

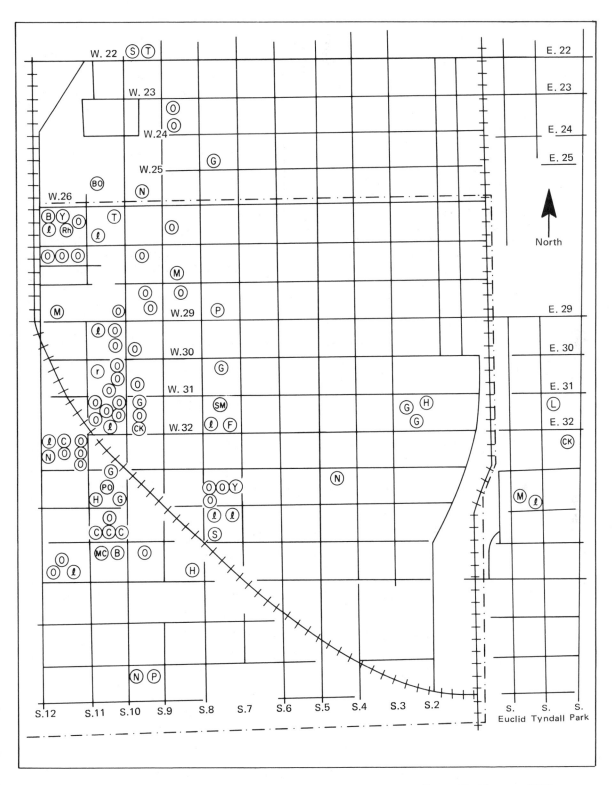

Figure 14. Native American-Papagoville Variant, Occupations According to Residence – 1959

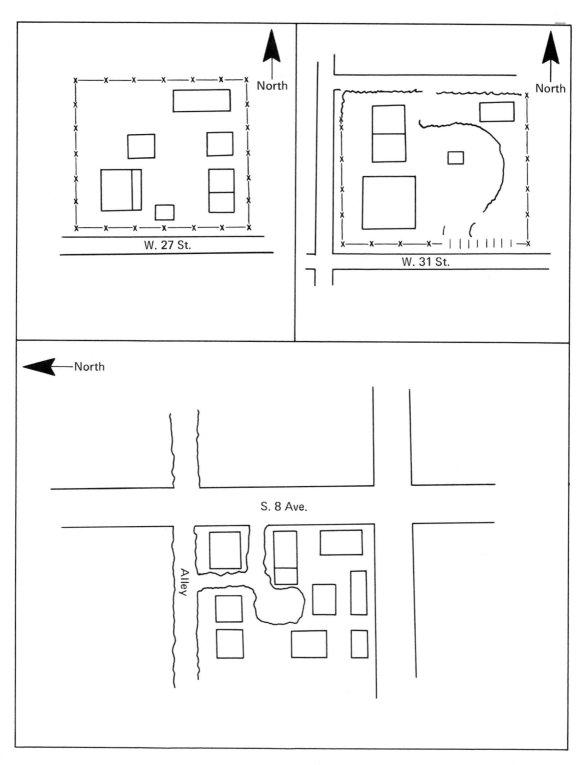

Figure 15. Papagoville Urban Family Residence Compounds

There are residence arrangements available in the Papagoville area for Papago individuals who are isolated or detached from some form of residence compound. Low-rent trailer courts and cottages provide such arrangements. However, it is possible that these may also constitute residence compounds for urban family clusters.

It has been possible to identify 87 Papago men through the method mentioned earlier. These individuals are attached to 66 distinct households which contain 291 individuals. Again this falls significantly short of the actual number of Papagos concentrated in the area, but the patterns are suggestive for purposes of generalization. Of the households identified, 23 (35 percent) are home owners. Undoubtedly a larger number of unemployed or spottily employed individuals are attached to these and similar households and have not been reckoned. The high incidence of "no occupation indicated," "labor," "yard work," and "construction" occupational roles suggests that there are likely many other individuals of similar status that enumerators may have missed, considering the turnover in these kinds of jobs.

At any rate, this concentration of Papagos consists of a smaller number of more permanently employed men or women and a larger number of "hangers-on" whose economic contributions to the households are less substantial due to the spotty nature of the work available to them or to which they avail themselves. In many cases, women, working as domestics in homes and hotels, provide the only substantial means of income. Figure 14 indicates the concentration of Papago households to the west of South 6th Avenue, between South 7th and South 12th avenues. For those whose occupations are indicated, construction jobs, common labor jobs, yard, nursery and hotel work are found to be very common. Those indicating no employment appear to be attached to households where there are individuals with permanent jobs. This area comprises those Papago individuals who still largely persist in those occupational roles which have been referred to as stereotypic Papago work roles. While they are represented, there seem to be fewer higher status occupations held by Papagos in this area. There are some more highly stabilized jobs, although still stereotypic, such as ground maintenance work. The outer extremities of the area, to the north, east, and south, suggest work roles that on the whole are more stabilized. Although the Tucson directory data do not reveal the importance of farm

work as a temporary safety valve when nothing else is available to Tucson Papagos, it undoubtedly is a source of work for many of those listed as "laborers" or those indicating no jobs.

It is possible to perceive the basic residence arrangement as being predominantly of the urban family cluster type, with some facsimile of the described residence compound housing a number of related Papago nuclear families or at least providing an arrangement that makes interaction with other Papagos and Papago families the prevailing form of social life.

With the residence compound functioning as a unit that absorbs reservation relatives, there is a vital link with both Native and Native Modified reservation individuals; although the units themselves contain individuals who are predominantly of the Anglo Modified type. This is to say that while the influences of the aged, more conservative segment and the younger, more active "native-core" segment of the reservation are an ever-present influence on the urban enclave, the majority have been sufficiently identified with the values of the urban setting in which they live. It is highly questionable whether there are any who could be classified as Anglo Marginal since cultural identification is still largely Papago. De-identification from Papago culture would be a difficult undertaking in this area of high Papago concentration. The individuals may, however, desire a fuller participation in certain aspects of Anglo culture which is not possible, either due to barriers erected by Anglo institutions and values or due to pressures of conforming behavior engendered by the members of the ethnic enclave. While the occupational statuses may remain somewhat low in terms of standards operating in a highly affluent and highly mobile society, the Native American-Papagoville sector provides an understandable degree of emotional security because it offers individuals relationships with others like themselves and certain rather well defined roles for adapting to an urban environment.

Suburban Variant

This type of urban complex encompasses Papagos who reside in predominantly non-Indian neighborhoods and who have assumed or are in the process of assuming middle class statuses. These individuals, although they may have originated in an area of high Papago concentration, characterized generally by a much "lower" social stratum, are now bent toward a new stratum of destination. Figure 16 reveals rather clearly the "higher" occupational statuses which characterize the heads of these households. For 20 individuals identified, there are 18 households consisting of 64 individuals. The occupations represented are either highly stabilized unskilled or semiskilled statuses or are within the highest range of Tucson Papago skills, i.e., mechanics, electricians, and iron workers. What is especially noticeable is the lack of the more stereotyped occupational roles that characterize Papagos in the Papagoville complex. Fifty percent of the householders are home owners and reside in neighborhoods with houses of considerably higher value than those found in the Papagoville and Old Pueblo areas.

There is a more obvious manifestation of acquiescence to many of the values and social relationships characteristic of the Anglo middle class. Sodality memberships linked to non-Papago activities are more prevalent; there is closer communication with non-Papagos in a variety of social situations; and the contacts with the more concentrated Papago enclave or reservation villages have been significantly reduced. The demands of the achieved occupational and associated social statuses have made relationships with non-Papagos more necessary, thus isolating much of their activity from Papagos and things Papago.

The individuals within the suburban segment have not, however, de-identified with Papago culture. Some of them form, instead, a core of Anglo-Modified Papagos with an express interest in the economic and social betterment of Papago people generally. They are not Anglo Marginals whose only deterrent to complete de-identification is their obvious ancestry. They form an intelligentsia, a more affluent segment of Papagos who express some administrative concern for the low status of many Tucson Papagos. Yet their kinship ties with other Papagos help them to retain their identification with their cultural group and to express emotional attachments when members of the cultural group have been slighted.

These individuals are from more isolated urban Papago families, those which intermingle in predominantly Anglo and Mexican middle class neighborhoods. Their children are highly Anglo-oriented, and many attend schools where there are few or no Indian children. Finally, there is little left of anything resembling an "active native core."

Structural Characteristics

This type of adaptive environment or occupational complex, while essentially an urban environment, does not necessarily consist of individuals who are totally dependent on urban occupations. On the other hand, it is unlikely that urban dwellers can live totally on what they are able to earn in seasonal farm labor. Unless the farm is immediate to the city limits, it is probable that most farm labor performed by urban Papagos is seasonal; otherwise residence on the farm would be more likely. Therefore, urban dwellers who rely on farm labor must be attached to some urban residence where one or more individuals are dependent upon income from some form of urban occupation. The reliance on farm labor by individuals in an urban household is only supplemental to the urban work activity. Perhaps those who rely part of the time on urban jobs also depend on seasonal farm jobs. On the whole, however, farm labor is not a desired or preferred pattern but is performed out of necessity. Choice of urban residence and utilization of urban institutions is a manifest expression of preference for urban work roles, and when the latter are available, they are preferred to unskilled farm labor.

Individuals in an urban complex of institutions may or may not manifest an overall occupational history which includes some farm labor. In either case, urban occupational roles are preferred when they are available or are of a desired kind.

An urban occupational complex consists of a nucleus or enclave of Papagos who have an extended history of urban, nonfarm residence and occupation. Some Papagos are totally urban oriented in that they are second or third generation urban Papagos, although kinship may link them to rural or reservation peoples and institutions.

Individuals attached to an urban complex either participate or attempt to participate in one or a whole range of occupations which have taken on a traditional character for members of the ethnic group. Only the town or city can provide an ample demand for these laborers. A smaller number, who have balanced training, motivational, and attitudinal factors, have been able to assume more skilled roles. However, the demand for more peripheral role elements, associated with the maintenance of higher occupational statuses, encourages a certain degree of assimilation of Anglo cultural values and perhaps

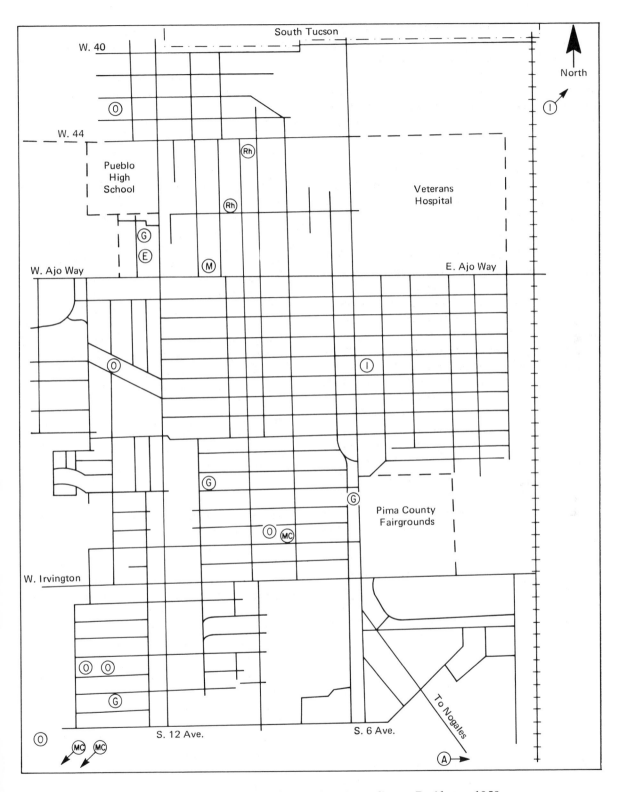

Figure 16. Suburban Variant, Occupations According to Residence, 1959

necessitates a de-identification with the lower stratum Papago community although not with Papago culture.

By virtue of urban residence and urban occupation, dwellers in an urban complex are almost totally dependent on urban institutions and their services. This reduces the extent of dependence on reservation structures; and even during periods of economic or occupational difficulty, the dependence on the urban complex is still largely intact. The more recently oriented rural or reservation Papagos may, however, return to the farms or the reservation at such times, although the individuals who comprise the core of urban Papagos are so oriented that their roles remain largely urban in character.

Occupational roles are still largely those that characterize a lower social stratum and thereby restrict the extent to which individuals can participate in certain institutions and values characteristic of an affluent society. The settlement patterns and the institutionalized occupational and other social roles tend to reinforce each other. Together, residence and occupation function to preserve identification with Papago culture in an urban environment that could otherwise serve to disorient individuals faced with new kinds of roles and social relations. At the same time, there is an available means for escaping or weaning oneself away from the ethnic community while maintaining an identification with Papago culture. Occupation becomes this means of detachment because higher occupational statuses demand new kinds of role behavior, including an increase in the peripheral role elements or the extra-job implications of higher occupational statuses. The ethnic community, if it supports essentially lower stratum occupational role behaviors, is a barrier to upwardly mobile Papagos. Therefore, certain occupational statuses insist on detachments from ethnic communities and identification with communities or neighborhoods which comprise individuals and families who have assimilated these values. Without this detachment, the ethnic community comes to represent a threat to the expectations parents might have for their children.

Occupational complexes in the urban environment are, therefore, largely residentially based in that occupations are instrumental in restricting individuals to certain kinds of residence; and residence in turn restricts individuals to a certain range of occupations. Restriction to a certain residence pattern by virtue of restrictions to certain kinds of occupations, further sets the boundaries as to the kinds of institutions or the kinds of social life in which people participate.

Range of Variation in Occupational Statuses and Roles

There has not yet been a complete study of the kinds of jobs and the ranges of skill which Papagos in urban areas represent. Thorough studies are needed not only for the immediate urban centers of Tucson and Phoenix but for the many relocation cities where Papagos are known to be working.

Two studies have been made which are helpful in setting a broader scope for Papago employment in urban occupations. A report to the Arizona Commission of Indian Affairs (1957: 45) provides employment data for 125 Tucson men from the 256 separate households identified. Table 20 summarizes the data obtained in the enumeration referred to in the 1957 report.

For a different point of view, Metsler (n.d.), in Table 9 of his manuscript, provides data of types of work done by Papagos in Tucson during 1959-60. His data are interesting because they were derived from a sample of firms, thus providing an institutional perspective. Table 21 provides a basis for comparison with the data summarized in Table 20.

Disregarding the overlap of categories due to the different foci of the two studies, it is possible to get a range of Papago occupational roles. Each study was able to expose occupational roles that the other either failed to disclose or lumped into some other category. Metzler's study seems to have concentrated on more stabilized employment statuses as they have become established through relatively successful attachment to firms.[3] As Metzler (n.d.: 96-7) notes, two-thirds of those Papago employees attached to the firms in his sample had very acceptable attendance records, indicating that these firms seem to hire only those with records of temperance and reliability. Those who cannot fulfill these expectations move toward casual labor, a category Metzler's survey ignores. The 1957 study allows for "casual labor" and "agricultural labor" categories, thus picking up some of the work force that Metzler's study of firms seems to by-pass, since the former study focused on the report occupations of household members.

---

[3] Metzler's sample consisted of 462 firms hiring 6,960 workers. Thirty-five of these firms employed Papagos at the time of his survey.

TABLE 20

Occupational Statuses of 125* Tucson Papagos, 1957

Skilled		Semiskilled		Clerical		Unskilled	
Carpenter	1	Construction labor†	12	Clerk typist	2	Gardener	19
Cook	1	Lumber yard labor	3	Stock clerk	1	Agricultural worker	6
Iron worker	1	Janitor, porter	2			Casual labor	46‡
Welder	1	Maintenance	2				
Mechanic	4	Truck driver	2				
Electronics	2	Miner	2				
Silversmith	1	Railroad maintenance	3				
Supervisor	1	Auto finisher	1				
	12		27		3		71

*Twelve were listed as unemployed.

†Cement finishers, plumbers' helpers.

‡Twenty-six were not confined to one type of work but performed several kinds — cotton harvest labor, track gang, construction, and yard work.

TABLE 21

Types of Work Done by 115 Tucson Papagos as Reported by Tucson Firms, 1959-60

Six Construction Firms

Common laborers	50
Machine operators	15
Supervisor	1
Maintenance man	1
Other specialized	3
	70

Six Manufacturing Firms

Laborers	3
Bottlers	2
Truck drivers	1
	6

Five Public Agencies

Maintenance	2
Gardeners	2
Truck drivers	3
Specialized labor	3
	10

Three Hospitals

Unspecified	3
	3

Four Hotels

Carpet men	2
Chef	1
Other	2
	5

Two Nurseries

Labor	13
Truck drivers	6
	19

Two Stores

Porter	1
	1

Seven Domestic Firms

Live-in yard work	1
	1

Using the 1958-59 Tucson City Directory data, which enumerate individuals according to both residence and occupation, Papago householders' specified occupations can be grouped into occupational institution categories as a further kind of comparison. Table 22 provides these data.

Although none of the tables provide a complete or consistent picture of occupational roles for Tucson Papagos, they are suggestive as to the range of roles that characterize Papago occupations. A complete study is still very much needed. The general "labor," "casual labor," "no information available," "unemployed" categories are in particular need of clarification, although presumably they can serve as catch-all categories for Papagos without any steady occupations.

In the recent Papago Employment Survey (1965), urban-oriented Papagos, largely from Tucson, seem to portray the same range of occupational statuses already discussed, except that Papagos on relocation tend to be the more highly skilled or trained. The ethnography of Papago relocation is another much needed area of research. The Navajo Urban Relocation Research Project of the University of Colorado in its study of urban migration processes as they impinge on Navajo adjustment in Denver[4] is a good example of the type of research needed.

In studying the field schedules of the Papago Employment Survey, it was possible to identify only nine Papagos over 35 years of age who could be said to represent predominant nonfarm employment histories. Of course, many in the sample were Tucson Papagos, a large number consisting of young men whose employment histories have not yet crystalliz into what could be referred to as a steady or stable pattern.

[4] A symposium on Navajo Urban Migration was conducted at the 1965 Denver meetings of the American Anthropological Association.

TABLE 22

Tucson Papago Laborers According to Occupational Institution Types, 1959

Type of Occupational Institution	Roles	Number of Papagos
Block, brick, sand and gravel companies	Machine operator Repairman Laborer Janitor	4
Construction companies	Plasterers (2) Maintenance man Laborers (3)	6
Distributing companies	Truck drivers	2
Farms and ranches	Farm laborer Ranch hand (2) Cattle inspector	4
Homes	Yard workers	2
Hotels	Cook Janitor Laborer (2)	4
Industrial-manufacturing companies	Mechanics (3) Iron workers (2) Electrician	6
Labor, unspecified	Laborers	10

Table 22 - continued

Type of Occupational Institution	Roles	Number of Papagos
Laundries	Wash man Laborer	2
Mines (other than Ajo)	Oiler Laborers (4)	5
Nurseries	Landscapers	4
Public agencies and businesses	Ground maintenance man (5) Gardeners (8) Post Office mechanic	14
Railroads	Truckman Porter	2
Restaurants	Cook	1
Stores	Bowling alley laborer Service station attendant Poultry house laborer Service manager — garage Stock clerk Ice man	6
— —	Retired	2
— —	No employment reported	46
		120

6. FIVE PAPAGO CAREERS

The discussion so far has dealt with cultural behavior as viewed from the outside. The best of anthropological tradition, on the other hand, has provided a methodological approach whereby anthropologists can hope to penetrate, albeit most superficially, the native or inside view of things so that the inside view might ultimately be formulated into scientific data — the outside view.

As Redfield (1960:82) expresses it, an ethnographer might be so successful in getting the native's inside view that he is unable to communicate it in the language of those who look in from the outside — those belonging to an alien "culture" such as that of the scientific community. In such a situation, it would be highly successful ethnography but could well be a failure as a scientific contribution. But failure to obtain the inside view of a culture, as perceived by individuals within that culture, is equally a loss to science, since social life and cultural behavior must certainly be something more than the meagre categories that scientists are able to abstract from them.

In the preceding chapters, general categories and abstract models have attempted to provide the "outside" view of a sociocultural phenomenon. Data from a variety of sources have been brought together, in the language of a science, as a way of portraying an outside perspective relative to Papago patterns of occupation and residence. Up to this point, however, nothing has been presented that approaches the inside view.

Redfield (1960: 84) would insist that while the "scaffolding of ideas that guides the investigator is composed of relationships, groups, institutions," the investigator, as an outside student of a typical human career, "must stay with the states of mind of somebody in the community as these states of mind range over many experiences and many phases of a single human life."

Following Redfield's (1960: 93) thoughts further:

The "ethnographical dilemma" is the scientist's form of the problem encountered in our common-sense life as the problem of "intercultural understanding." How are we to understand another people through definitions of experience that are different from those we are trying to understand? Ultimately it is the problem of communication and understanding between any two human beings. In all these cases it seems to us that in some circumstances understanding is in fact reached. And in all of them the way to understanding seems to lie through an alternation of talking and listening.

Simply put, the intent of this study is addressed to the problem of understanding Papago adaptation to off-reservation jobs and the social fields these jobs thereby create. It has seemed that the best way to approach this understanding would be to "stay with the states of mind" of a few Papago "somebodies" as they face a range of experiences in the course of their participation in occupational social fields. What social roles are they performing? How do they see themselves in these roles? What successes or failures do they see? What kinds of fulfillment? What kinds of frustration? Can adaptation to certain kinds of roles relate to successes or failures in certain kinds of occupational role performance?

The next two chapters will seek to bring together some of the basic data that have been derived from rather close and extended interaction with a few Papago men representing each occupational complex type abstracted in the preceding chapters. The field approach, from which the data for the discussion to follow have been derived, has followed that suggested by Leeds (1965: 385), that is, "that the most incisive way to discover the intimate workings of the system was to trace the histories of individuals as they moved through their careers, establishing connections and moving from organized entity to organized entity." This is remarkably similar to that proposed by Mayer (1962: 577) and Fortes (1936: 46) as discussed in Chapter 1. By presenting a thumbnail sketch of a Papago worker's occupational career and by charting his social genealogy or the mapping of his personal connections and roles (Leeds 1965: 385), it becomes possible to describe the fundamental aspects of social institutions as they impinge on the role behavior of many Papagos facing similar socially structured fields.

In this chapter, a few very brief occupational careers representing each occupational complex type will be presented. These career histories also will provide the cultural backgrounds of the individual Papagos, that is, the types of cultural experience and the types of acculturation categories (native, native modified, Anglo modified, or Anglo marginal) which characterized their families of orientation. The personal histories will also attempt to include the occupational careers of members of their extended families, that is, as far as these became known. Also, the career histories will attempt to include the highlight experiences which have specific bearing on personal adaptation to the occupational social field.

In Chapter 7 there will be an attempt to identify in these cases the crucial social roles that have some apparent relationship to the kinds of adaptations or accommodations taking place in the process of occupational adaptation. The discussion will focus on how certain social roles are perceived by the individual and how they are enacted, resulting in either role conflict,

role alienation, role accommodation, or role enhancement. The social genealogies will be mapped to indicate the personal apprehension and enactment of a variety of occupational, kinship, leadership, ceremonial, sodality, friendship, and a host of other Papago and Anglo institutional roles. It is not only a matter of identifying these roles, however. An even more important concern is to account for the interplay of these roles in the personality organizations of Papago workers and the relationships the interplay may have to adaptive processes.

Finally, the discussion will conclude with the identification of the cases in terms of their acculturative types and a statement of prognosis as to the direction of change for the individual cases.

COMMERCIAL FARM OCCUPATIONAL COMPLEX

The Case of Alonzo Jose[1]

Alonzo Jose is a 64-year-old Papago from the village of Ali Chukson in the Baboquivari District of the Sells Reservation. Al is living in a long adobe house that is part of a two-house camp lying on farm property being leased by the Barnes' farm near Sahuarita, Arizona. He has been a steady farm hand for Mr. Barnes since 1960, having come from a similar job on a much larger farm near Coolidge, Arizona. Al, his Topawa wife Juliana, and his youngest son Albert's daughter Angela, age 6, live in two of the house's five rooms.

Al is still in excellent health and claims to be feeling like a young man, although he says he has not been to a doctor since his work for the government on the reservation in the 1940s. His English is pretty good, although it is muffled by the absence of some front teeth, and his thinking gets bogged down if one goes too fast or is not careful in keeping conversation relatively simple and about things with which he is familiar. He is friendly, hospitable, and outgoing with an occasional flair for wit and humor.

Al's father was a flood farmer at Ali Chukson and had a few head of cattle and some horses. Seldom did his father have occasion to leave the reservation; so

most of Al's early years, when he was not away at school, were spent in the vicinity of Ali Chukson. Since most of his relatives lived in Topawa, Ali Chukson, or other villages close by, Al says he never had any reason to stray very far from home. He never came off the reservation to live until he was a grown man, after he had married and had a family. On special occasions as a boy or as a young man, he would ride over on horseback to such places as Topawa, Gu Oidak, Havana Nakya, and Santa Rosa to attend the dances and fiestas. He recalls the many people and the fun of these festivities.

His father never did any wage work off the reservation, but Al remembers when he used to come with his father to Tucson with a wagon load of wood or chunks of home-made cheese to sell. Sometimes the trips occurred once a month, sometimes not more than once a year. They would take the old wagon trail straight across to Tucson, sometimes stopping at San Xavier to sell cheese. Most of the time they went directly to a Chinaman who had a store a block or so from a big church, near 22nd Street and Stone Avenue. There was just a bunch of Indian houses there then, just south of Congress Avenue where a lot of big buildings are now. The Chinaman's store on West 18th Street was always surrounded by a lot of wagons belonging to Indians and Mexicans. Al's father had credit at the store and sold his cheese to the Chinaman or else made his own rounds to the houses of the Indians and Mexicans. Al considers

---

[1] The personal names used in all cases are fictitious.

these experiences as being very enjoyable and interesting for a boy so young.

Al carries a lot of vivid memories of stories told by his grandfathers and grandmothers (the old folks) about the Apaches and Mexicans, and Papago heroics. He still enjoys talking about them. He also received the familiar precautions to be careful around strangers and animals. When they would camp up in the mountains, the old men would tell stories at night, and every little noise in the darkness beyond camp was identified as possible Apaches still lurking about (a good way to keep the children close to camp at night).

During Al's boyhood, adult tasks were gradually learned — carrying wood and water; digging post holes and making fence posts; walking a plow in the fields; planting, cultivating, and harvesting the corn, beans, wheat, and melons; rounding up cattle; milking; making cheese; and going to Tucson to sell wood, cheese, or perhaps the products of their fields, or a cow for two gold pieces ($40). But, for boys, work assigned or expected becomes an excuse for play and fun; when it ceases to be that, it is better to head for the desert before someone thinks of a job to do. There is work to be done, but only when necessary. There will be time, when one is older, to work. Thus, while there was always work to do, Al had a leisurely attitude toward work. In his own words, "I used to just play around, then get hungry and come around the house, then go play again." Childhood was a time for doing chores; but mostly it was a time for standing aside or going along and watching how the older ones did it, for some day work would be an inevitable part of life. One must learn to work even though one does not have to do it immediately.

In 1914, Al, at the age of 12, had his first introduction to school when a Papago lady came to the village and taught a group of a dozen or more children in a little ocotillo schoolhouse built next to the church.[2] This prepared him for his new experience at a Franciscan mission school up on the Navaho reservation, which he attended from 1915 to 1922. He carries a few pleasant and a number of less than pleasant memories of his experiences there. Foremost of his fears was the fact that there were going to be Apaches there, and he had heard so much of the mean Apaches that he was fearful of running into one. Later he found some friends among them, but he claims that his apprehension of Apache temperament

was confirmed a time or two. At first he was the only Papago at the mission school, and he correctly perceived that this arrangement was a device to wean him away from his reliance on his own language.

His parents at first opposed the priests for taking him away, but after awhile they got used to it. By the time Al's parents were thinking about sending him back to school, the priest told him he should now stay and help his father. In addition to his farming and ranching activities, Al's father was a *makai*, or Papago medicine man. According to Al, his father had a good reputation and had a considerable clientele of Tucson Mexicans as well as Indians who came to see him, have him sing all night, determine the nature of the illness, and give them things to make them well. As Al recalls,

He must have been good because a lot of people came to him. He would make them better. They would come to get medicines from him, like herbs or roots and stuff like that. I don't know why I never learned that from him — that is the way some of the Indian doctors learn, from their fathers, but I never learned much of that from my father. They are different than white doctors. They don't ask for money — whenever you can pay, you give a little, sometimes a quarter.[3]

Al was away from home and kin for several important years while at school and came back only once in the seven years he was there. The priests brought him back for two weeks one summer, then took him back to school. At the school, Al learned arithmetic, history, geography, and a lot about how he was supposed to be a good Catholic. They also taught him tailoring and carpentry; but these were not practical when he got back home, since there were no machines or tools available. He also got interested in games familiar to Anglos, games that were not too dissimilar from the foot races and kick ball games that he so much enjoyed at home. Al also learned to play the

---

[2]The school at Lourdes, or Ali Chukson, was one of the first two Franciscan mission schools established in the Papagueria or present Sells Reservation. This school and one at Topawa were begun in 1912 (Officer 1956: 107).

[3]This is either a virtuous feature of the more serious Papago *makai*, that is, an aspect of "ideal" culture, or the pattern refers to an earlier value about the Papago medicine man before the "age of affluence." Some *makai* now receive for payment the equivalent of an M.D.'s office call. Al's mother's brother, still living in a nearby village, is one of the most reputable *makai* on the reservation.

saxaphone and the cornet, handy for joining an orchestral group at a fiesta.

But school ended; and he was back at his home village, now 20 years old, back to plowing, planting, harvesting, and rounding up cattle. In 1926, at the age of 24, Al brought his young wife of 17 to his father's place at Ali Chukson. Children came in 1928, 1929, 1931, and 1936, and there were now the responsibilities of keeping a family. He inherited about 15 acres of land from his father, but the horses and cattle were all sold during "bad times," when it "got so dry that we couldn't feed them or water them." Al continued to cultivate the land intermittently until around 1942, but since that time his fields have been idle.

Fortunately, the government began its program on the reservation in the early 1930s; and Al, leaving his family at Ali Chukson, hopped the government truck and went away to work on mountain trails, or to help build charcos. During this period he lived in tent villages and did his own cooking, although some of the men took their families. Al would take the truck to Sells on weekends and hoof it the remaining six miles home, and sometimes he would stay home for a week or so and attend to other chores. In 1935 Al started driving heavy equipment. He learned to operate a variety of machinery — bulldozers, caterpillars, "razor blades," trucks, and tractors — working over much of the reservation. He continued working for the government until around 1943, when his attention turned almost exclusively to off-reservation wage work.

In 1943, a big truck and trailer came down to the Sells vicinity and took a load of seasonal workers to a little farm camp about 10 or 12 miles northwest of Stanfield, Arizona. After that first season, Al and his family came back to his home village until the next cotton harvest. It was after the 1944 season was over that the farm operator, finding out that Al was an experienced equipment operator, asked him to stay on as a permanent hand. Al drove a tractor at this particular farm until 1947 when the operator lost his lease. Al immediately went to work at another farm two and a half miles northwest of Stanfield, living in the farm camp. The children started attending the school in Stanfield, and Al got his first experience as an irrigator. In 1949, the family decided that they wanted to go home for a while, so Al left his job at the Stanfield farm. His older children also had been

working in the fields chopping weeds, and enough money had been saved to last for a while. Before this time, they just went back when work in the fields was slack.

The family stayed at Little Tucson (Ali Chukson) until 1951 when it went to a tent cotton camp near La Palma, Arizona, north of Eloy. When the cotton picking was over, the operator asked Al if he could drive a D-4 tractor cat; when Al said he could, he was asked to stay on. The family lived in two tents at this camp for about a year, then moved to a camp north of Coolidge, where Al worked as an irrigator and driver for the same operator. By this time the two oldest boys were irrigating and driving for the same man on a part-time basis. On occasional breaks, the family would return home. In 1953, Al had some differences with a foreman and "just pulled out."

There was a farm near Three Points that he heard needed an irrigator and cultivator, so he moved his family into an old trailer house on that farm and labored there about a year. The lady who operated the farm left farming, and since Al was "feeling sick," the family returned to Little Tucson until they again went up to Coolidge in 1955 to work for the same operator, who had since gotten a new foreman. Al worked there until 1959, also putting in a little work as an irrigator and general hand for another Coolidge farm in 1956.

Al's youngest son was working at Barnes' farm in the Continental-Sahuarita area in 1959, and when Al came down to visit, Mr. Barnes asked him to work for him. Al returned to Coolidge for a couple of months but then decided to take Mr. Barnes up on it since the pay was the same, it was closer to home, and the house was a better one. Al has worked as a steady hand since 1960 for Mr. Barnes, while his sons have since continued to float around to different farms or return to the reservation.

In 1966, the oldest son Carlos was living at Sells, inactive since he fell from a hay rack while employed at the Sells store two years earlier. He and his family are living off a monthly disability allotment. A second son, Emetrio, since November, 1965, has been driving a tractor on a farm northwest of Marana; and, Albert, the youngest son, and his family, with the exception of the youngest daughter, are in Al's place back at Ali Chukson, where Albert is "trying to get a job with the agency." A daughter, Mariana, lives with her husband at Chiawuli Tak (Fresnal Village). Her husband is a cattleman and farms at Supi Oidak.

Al, who is a year away from full retirement age, has this to say about his plans:

I still would like to work yet; I still feel young. I'm not ready to quit yet, that's why they keep me here; they like my work. I want to work even after I get my social security. How much will they let me make? I don't know how long I can work yet but I feel good now and I want to keep at it. Someday I'll go back to Little Tucson, but I want to try and farm it.

AJO MINE OCCUPATIONAL COMPLEX

The Case of Raymond Victor

Raymond Victor, a 45-year-old Papago, has been a regular employee of the Phelps Dodge Corporation at the Ajo open pit copper mine since 1947. Raymond, his wife Amelia, from Kom Vo in the Pisinimo District, three daughters, and a son live in a four-room frame house, built by the company, at the foot of a "slag" heap in the southern-most part of Ajo Indian community. The oldest son, Gerald, also an employee at the mine, lives with his wife and infant son in a company house across the street. Another son, Benson, is attending Haskell Indian Institute at Lawrence, Kansas; while the oldest daughter is in her first year of high school at St. John's mission boarding school for Indians on the Gila River Pima Reservation south of Phoenix.

Raymond is a friendly man and fairly articulate in English, considering that he had only seven years of school. His wife, on the other hand, speaks hardly any English and is much more "Papago" in terms of her attitudes, beliefs, social roles, and behavior.

Raymond was born in 1920 at the village of Lower Covered Wells 12 miles south of the Santa Rosa villages. The former village, Chu'wuk ("rotten place"), at the site of the present village, was a well village for the Santa Rosa people before the turn of the century, and some of the houses in the village today are used by Santa Rosa people on round-ups or during festivities. Raymond's father Juan, a ceremonial and civic leader in the village before his death in 1957, came from Sikul Himatk, seven miles to the southeast, a village related to other Santa Rosa villages. Up to the time he was six, Raymond lived at Gurli Put Vo, six miles to the northeast of Covered Wells. Thereafter, the family made its more permanent home at Covered Wells, although a summer house near the field village of Gurli Put Vo was maintained until Raymond's father died. The family's cactus camp or *wha'to* has been maintained to this day just a little way to the west of the summer field village. Raymond still has fields and a few head of cattle, which he inherited from his father, at Gurli Put Vo, although his steady job at the Ajo mine does not give him much time to give to these concerns. Relatives care for what remains of the herd.

Juan Victor, Raymond's father, was a very busy man in village and district affairs besides having his own fields and cattle to care for. Raymond grew up anticipating that someday he would have to assume some of the same responsibilities, since his father held this up to him many times. Juan Victor used to lead the rain dances and songs at the wine feasts at Covered Wells, but he was also very close to the Franciscan Fathers, who had established a mission church and school in the village. Having deep attachments to many aspects of Papago custom as well as to the innovations of church fathers and government workers, Juan Victor was therefore a controversial figure to those who felt his progressive ideas were detrimental to some of the customs. In his later years, Juan was able to re-establish some of these relationships that had grown brittle, as he became more conservative regarding certain customs.

Raymond has many rich memories of his childhood experiences, and he enjoys talking about them. His "grandfather" (father's uncle) told serial stories, such as the one about the good hunter or the one about the eagle who killed many people. If anyone got ahead of the story or interrupted during its telling, the story would end, leaving a group of disappointed youngsters.

Raymond, much to the surprise of his elderly mother, still remembers a two-day wagon trip to Tucson with his father in 1925 when they took a load of chickens to sell to the Mexicans and Indians living on the outskirts of Tucson. They stopped two different nights along the way in villages where there were relatives.

When Raymond was about eight, his father taught him how to trace the tracks of horses and how to hobble the horses. About the same time he also began accompanying his father to the fields. He recalls how he held onto the lower brace of the old wooden plow as his father held the upper brace, and how the two of them followed the horses and the plow through the fields. Only when he had enough weight did his father let him do it alone. Raymond also followed his father as he plowed, planting the corn seeds. Then there were always weeds to hoe.

Sneaking away from chores to play with siblings was common, but in Raymond's household it could not be done without punishment of some kind, even if only a good talking to. Whenever older people or visitors came around, Raymond was taught to water the horses and to stay quietly in the background. On one occasion his father "hobbled" Raymond and his first cousin together when they got too noisy during a visit from relatives.

Raymond recalls that when he was just a little boy his father's family and some of his father's siblings' families went up in a wagon convoy to Mesa, Goodyear, Gilbert, and Tempe to pick cotton. They also camped at Guadalupe village, near Chandler, among the Yaquis. They had been doing this for a number of years up until 1927 when his father was able to buy some cattle and devote all his time to farming and ranching.

In 1927, Raymond was told that the priests were going to take him away to go to school at St. John's. It was a very sad time, and when the truck came he was put on it in spite of his crying protests. Raymond remembers how lost and homesick he was. When he came home for the next summer he said he would not go back. But he did. However, in November of the same year, he was brought home to go to school at Covered Wells, as the Ajo road was being built through the village, and a school was started for the children attached to the nearby workers' camp. The camp eventually moved on, so in September of 1929 he was back at St. John's.

It was not long before he ran away from the boarding school along with an older cousin and was permitted to stay home to attend the new school next to the mission church. In the familiar surroundings of home, Raymond was able to finish seventh grade. He says he learned a great deal from a very strict old man and can relate many of his experiences with this old teacher.

At the age of 14 he had to drop out of school in order to take on more of the work for his father, who was losing his sight. Although at that time he did not regret dropping out, he now regrets that this is all the education he was able to get.

In addition to the work in the fields or doing work around the mission and school, Raymond went to spend a couple of weeks for three successive summers with a half-sister and her husband in Los Angeles. On the last trip, when he was about 15, he stayed three whole months as a gardener and caretaker at a home where his half-sister arranged for him to "live-in." However, he got homesick and decided to return to Covered Wells.

In 1937, Raymond's parents moved the family to the village of Many Lizards at Santa Rosa, since his father's fields were not getting enough rain. Juan Victor rented a little house next to St. Elizabeth's Church and planted in fields belonging to his collateral relatives. Raymond went over to Ajo about this time (May, 1937) and worked on the track gang at the mine until August, when he returned to the family at Santa Rosa. There he started driving the mission school bus until the end of the semester, although the family moved back to Covered Wells by October.

In 1939 the family went in a contractor's truck to a cotton farm near Eloy and lived in a tent camp at that farm. After the harvest, they returned home. In January of 1940 Raymond married his wife Amelia at the Catholic Mission at Pisinimo, and by August he was still unable to get a steady job. His father had worked for an old couple north of Eleven Mile Corner when Raymond was a baby, and this old couple notified Raymond in August of 1940 that a neighboring farm needed a steady hand and irrigator. Raymond, his new bride, and his whole family made the trip up, since the other members of the family intended to pick cotton. In October, his wife caught pneumonia and had to be taken to the Sells hospital. On her release, around All Souls' Day, he brought his wife home from the hospital to Covered Wells and his family returned from the cotton farm.

In November, 1940, Raymond's father's brother-in-law from Santa Rosa told them of a farm near La Palma, Arizona, where they had been working for a few years. Raymond and his wife joined his father's family in the seasonal trips to this farm in 1940 and again in 1941. In the spring of 1942, Raymond was asked by a church brother to accompany him to Ajo to help rebuild the Ajo Indian village church that had burned down. By June the work was completed, and the lay brother helped him get a job as a clean-up man, and, eventually, as a sampler at the Ajo mine mill. He got tired of the job and wanted to go home, so quit his job at the mine in July of 1943 in time to join the family in its seasonal trip to the La Palma farm. When the cotton season was over, Raymond and his wife stayed on and Raymond irrigated at the same farm until May, when he was drafted into the Army.

A friend of his from Sells was drafted with him, and they remained together through basic training and for part of the time in Italy, where Raymond served as an infantryman, a volunteer litter bearer, a member of a medium tank crew, and finally as a member of a heavy artillery division. While in Italy he ran into another Papago friend from Supi Oidak.

It was while Raymond was in the service that he began to think about the necessity of getting a steady job and supporting his family. Up to that time it was a little work here and there, then back to Covered Wells.

When he got back home, in January, 1946, Raymond joined his family at the farm in La Palma. When the cotton season was over, he got a job as an irrigator at a farm near Casa Grande and had worked there about a month when his father came to the farm and asked him to come home. Raymond willingly told his boss that he was leaving and went back with his father to Covered Wells. He worked for a short time at the Covered Wells store as a clerk, then was persuaded by a government lady to go somewhere to get a steady job and start qualifying for

social security. In December of 1946, he decided to go once again to the Ajo mine, where he was offered his old job back at the mill. Since he would have had to wait several days, he decided to take a track labor job instead, in order to get to work right away.

In May of 1947, Raymond became a mine pipe laborer and has been with a pipe gang ever since, gradually achieving the highest pay grade possible in this category of work.

Through the years that he has been employed at the mine, Raymond has maintained two residences — his home at Covered Wells and his rented house in Ajo Indian village. Whenever there is a shutdown, day off, or vacation, the whole family goes back to the reservation village. Raymond has the following to say about his job at Ajo and his prospects for the future:

I plan to go out there [Covered Wells] when I am done here. That's why I've never tried to buy here. I want to go back. I've always wanted to go back when in school, working in Los Angeles, at the mine, in the service. I knew I had to get away in order to make a living, but I intend to go back for good when I am done here. I've talked to the boy about it. If he makes good at Haskell in auto mechanics we'll try to start a garage and filling station back home. I had a little of this when I worked for the Jackson's [at the Covered Wells Store]. The first thing I like about it is like I said, I want to be at home. We could also manage other things like farming along with it. I guess it's in *my* blood, too. I want to be able to do this before I get all involved over here and before I get too old.

OSCILLATING FARM-NONFARM OCCUPATIONAL COMPLEX

The Case of Paul Antonio

Paul Antonio is a 45-year-old Papago from Pan Tak (Coyote Sits), a reputedly old village nestled at the western foot of the Coyote Mountains in the eastern portion of the Sells Reservation. Paul has kinship ties to the villages of Sil Nakya and Palo Verde of the Santa Rosa complex through his parents. Pan Tak people have also had connections with the San Xavier Papagos for a long time, and Paul has many relatives in the San Xavier villages.

Paul is one without a clear commitment to either an urban or rural way of life and reveals a great deal

of ambivalence relative to this uncommitted style of life. Paul presently is temporarily separated from his wife Margaret and is living in South Tucson. He has recently been spending a lot of time in jail on a series of drunk charges but occasionally gets in a few days of work with one of Tucson's larger nurseries. Margaret and their six children have recently moved to a one-room adobe house in the village of Bac at San Xavier, where she is drawing a monthly Aid to Dependent Children check, although her husband makes an occasional appearance at the house. Court authorities have been trying to locate Paul in order to enforce his responsibility to the family.

Despite Paul's present apparent irresponsibility toward his family, himself, or his job, there is a pattern to his career, and the present situation is a part of the overall pattern in that it is temporary and has happened before.

Paul is, when sober, very quiet and a difficult person with whom to converse, although he is not unfriendly in his introversion. His response verges on shyness and solitude. However, when Paul is braced with a moderate amount of alcohol, he becomes an extremely talkative and gregarious person. Unfortunately, the moderate stage is an impermanent point on a continuum of consumption which leads inevitably to extreme intoxication once Paul begins to drink, whereupon he is finally rendered incoherent and sometimes verbally hostile. Therefore, unlike Al and Raymond, Paul has been an extremely unpredictable informant.

Paul grew up in Pan Tak, and most of his early years were spent in the association of relatives from his home village, the sister village of Viopuli (San Pedro), or the San Xavier group. His father, who was killed in a highway accident near Sells in 1954, spent most of his adult lifetime at Pan Tak, working his own land, flood farming, or occasionally making trips to Tucson for economic ventures. Paul recalls his father never having any cattle, and before Paul's time his father irrigated and farmed land belonging to him at San Xavier. Paul remembers his father on one occasion telling of going to a farm near Marana to work, but this was before Paul's time. There were infrequent wagon trips to Tucson for the purpose of selling wood, and returning with a load of merchandise. A more common family activity was the wheat harvest at San Xavier, when the whole family would spend three months hand cutting wheat and returning to Pan Tak with a share of the wheat as its recompense. His father had a summer house in the village of Many Ants just west of the mission. The only other wage work Paul remembers his father engaging in was road construction near Marana and Picacho many years ago; he never did any CCC work on the reservation. As Paul puts it, "He was just a farmer."

Paul remembers as a boy bringing in a wagon load of wood from the desert to the house or making the mile-and-a-half trip to Coyote Spring on the western slope of the Coyote Mountains to get water and haul it back to the house. Sometimes there was digging and chopping in his father's fields.

Paul recalls that the thing he liked to do most as a boy was to go off by himself, with his .22 rifle, and hunt rabbits, deer, and wild hogs. He says he knows just how high all those mountains are because he used to go all over them when he hunted. He would still like to go out and hunt if he had a gun. Also among his most vivid memories are the occasional wagon trips to Mexico to attend the Magdalena fiesta. Deep in the recesses of Paul's memory about his childhood experience, a cognitive area difficult to tap, lies his identification with the Papago past — an affective link with Papago tradition that is part of his personality "mazeway." Only while in an inebriated state did Paul volunteer a hint of this affective link: "All of us Indians know what's what — no, the old people used to tell us what's what and we knew everything we needed to know. But the old people don't know what's what any more. Things have changed. It's not like it used to be. . . now we have to come over here and the people forget everything."

Paul's father, Averisto Antonio, initiated the off-reservation work pattern with his brief experience at a farm near Marana and in working on the construction of roads in the vicinities of Marana and Picacho. Most of his life was spent, however, at either San Xavier or, later, Pan Tak. Paul's older brothers, Lalo and Juan, spent their earliest years at San Xavier, but by the time Paul was born, the family had moved back to Pan Tak, although Juan stayed with relatives at San Xavier in order to attend school there, and Lalo was sent through the eighth grade at St. John's. Paul, his older sister Catherine, and another brother, Ronald, had to ride by truck to a little white schoolhouse at Three Points; but, when the Santa Rosa Ranch school was built, Paul and Catherine were able to complete the sixth grade there. Paul does not remember much about school except that he learned English, how to read, and the elemental things one learns in grade school. He says he quit when he was around 15 in order to "work and help out the family."

In 1936, he went to Ajo with his brother Juan and tried to get a job at the mine. Juan got a job, but Paul was too young and was turned down. Their oldest brother Lalo had gone over in 1934 when operations resumed after the depression and was working there at the time. Lalo worked intermittently at the mine through 1948, at which time he stabilized his employment, and maintained a very good record of dependability until his sudden death in 1958. Juan, however, left the mine in May, 1937, 14 months after he started.

In the late summer of 1937, the Pima Farms of Cortaro, in the Marana area, sent trucks to the reservation to contract Papago cotton pickers, and the truck stopped at Pan Tak village. As Paul reflects, "A contractor came by my village in a truck and took us [his brothers Juan and Ronald and his sister Catherine] over there. I don't remember, but I guess that was the first contractor's truck to come to our village so I just went on it." They stayed in a tent camp at the farm from September through November, with Catherine doing the cooking for the three brothers.

From 1938 to 1940, Paul and his three older brothers were able to work for the government chopping trees, making fence posts, building corrals, and putting up fences around the wells and charcos. A government truck came to the village; and, when enough men were hired to comprise a crew (eight to ten men), it would be assigned to certain villages in the district. Paul always had at least one of his brothers in the same crew. They would live in a tent camp in the area in which they were working and return to Pan Tak on weekends. For the first three months, they just chopped trees; then work stopped for awhile, and they went back home. Later Paul and his brothers went back with their respective crews to put up the fences at the various villages. Paul says he got $45 every tenth of the month for a 40-hour per week work schedule.

In June, 1941, Paul's brother Lalo wrote him from Ajo to tell him that the mine was hiring men; so Paul hopped a mail truck, rode over to Ajo, and got hired as a track laborer. Paul first stayed with his brother and his wife in the Clarkston settlement, but a little later they moved into one of the new company houses in the Indian community. In April of 1942 Paul was discharged for coming to work drunk. He therefore went back to Pan Tak and remained idle until he was drafted into the Army in 1943.

Paul spent 34 months in the service, receiving his basic training and heavy artillery training at Ft. Sill, Oklahoma. He was stationed for a few months at Camp House, Texas, and then was shipped out for overseas duty in the European theater, going by way of Scotland, England, France, Belgium, Holland, and finally to Germany. He was a machine gunner in service battery and was also attached to munitions supply, following up the front lines with ammunition.

When Paul was given his honorable discharge in 1946, he returned to Pan Tak for a period of a year. In 1947, he came to live in Tucson with relatives on West 31st Street. He worked for a short time at a nursery, then a friend got him a job making cement blocks at a cement block factory. Paul was at the block plant almost two years, then decided to quit. It was during this time that he married Margaret Lopez, a Santa Rosa girl who grew up in Tucson. They lived in a series of rented houses or rooms in the West 29th, West 30th, and West 31st streets neighborhood.

In 1950, he answered a newspaper ad and got a job at another Tucson nursery, working off and on at this place until 1953. On this job he got acquainted with much of the city and made contacts that have since helped him when he has gone out on his own doing yard work. Paul was instrumental in getting his brother Juan a job at the same nursery. They got experience planting shrubbery, and pruning and trimming trees. Paul left the nursery for "lots of reasons" and got a job at another nursery in Tucson, where he worked for a short period.

In the summer of 1953, Paul ran into a "friend" on the streets in South Tucson who told him about some work up in Eloy, so he went up on a bus to find out about the farm and where the family would stay. He then came back for his family and took them to the farm camp near Eloy, where Paul, Margaret, and their two small children stayed for about a year, although making periodic trips back to Tucson. It, was at this farm, a mile south of Eloy, that Paul first learned how to start and operate the irrigation pumps and to put up the hoses. He was becoming acquainted with the duties required of a steady hand.

In the summer of 1954, the family moved south to Sahuarita with a Negro contractor to chop cotton. This took Paul and his family closer to home. During the chopping season Paul kept himself busy; but during the picking season, he preferred to try finding some yard work in Tucson since he did not like to pick cotton. For the next two years, Paul followed a similar pattern, that is, working as a chopper and irrigator at two different farms in Sahuarita but returning daily for occasional yard jobs in Tucson when the water was not pumping.

In 1957, a brother-in-law from the Florence Indian village, who was working in the Florence area and who was well acquainted with a number of farms, came to tell him of an opening for a general hand and tractor driver. Paul, his wife, and three children moved to the camp on this particular farm and remained there, cultivating and irrigating, until Paul was "laid off." While Paul was in Florence, his wife gave birth to a fourth child, a daughter, at the Sacaton Indian hospital.

In 1958, the family returned to Tucson and rented a rear apartment on West 31st Street. Paul was able to get work at one of the nurseries at which he had worked during 1950-53. He soon got mad at the boss over an argument they had and quit his job. The family again headed south to the Sahuarita camp, where Paul got in on some of the chopping season. A foreman that he had had on one of his prior jobs near Sahuraita asked him if he would like to irrigate, and Paul said he would. Paul worked somewhat regularly for this large cotton farming corporation until June of 1964 when he was "laid off."

He knew some fellows who were working for the Barnes' farm farther south at Continental so immediately went to work as an irrigator there. Paul moved his family to a "duplex" farm house about a mile north of the Barnes' camp. Paul maintained his household at this residence until October of 1965, when he left his job and his family and moved to Tucson, where he lived in a low-rent trailer court. His family, in the meantime, began drawing Aid to Dependent Children on the basis that he had abandoned the family.

During this period in Tucson, Paul was able to pick up a few yard jobs and ended up in jail a few times on drunk and disorderly charges. Over the past several years, even while at the farms in Continental and Sahuarita, Paul had kept in touch with five or six regular customers for doing yard work. Yard work and nursery work could be counted on when the pumps were shut off at the farms, although most of that time he maintained residence for himself and the family at the farm camps and "commuted" by bus to Tucson.

At the beginning of 1966, Paul rejoined his family and moved them to a small place at the village of Bac at San Xavier. He had arranged to start irrigating for a farmer who was leasing Papago land but instead found a job at another Tucson nursery, one that he had never worked at before. Shortly after starting to work there, Paul got a series of drunk and drunk driving charges and once again "abandoned" his family. Paul then lived with a cousin on South 5th Avenue; and his whereabouts was supposedly "unknown" to his family, which went back on welfare.

There are some aspects of role which help to explain Paul's oscillating pattern of occupational commitment and his propensity to high turnover. These will be discussed in the next chapter. Paul has this to say about his work:

I came off the reservation about 1947 because there were no jobs on the reservation and a man has to work. It is my home and if I ever got laid off work and couldn't get any more, I would go back. I liked my job with the nursery best because I like that kind of work best, like planting trees, bushes, plants, and taking care of lawns. I would also like to drive a tractor, but there are no openings. I've irrigated and chopped and picked cotton, and I have also made cement blocks. Maybe I could do any kind of work if somebody would show me and give me a chance; I think I could do it.

URBAN, NONFARM OCCUPATIONAL COMPLEX

The Case of Christopher Xavier

Chris Xavier is a 54-year old Papago man from Topawa village in the southeastern portion of the Sells Reservation. His elderly mother still lives on the family lands at Topawa and receives a monthly Old Age Assistance check from the government. Chris seldom gets back to Topawa; but on special occasions his mother comes to visit relatives at San Xavier, and he sees her there.

Chris has twin brothers, Antone and Patricio, who live at Topawa with their mother and care for the family cattle and horses. Another brother, Mark, lives in Topawa and works for the Bureau of Indian Affairs at some kind of work Chris does not know about. One brother, Phillip, spends most of his time at Topawa, but for the past couple of years has gone to pick cotton in the Eloy area for two or three months. Morris, another brother, now works in the cotton fields around Tucson and lives with either Chris or with the youngest of the Xavier brothers, Lester, at different places in downtown Tucson. Morris and Chris frequently are inmates together at the city jail. Lester has lived at San Xavier with relatives but most recently has been living at a cotton camp dormitory in Tucson and riding out daily to the fields. Lester has done a variety of work in Tucson, such as construction labor and yard work. There is one other brother, Jim, who was working in California the last Chris had heard. Chris has one sister, Martha, who lives in Tucson or at San Xavier on occasion.

Chris actually has little prolonged contact with the extended family, except when he sees them on the streets of Tucson or in jail, and is never sure where they are or what they might be doing. Chris is a regular inhabitant of the Tucson jail, having well over 500 arrests for drunkenness. He actually gives the city jail annex as his address, in addition to a flop house hotel on West Broadway, but he is more often in jail than not. Chris also has lived at a number of rooming houses in the downtown area, as he most recently has been doing, for $7 a week.

Chris says that he does yard work or any other odd jobs for whoever wants the work done. He knows people around town and goes occasionally to see if they have work for him or if they know someone who does. A certain few places close to the downtown area have him check with them every two weeks to clean around the yard and mow the lawn. Most of these jobs last a day or two at the most, but they do give Chris a little cash. It is likely that Chris, his brothers, and his friends lean on each other as much as possible for living quarters, meals, and above all, drinking money. The jail has become the most reliable source for the "bread and butter" aspects of life, and Chris has come to look upon the jail as his most secure living arrangement.

The early years were largely spent on the reservation on the family lands, where a few head of cattle have been maintained to this day. Therefore Chris was accustomed to the kind of life that ranching provides. He attended the Catholic mission school at Topawa through the sixth grade and had started into the seventh grade when he decided to drop out at the age of 16.

Chris remembers that his first wage job was working at the Ajo mine as a mill laborer, loading heavy rocks containing ore onto metal rollers so the rocks could be rolled to the crusher. The going rate of pay then was $80 for two weeks' work. Chris claims this was the hardest job he has ever had, but the money looked so good to him that he bought a new riding saddle and had the date (1928) branded on it. He remembers staying at the mine about a year and a half.

After he quit his job at the mine, he went to Fontana, California, in 1930 to work in the citrus groves. His work entailed driving a tractor and sometimes irrigating. Chris was in California about three years, then came back to Topawa and started driving a school bus for the agency schools. In the mid-thirties, Chris quit his job as a bus driver and worked on the CCC program, building roads and charcos, and cutting fence posts. After the program ended, Chris joined a Southern Pacific section gang at Benson and moved around over a large area — Cochise, Amado, Mesa, and Gila Bend — laying tracks and repairing ties. Around 1940, he returned to Topawa and sometime shortly after that married a girl from his village.

In 1941, Chris left the reservation for good to live in Tucson, and has not lived in Topawa since that time, although he has gone back for brief visits. In 1942, a son was born, and in 1944 a daughter. Chris's children have since grown, and Chris has been estranged from his wife for several years. She has since remarried and lives with her present husband in Sahuarita, Arizona. Chris presumes his daughter[4] is with her mother, but he has not heard from them for some time. He has heard that his son was working in California somewhere, but he could not remember what he was doing.

Chris has had somewhat the same pattern for the past 20 years — doing yard work, going out on a contractor's bus to pick or chop cotton, living in rooming houses and cheap hotels, or getting drunk on the streets and ending up in jail. When he is out of jail, he is most frequently seen around the bars in the vicinity of West Congress and usually gets back in jail as quickly as he gets out. Chris is not unaware of what has happened to him and has this to say about his occupational career:

The sergeant has said if I could quit drinking, I could handle any number of good jobs — like cooking or at a laundry. I have even been doing typing here at the annex [jail] . I would like to have other jobs because they are more steady than yard work. If I could just leave it alone I would be O.K. My resistance is good while I am in here, but as soon as I get down town and get a drink, I'm back here again. I want to find work that gives me more to do than yard work. If I could find a job, like I have here in the laundry, on the outside and could keep from drinking, that would be better.

---

[4]The Bureau of Ethnic Research Papago register indicates the daughter died in 1960, but Chris has not had recent enough contact to know.

The Case of Anthony Cypriano

Anthony Cypriano, a man of 50 years, is ecologically (but not sentimentally) separated from a Papago residence complex or neighborhood. The value orientations which he has assimilated do not seem to be congruous with those that prevail in the Papago neighborhood clusters; therefore, Anthony has moved his family into a middle class suburban area in the southernmost part of Tucson. Anthony, his wife Ethel, and their six children live in a five-room house which is similar to the many other houses in this typically middle class suburban neighborhood. The children attend schools in the general vicinity, schools which have very few Papagos in attendance because there are few Papago families in the neighborhood.

Anthony's parents came from the villages of Pozo Verde and Many Dogs on the Mexican side of the border, but they came to Tucson several years before Anthony was born. His parents also had resided at Sells, and Anthony has some relatives there. Anthony's wife also has relatives at Sells, so the family goes over to Sells on infrequent occasions. Anthony's mother has been a domestic worker in Tucson homes for many years and maintains her own home on West 27th Street in South Tucson. Anthony grew up in this South Tucson neighborhood; but, by the time he was of school age, his parents had arranged to send him to Sherman, the government Indian school at Riverside, California.

Anthony received his entire academic and vocational education at Sherman, with the exception of one year, in which it was decided that he would remain at home and attend one of the local high schools. Anthony says that at Sherman in the earlier grades he was permitted to rotate in the learning of various trades, such as machine shop, electrical work, plumbing, welding, and cooking. In the last two years in the vocational high school, following his one year at Tucson High School, he was permitted to specialize in a vocational area of his choice; Anthony chose cooking as his field of special interest. The purpose of the training was to prepare each student for a number of different trades and then try to guide them according to individual interests and the abilities shown. By the time he was in his last year, Anthony was supervising the kitchen work of other students.

Sherman was an important experience in Anthony's life. He has high praise for his instructors and credits them for the attention they gave him and their encouragement to stick with it and plan for his future, especially during those times when he was not looking ahead. When Anthony attended Sherman it was an accredited school with high standards, but he thinks that a large influx of Navahos after the war caused the school to deteriorate some in its standards. However, Anthony still thinks Sherman is one of the best; he is glad his mother encouraged him to stay. While Anthony was at Sherman he would work at a farm on weekends, cleaning out poultry shacks, mowing hay, or sorting oranges for 65 cents an hour. He was actually under-age, but it did give him some extra money.

His mother and his instructors continually tried to impress on Anthony that the government was not to be expected to feed him. He would have to get out and make it by his own effort. When he was about 16, that is, during the summer prior to his last year at Sherman, Anthony was getting interested in joining the Navy and began to think about going in after he finished at Sherman. He therefore got the idea, along with a Mission Indian friend, of signing up as a cook on a merchant tanker that made round trips to Honolulu. Anthony spent the entire summer of 1931 on the ocean, working for $65 a month with free room and board plus insurance coverage. The experience broke any notion Anthony had of being in the Navy; as he says, "It was like being in jail." He went back to Sherman after the summer was over, but his Mission Indian friend stayed on a liner and did not return to school.

After Anthony graduated from Sherman, he returned to Tucson and got a job as a baker's helper in a Tucson hotel, a job which he kept until 1940. He then started taking night courses at Tucson High School to learn sheet metal working. It was his plan to go to Los Angeles on completing the course, but one night the instructor at the class told the whole class that sheet metal workers were needed badly at the Army Air Force base due to the war effort. Anthony never did do sheet metal work, however, and went to work on the hangar line instead. Shortly after starting to work at the base (1942), Anthony was called into the military service and assigned to the Army Air Force as an aircraft mechanic. In addition, he received training in radar operations at Tampa, Florida (Drew Field), then was sent to the Southwest Pacific where he served three years in Australia and the Philippines. Anthony says he was almost talked into being a cook but he did not want that; he did not pass the test anyway. This gave him the chance to go to radar school; and some of his duty was as a radar operator, although most of it was in the capacity of aircraft mechanic.

On his active duty release in 1946, Anthony returned to his former job at the air base as an aircraft mechanic on the flight line while maintaining a reserve status with the Army Air Force. In 1948, Anthony married and moved from his mother's home on West 27th Street to a rented place on West 28th Street, about five blocks from his childhood home. In 1949, Anthony was advanced to the supervisory position of crew chief, a job that he has held up to the present with the exception of a brief period of active duty during the Korean conflict.

In 1952, Anthony was activated, despite having three dependents, because of his experience as a radarman and mechanic. He was sent to San Francisco and did some aircraft mechanic work while awaiting an overseas assignment. However, his wife gave birth to a fourth dependent, thus invoking the military ruling that he be released. Anthony says that he wanted to go overseas if he had to go in at all, but he never made it; instead, he spent all eight months on the West Coast in the San Francisco Bay area.

In 1953, Anthony returned to his Tucson home and his former job at the air base. Since 1955, Anthony has been living in a Tucson suburban home, about five miles south of the Native American-Papagoville area. He works in what is referred to as process "N", leading a crew of eight mechanics in repairing incoming aircraft. Anthony works a regular eight-hour day for five days a week at the rate of $3.50 an hour. This amounts to a gross income of about $7,200 a year. Anthony is still paying for his modestly furnished home through his GI loan.

Anthony has high aspirations for his children. He has had an opportunity to learn a number of trades and had a number of jobs he would like to have tried. He has enjoyed his work as a mechanic, especially when working on jets, but Anthony has even higher aspirations for his children. Anthony perceives that one of the greatest disadvantages that befalls young people is that they "drop out of school too early and cannot see far enough ahead for their own good. The parents don't push them; the kids try but their parents are not educated, though it is not their fault, and they do not get their children going. Instead, early marriages, or cars, girl friends, drinking, and running around become more important."

Anthony has been somewhat of a leader in local Papago affairs, although his direct participation at the Tucson Indian Center is never conspicuous and is usually quite unpredictable. He seems to throw more of his individual attention toward his own children and takes a positive role in directing their extra-home activities. Anthony says he knows of a lot of capable Papagos who try to go on to school, but they soon get discouraged or restless and drop out. As Anthony reflects,

They do not have the benefit of those closest to them who have been through successful adjustments and therefore they find it hard to think in terms of long-range plans. Many of their parents do not have the schooling and have little experience in thinking and planning ahead. That kind of thing has not been a part of their life and it is still so much of their way that it is hard for others to get them thinking ahead. My brother was like that; he would have had eight to ten jobs, some of them real good ones, but usually left them for some reason. He went through junior high in Tucson but didn't have the benefits of Sherman.

Anthony thinks that Papago (and other) parents are too permissive and let their children start running with girls too soon, or driving cars and drinking. He is trying to control these with his own children: "The parents must play a part in their children's adjustments — hold things up to them and try to hold them to these things."

Anthony hopes his children go farther than he has gone. When they suggest they want to work at what he does, Anthony says, "Oh no you're not." As it is, his boys are interested in school, athletics, and a number of extra-class activities. They show interest in a number of hobbies and crafts and are already beginning to voice their ambitions — to be a coach, to attend the university, to be an artist, etc. Anthony talks at times with the school counselors about the children. The boys have been out selling magazines and mowing lawns in order to save for some of their future interests.

Papago as a language is waning in the Cypriano home. Anthony and his wife speak it on occasion. The oldest boy (17) understands some with difficulty but cannot speak it. None of the other children can speak Papago; therefore, English is the first language in this household. A strong concern for Papagos improving themselves is maintained by Anthony, and he takes some leadership to help promote this improvement. As a Papago he identifies with Papago culture in terms of trying to aid in the accommodation of Papagos to the value demands of the present social order.

7. OCCUPATIONAL ROLES AND OTHER SOCIAL ROLES: A ROLE ANALYSIS OF INDIVIDUAL CASES

This study suggests that the most meaningful social field in which Papago men confront change-inducing situations is the occupational structure that orients them to a whole complex of institutions in which social roles must be properly perceived and performed. Occupations become the centers of activity that bring a number of strategic social roles together, and the interplay of these roles in the social personality of the individual is expected to dramatize the kind of adaptation the individual is making to an occupational complex. When the individual learns social roles derived from participation in two different cultural systems, these roles must be brought into some kind of accommodation, particularly if the demands of role are incongruous in the two different systems.

Figure 1 in Chapter 1 shows the occupational social field. An individual Papago, with the particular social roles that characterize the nature and extent of his participation in Papago institutions, is perceived as assuming involvement in a particular occupational complex. In so doing, he becomes attached to some kind of kinship unit or some substitute residence unit. This residence unit is part of a larger neighborhood or settlement unit. It is the attachment to a particular occupational status in an occupational institution that largely encourages a certain kind of residence pattern, and a particular type of living arrangement exposes the individual to certain other institutions. In other words, the accustomed role behaviors, which are directed by the cognitive residues of his past role perceptions (Wallace 1961a: 16), come into a direct interplay with current perceptions of occupational and other social roles demanded by involvement in institutions other than those for which his past cultural participation has prepared him. This interplay of familiar role involvements, due to the individual's particular cultural experience, and less familiar role involvements, due to their not being a part of the individual's customary cultural experience, determine whether or not certain occupational roles can be carried out effectively.

The theoretical model of the occupational complex, therefore, is an aid in identifying the crucial role involvements and how the interplay of these roles, as they are perceived and as they are enacted, determine the adaptation of the individual to his occupational role. The discussion now turns to some of these role involvements and how they are perceived, organized, and enacted in the life styles of individual Papago men. Of course, it is possible to deal with only a few of the many role involvements that these individuals face in the particular social fields in which a large part of their interaction takes place. Tracing these crucial role confrontations in a few individuals is suggestive of what likely occurs in the broader aspect of cultural abandonment, for it is the abandonment of culturally induced roles and their performance that is the crux of cultural abandonment. It is the abandoning of traditional role behaviors and the acquisition of new role performances which, if a shared experience for all members of a cultural group, lead to the demise of a culture. Or it is the accommodation of new roles to traditional roles or vice versa that permits cultural reformulation or revitalization that leads to new configurations of a culture.

If what is happening in the life styles of individuals is significant, it should have some projected implications for Papago cultural reformulation as a broader phenomenon; it should reveal processes of change as they occur in individual personalities confronting situations of cross-cultural contact. If the occupational field is a social environment consisting of mutually predictable roles and shared experiences and individual Papago mazeways are thereby organized into a kind of collective representation, what has happened or is happening to individual Papagos can be expected to have occurred or to be occurring in the lives of many. The following discussion looks at a few of the crucial role confrontations, experienced by Papago informants, as they have bearing on the carrying out of occupational roles.

An occupational complex as a social field introduces an individual to a number of socially structured relationships, including a set of occupational role elements that must be brought into conjunction with each other and integrated into the total social personality. It is postulated that certain kinds of occupations are conducive to certain kinds of social arrangements. Further, occupations present social situations for the confrontation of social roles, which are more clearly established in the social personality, and social roles that by virtue of their newness are less well defined. In addition, intracultural socialization is sometimes conducive to the inadequate learning of ideal social roles, and an individual's own culture introduces him to social roles that are not always compatible. Therefore, the cross-cultural setting may present further complications in organizing a reasonably well integrated social personality and thereby retard a satisfactory social and emotional adjustment. On the other hand, the cross-cultural contact situation may actually help in the adjustment process by providing new roles that might be more readily incorporated into the social personality than those the individual confronts in his original cultural community.

By and large, the cross-cultural setting initially is one in which diverse social roles must be accommodated to each other in some manner. Once an accommodation is satisfactorily attained, the social personality is then capable of emotionally satisfying behavior within the appropriate range of permissible behavior in the new sociocultural orientation. Transitional peoples in the process of adapting familiar roles to the necessary array of new roles are often confronted with role stress that makes a completely satisfactory emotional adjustment somewhat complicated.

KINSHIP ROLES

One of the most vital areas of social life affected by the cross-cultural social situation is that of family life and kinship relationships. The resettlement of individuals and families into new living arrangements away from their kinship villages tends to modify the structure of family units and to alter the social relationships of related individuals. There are four basic questions pertaining to kinship involvements for which answers will be sought from the Papago case materials.

1. How does the residence unit associated with a Papago worker's occupation facilitate the kinship relationships that have been the most meaningful to him?

2. How does the residence unit relate to the ecology of sentiment, or where does the sentimental or affective domain of an individual lie relative to kin and kind?

3. To what extent does the occupational setting permit or restrict family involvement?

4. What are the explicit or implicit satisfactions or dissatisfactions that the Papago worker has regarding the family arrangement within the job complex?

Alonzo Jose

Alonzo Jose's off-reservation living arrangement seems to be quite amenable to kinship relationships.

The adobe dwelling, a five-room structure, is somewhat useful since it permits some extra space for periodically accommodating any of his sons or members of their nuclear families.

The rural residence that characterizes Al's predominant pattern, while not totally comparable to the reservation village arrangement, is strikingly similar to the manner in which his household residence pattern has always functioned. His family residence pattern follows what may be referred to as a family accretion-depletion cycle. The reservation residence has been a relatively insignificant one for a number of years, and Al's three adobe houses are badly in need of repair, although they are equipped to facilitate any of his family or their families on infrequent occasions. The adobe house provided by the farm where he now works is in much better repair, more adequately furnished, more accessible to stores, and is provided with water and electricity. Presently it is the more permanent arrangement since it is where the wages are, yet any residential arrangement that Al has assumed seems to have followed this accretion-depletion cycle.

The accretion-depletion cycle refers to a situation where the father's residence, wherever it may be at any one time, functions as a kind of central household that can numerically expand or contract, depending on the particular facilities available and circumstances that may prompt certain family members to attach to or withdraw from the household unit. In other words, at times Al's residence unit is what has been referred to earlier as a "rural family isolate," consisting of just himself and his spouse. On other occasions, however, such as during the peak of the harvest season, the living facilities are adequate to allow for some expansion in number. When the number of consanguineal or affinal relatives increases, there is a kind of rural family cluster in that there are members of several related nuclear families living either under a common roof or in adjacent structures, sharing a common kitchen. Wherever Al has lived off-reservation, whether in Stanfield, La Palma, Coolidge, or Sahuarita, his sons have always managed to stick close by and, on occasion, move in with their father, either alone or bringing with them their own nuclear families.

Of course, the arrangements never have been totally adequate to accommodate all the sons and their growing families at one time. However, the need to rely on the father's stable household is never simultaneously the case for all of his sons. When one may have the need to do so, the others may have worked out satisfactory arrangements elsewhere; but any one of them, throughout the course of a year, may have occasion to depend on the father's household. The situation at times works an extra burden on Al, one that he assumes willingly, even if "there is just too many to try and take care of."

The pattern is very understandable when it is considered that Al's first work on the farm came as his sons were growing up. They grew up around where their father worked in the fields, eventually working for the same farms their father happened to be working for or, if not, finding some kind of work on other farms in the area. Thus, while one son may go back to the reservation home for a period of idleness and another may go to his wife's relatives, at least one may live with or near the father.

While Al's expressed sentiments make reference to his home on the reservation, they are expressed in terms of past and future, either recollecting past experiences with now deceased relatives or projecting toward the near future when he reaches full retirement and can once again enjoy the fruits of his own land. As Al says,

I want to build another house there when I can. I would also like to farm it again. I am building fences now when I go over. They have bad summers over there now like the last one [1964]. You can't irrigate like here, you just have to watch the rain and know how to use it. That's why they had those wine feasts back then; I guess they worked because they used to have more rains then and do more farming than they do now. There is nothing but cholla, cactus, and bones over there now.

Al's present arrangement is more practicable than returning home, and even during idle periods he spends most of his time around the farm, since it is accessible to the Sahuarita commercial services and bus services to Tucson. The residence arrangement seems very amenable to the maintenance of familial ties in that Al's household is available to incorporate a son out of work, or a son working at the same farm, or some other member of the extended family who needs to rely on the stability of Al's household. It may not be as adequate for kinship purposes as the home on the reservation, but it has the advantage of an accessible job and a somewhat dependable income, which frequently benefits more than just Al or his wife.

Al regrets that all the boys drink too much and therefore end up jumping from one farm to another or going back to the reservation to lie around until they can get work some place else. Despite these shortcomings, Al seems quite content with his present job and residence and intends to stick it out until he retires. He works hard and earns the praise of his employer for his dependability. One of Al's foremen condemns Al's sons for taking advantage of their father's hard work. Yet Al fulfills his obligations as a father and succeeds in maintaining an apparently happy disposition about his work and toward his family.

Raymond Victor

For Raymond Victor, as for many Ajo Papagos, the Ajo residence within a company-directed Indian village provides a context for maintaining his nuclear family. While there are other relatives, they are largely scattered over the community and function within independent nuclear families. The physical facilities do not lend themselves to the kind of living arrangements which characterize reservation villages. The confined areas, the small houses, and restrictions against building their own structures do not permit Raymond or other Ajo Papagos to extend their facilities to take in kin who might be dependent on them. While certain families have informally appropriated certain sections of the village for their exclusive usage, company policy and the layout of the village do not permit this to any great extent. Considering this inadequacy, it is no wonder that Raymond, who is deeply committed to his relatives, saying, "we really couldn't get along without our relatives," finds Ajo a necessary but not totally desirable living arrangement. It is, however, a stable and functional living arrangement, since family members have access to the services of certain Ajo institutions, such as schools, stores, and recreational facilities.

The reservation village on the other hand is a place where Raymond says he is related to everyone in some way or other. His home there is part of a larger extended family complex of residences where his mother, a brother and his family, a sister, her husband, and their family, and Raymond's family occupy a cluster of adobe houses surrounded by house complexes belonging to more distant collateral relatives. The extended family compound has shared a common kitchen for many years, and in the past it consisted of 11 or 12 individual families, where the women all worked together in the preparation and serving of meals. Raymond conveys the significance of the corporate kitchen: "We usually all ate together as a group at my mother's kitchen until we started our own kitchen just this summer [1965] a few weeks ago. We have always eaten as a big group and when we set up our own kitchen my mother objected strongly. She just wasn't used to that kind of thing, but with all of the children we just had to do it."

The experience at the Ajo residence probably has affected this new eating arrangement. The extended family relationships have, however, despite this eating group fission, remained largely intact; and Raymond thinks in terms of this larger context of kin.

At every opportunity he returns to his home on the reservation; and since it lies only 50 miles from his occupational residence, shutdowns and vacations permit him to load his whole family onto the truck and head for home as many other Ajo Papago families do. Evidence of the strong sentiment for his reservation home can be seen in his expectations for his children and their children. Raymond sees the day when they can bring their attained skills and educations home to the reservation in order to be of some service to the tribe. In order to do this "they will also

have to learn to be open with people and active in their districts and communities."

The Ajo arrangement is an expedient one, largely detached from Raymond's network of relatives but functional primarily for the nuclear family. The arrangement does benefit the extended family economically, as Raymond frequently takes food and merchandise to his mother and brother. The reservation residence is the object of sentiment and remains the unit toward which the present activities are oriented. The latter residence is a permanent domain of sentiment and more fixed roles and relationships; the Ajo residence exists to insure the maintenance and perpetuation of the reservation family residence unit as well as his own nuclear family. Yet the Ajo residence has been the predominant one for 20 years.

Permanent residence in Ajo tends to be devastating to traditional kinship relations. While a householder in the Ajo Indian community has ways of taking in a limited number of relatives to support, the perpetuation of an Ajo-based kin group beyond the nuclear family organization is curtailed due to the great difficulty of qualifying for employment at the mine as well as the problems inherent in the design of the village arrangement and the company's policies. Even the nuclear family cannot be sure that its members will be able to work at the mine, but the reservation residence compound always has ways to accommodate individuals whether they are working or not.

As a father, Raymond is concerned about his sons' futures:

I've always taught the boys to speak up and not be shy and afraid like some others are. That is the only way to get along with others and do things well. . . . The reservation has problems. I'd like to see some youngsters be put in a position to help out the tribe. I wish my kids could come to a point in their education where they could put their business to use on the reservation back home. We could use them on the reservation. I would like to be able to have them go home and work on some of the problems. . . . They could come back to the reservation and have a mechanical and electrical shop. That's my dream for my boys.

Raymond's hopes for his sons are in terms of the reservation community. The Ajo community can offer no complete assurance for occupational opportunities for the next generation. Raymond has taken some initiative in making plans for his children's educations and vocations, but he has still been an extremely permissive father in that the boys have been given the final choice in their decision making, even if Raymond has had something else in mind for them.

Raymond is not at all satisfied with the living arrangements at Ajo, as indicated by the following remarks:

The company had arranged to give houses to certain ones [Indians] and the most disappointing thing was these people 'they gave the [new] houses to were the ones who needed it least. They were the ones who had the least families. . . . The reason they got them, so I heard, was they had no kids so they were able to keep their houses nice and clean — it was because they had no little kids. . . . I told them if I was offered one I would turn them down. My kids were still too young and I had enough keeping the one I had in order with little kids around. The company said those who moved into the new houses had to get new appliances and furniture — I couldn't do that and many others couldn't manage that either. . . . It would help if they could build houses separately.

It is pretty clear, then, that present living conditions and the present mining company policies about Indian residences conflict with some of the basic realities of Papago kinship and family structure and sentiment. It is not the preferred arrangement and stands in the way of fulfilling the desired kinship roles. Papagos can accommodate to this inadequacy largely because company work operations are favorable to frequent returns to their kinship villages.

Paul Antonio

In contrast to the first two cases, the case of Paul Antonio reveals a pattern of periodic shifting about from one residence to another. As a result, some kind of modification of the kinship alignments that characterize the kinship-based society would be expected. Paul's case clearly indicates the significance of kinship ties with the extended family, but it reveals the extent to which the occupational commitments of the extended family have tended to weaken these ties and thereby create greater dependence on non-kin social alignments, or more correctly, to promulgate a stretching of the closer kinship ties to incorporate more distant kin, fictive kin, and friendship alliances. It is suggested here that Paul's pattern of occupation and residence is related to his growing dependence on other than kin.

Very clearly, the extended family, even as a part-time residence unit, has been totally nonexistent. Instead, Paul's unit has functioned largely as a rural

family isolate with all activities involving the nuclear family only. Paul leaves the family and hangs around Tucson for several days, returning unexpectedly from time to time. In town, Paul finds an anonymous atmosphere away from the tribal drinking restrictions and among friends with whom he drinks and with whom he stays.

Some of the San Xavier people were highly critical of Paul during the Feast of San Francisco. Paul was drunk when authorities tried to locate him regarding the death of his infant daughter, and the gossip lingered for several days among some of the San Xavier people. Tucson bars and drinking companions, on the other hand, are less repressive of some of Paul's habitual inclinations.

Paul's closest kin, other than his nuclear family, have been extremely scattered for a number of years, although it has not always been so. This outwardly appears to have diminished the importance of the extended family so far as close relationships are concerned, yet the dispersal has also been functional. With consanguineal and affinal relatives at San Xavier, Tucson, Sahuarita, Continental, and Florence, there is an informal network by which one member can be notified of a job opening at a place where another relative has been working. This is especially functional in terms of Paul's occupational pattern in that it provides a number of potential sources for work when a present job has exhausted itself. It has worked reciprocally for other male members of the kinship group as well. This breadth of kin distribution reveals itself in Paul's occupational pattern as well as the patterns of his brothers and a few of the affinal relatives known through the study. It has not been the extended family living as a residence unit but an extended family functioning as an occupational network.

While the extended family is still important in terms of feelings and relationships, the dispersed nature of Paul's and his relatives' residence patterns has evidenced a need for greater reliance on non-kin. At the birth of an infant, a friend of the family, a public health nurse met in the course of her contact with the cotton camp, had the privilege of naming the baby and buying its christening dress. Another lady, attached to the migrant ministry, was asked to care for the baby while Paul and his family made the trip to Magdalena. *Patrón*-like relationships develop between Paul and his employers, such as obtaining advancements in salary, putting up bail, providing a

set of gardening tools, and providing emergency
transportation. Surplus clothing, household items,
and other charity services by Anglo contacts, plus
dependence on public agencies have further played a
part in extending relationships beyond kin, who may
not be able or available to provide these kinds of
relationships and services. It is a matter of exploiting
any person or situation that would make the living
arrangements a little more secure.

With Alonzo Jose, while he has future plans
to return to his home and has a rich residue of
memory about his early days, the off-reservation
farm has served as a relatively stable arrangement
in which he has maintained good relationships with
employers, performed work he has liked and needed,
and has maintained an off-reservation "home base"
to incorporate his sons and their families when
necessary. With Raymond Victor, the domain of
sentiment clearly is the reservation village. Paul,
by contrast, has on single domain of sentiment,
and a great deal of ambivalence and individual
stress are readily apparent. The farm has been
an expedient and secure place to work in that
it renders the most support and care for his wife
and children. Paul says "it's too expensive" to
support a family in town, but he would rather
do nursery work in Tucson than anything else.
"By the time I get a house and pay rent and
move my family up here [Tucson], the money
I make would be gone. I get my house free
from Mr. Barnes, and it's better this way."

This was not the big problem to Margaret, Paul's
wife. While the family was still on the farm,
Margaret expressed the hope that Paul would not
be able to keep the car running, since he would
head for Tucson and most likely end up with
his friends, getting drunk, and not making it back
to work. Living in Tucson would present an even
greater threat to the family's economic well-being
than remaining on the farm, for on the farm
he had no way of going to town so often. Thus,
Paul and his wife, although expressing slightly different reasons, found certain features of the farm
to be the best economic arrangement.

However, Paul's relatives and friends at San Xavier
and Tucson are important to him. On one occasion
Paul had gone in to Tucson by bus to get some
relatives to help him move a recently purchased

second-hand washing machine. Margaret humorously
made reference to the situation:

Oh, I had to go get it myself. Here Paul took three
days trying to get it down here and never did. I
finally just went down to the store and asked the
butcher. He goes into Tucson quite a bit and I asked
him if he would help, and he brought it back for us. I
think he [Paul] just went into town and ran into
some of his friends. He probably went out to see his
relatives at the reservation [San Xavier] ; he has quite
a few of them out there. But he never could get the
machine down here.

Margaret also mentioned that once he gets among
his friends in Tucson, he is not sober very long,
because liquor is always available whether he has any
money or not.

Tucson, then, is a place where Paul seeks out
drinking companionship and all the rewards and
enjoyments related to drinking group behavior.
Tucson is a source of ambivalence because it
represents a source of enjoyment, escape, and male
companionship, and also constitutes a threat to the
economic and emotional solidarity of his nuclear
family.

Paul's children are always happy to see him when
he returns from town or work or a few days in jail,
and Paul's behavior toward his children and wife
reveals his affection for them. The pull of nuclear
family obligations and obligations to friends and
more distant relatives is a source of much conflict. On
one occasion he chose to attend the wake of a
recently deceased friend and fellow committeeman for
the Feast of Corpus Christi instead of sitting close to
his infant daughter's bedside when she was close to
death. His rationale for choosing the former
obligation was that there was little he could do to
change the course of events for his little daughter. In
the other situation he could take some liquor and
food to his friend's relatives to show them his
concern and help them to express esteem for the
deceased. Disregarding the unconscious motivations
for so choosing, it is this kind of rationale that
governs the relationships of people.

Paul's affective relationships are spread out over a
large area, and one residence associated with an
occupation may be antithetical to the meaningful
relationships that concern him elsewhere. If the
sentimental domain could be constricted into a more
concentrated spatial domain, as is true for the other
two cases, perhaps some of Paul's difficulties would

be reduced. On the other hand, it appears that Paul uses one set of obligations to run from another set of obligations.

It is now quite clear that Paul's recent "abandonment" of his family has been, in part, an implicitly understood arrangement between Paul and his wife. It permits Margaret to gain access to public economic assistance and grants Paul the freedom to maintain his ties with friends in Tucson, something which Margaret cannot influence anyway. While not acceptable to legal authorities, or to our Anglo sense of values regarding family care, and perhaps not totally so to either Paul or Margaret, occasional efforts on Paul's part to get conveniently lost from his nuclear family obligations actually aid the family economically when he is not able to do so. The efforts aid him in that he can maintain his relationships with friends in Tucson. This interplay of obligations, sentiments, and relationships has a profound effect on Paul's occupational pattern. His mobile occupational pattern is related to these non-occupational role involvements.

Paul's jobs have been a source of recruitment within his nuclear family. His 17-year-old son has been able to work for Mr. Barnes and, more recently, at the same nursery where his father has been working; although Dennis can do so only during summer vacations and on weekends, since he is still in school. This has, on many occasions, proven very helpful to the family. The family has had the assurance of some income even when Paul did not go to work; or when both father and son were working it meant additional income. It suggests a situation that might explain how stereotyped occupational roles are maintained through the next generation despite better educational preparations. One could predict that if Paul's reliability on the job and responsibility for the family progressively deteriorates, his son Dennis, who is already proving himself dependable on jobs with which he is familiar, will maintain occupational roles similar to those to which he has already been introduced. This most likely will be the case even if Dennis succeeds in incorporating other vocational values and expectations for himself as a result of his educational opportunities.

Paul seems confused or ambivalent about where he would prefer to live, as can be inferred from some of his behavior. He is drawn as much to festive activity and drinking situations with friends as he is to his job and to the needs of his wife and children, and he

often chooses the drinking associates. It is a manifestation of discontent and an inability to resolve some very definite role involvements that are antithetical to each other. As a result, his family appears to suffer from his choices.

Christopher Xavier

Christopher Xavier characterizes a way of life referred to earlier as a floating subculture within an urban setting. His chronic habitation of the city jail and his getting lost in the bigness and hubbub of downtown when not in jail have made Christopher's kinship involvements more difficult to trace. Only an intense acquaintance with his relationships in confinement and out of confinement would provide a truly clear insight into the role kinship still plays in Christopher's life style.

There is no family unit as far as a residence unit is concerned. Since Chris is mostly a jail resident, his cell or tank and tank mates comprise his most frequent residence unit. When he is released, Chris heads for the familiar territory downtown. He says he has a sleeping room in a downtown "hotel," but police authorities say that he is often found sleeping in an alley or behind a building. Chris sees two of his brothers frequently, either on the streets or in jail. He mentions he sees his mother infrequently when she comes in to San Xavier, and he can pick up by word of mouth what his other brothers might be doing or where they might be living. Chris has been separated from his wife and children for several years and has only vague ideas about where they might be or what they might be doing.

There is undoubtedly a residue of memory about his earlier life on the reservation, a way of life shared by many Papagos. However, Chris's long immersion in Tucson bars, and in the life on Tucson's streets and in flop houses clouds this aspect of his present mazeway. His only sober moments are spent with fellow inmates, jail personnel, and in the performing of tasks which characterize his roles as a jail trustee. Chris operates largely in two contrasting social fields — in the vicinity of Congress Avenue downtown and in the confines of the jail. The first is one of progressive inebriation; the second is one of drying out, sobering up, and serving an allotted period of time. There seems to be little departure from this pattern; the former style of life leads to the latter, and it is in the confines of the jail that Chris experiences his most secure role involvements. There is a place to sleep;

there are associations with people he has seen many times before; he has tasks to perform; he has the prestige of being one of the most steady occupants; and his physical needs are met, with one exception — alcohol. This is not to suggest that Chris only drinks to get a ticket to the city jail, but there is no question that Chris feels the most secure while in jail. Kinship ties do not seem significant to Chris's present style of life, although they may be related to some of the unconscious motivations and anxieties which lie behind his mode of living. Without a persistent contact with Chris, it has been difficult to do much more than infer that his style of life seems to rule out any intense involvement with kin, although the sentiments may be there.

Anthony Cypriano

The nuclear family is a basic unit for Anthony Cypriano. He has no living brothers or sisters, but his elderly mother still maintains her home in South Tucson. Anthony drops by to see her frequently to check on her well-being. He has some uncles on the reservation, but only on rare occasions does Anthony have any contact with them. Anthony's mother has gone back to pay respects to the dead on the first year after the loved ones' departures, and his wife Ethel sometimes makes trips to Kom Vaya and Sells to visit relatives.

While kinship ties are meaningful, the demands of Anthony's job, the involvements his family has in the neighborhood, the schools, the church, and the Tucson Indian Center; and the fact that his life has been spent in Tucson all contribute to the more Anglo-middle class character of his kinship connections. The kinds of expectations Anthony seems to hold for his children are very indicative of his having assimilated the value orientations of the Anglo society around him. These expectations tend to make the welfare of the nuclear family members of most concern; that is, there is a greater stress on individualism, self-improvement, and looking ahead.

In terms of Anthony's sentiment or affective relationship to space, there is no apparent sign of an ecological homeland that exists in his dreams, as is characteristic of the first three cases. Anthony's experience as a lifetime resident of Tucson, his experience at Sherman Indian School, his military experience, his relationships on his jobs, and a number of other experiences related to his lifetime pattern all bear witness to the fact that his has been a

non-reservation experience. Anthony makes no verbal claims of a village origin that corresponds with his parental origins but, instead, claims Tucson as his home. His lack of manifest sentiment toward a Papago homeland is not to be taken as a lack of sentiment regarding Papago culture, however.

There is very clear evidence of Anthony's concern for a new modern Papago culture, modified in terms of the kind of work Papagos are facing. Anthony therefore is able to enumerate features of the traditional ways of rearing children and how these features stand as obstacles to progress among Papagos. His concern is a most sympathetic kind of concern, where he is conscious of what he must do for his own children — what other Papago parents, by no fault of their own, have not been prepared to do.

Anthony is one of the leading figures in the Tucson Indian Center and occasionally takes turns supervising the activity. All the members of his family have participated in one way or another. The interest his children show in participating groups, in hobbies, in school, and in future plans manifests this concern for a new orientation, under adult guidance, for Papago youth. In order to ensure these accomplishments in his own children, Anthony must devote his energies toward his own nuclear family. But his concern for other Papago youth in Tucson is reflected in his interest in the center.

The kind of industry in which Anthony is employed is not geared to patronizing families as farms, nurseries, and to some extent the mine, have been able to do. The air base where Anthony works is a large, bureaucratic organization characteristic of a federally operated enterprise. Statuses and roles are defined on the basis of special technical competence, competitive entrance tests, and other qualifying mechanisms. If any of Anthony's sons would desire to be employed there, they would have to compete on the basis of technical competence. It is significant that when the oldest son expressed an interest in working where his father does, Anthony discouraged him and told him he expected the son to do even better than he himself has done. Anthony's involvement in his occupation and standard of living has oriented him to a system of values which will more readily aid his children in learning to prepare and compete for jobs in an urban, industrial society. So while his specific job holds no assurance for his children's participation at the same job, Anthony's involvement in a system of values, which helps him maintain his own occupational adjustment, will also have an impact on his offspring.

As can be noted in the case material presented earlier, Anthony is able to articulate his expectations for his children and what might need to be done by him in order to see some of these expectations fulfilled. He can specify what he wants for his children and what he does not want, and he can relate these expectations to actual behavior — what is appropriate behavior for his children and his relation to and

influence on their behavior. This contrasts with the more permissive and relaxed concern that both Paul Antonio and Alonzo Jose manifest when they picture their sons and grandsons occupied in much the same kind of work they have been doing. Raymond Victor's attitudes and expectations more closely approximate those of Anthony, with the exception that Raymond's orientation is toward a reservation and tribal involvement, while Anthony's thinking points toward making one's way in an urban society.

LEADERSHIP AND CEREMONIAL ROLES

Another important aspect of a Papago worker's social personality has to do with the roles he feels under obligation to perform in leadership and ceremonial contexts. If the occupational setting is a cross-cultural environment, it would seem appropriate to look for certain kinds of roles that an individual is under some compulsion to carry out in a Papago cultural community and what effect these activities have on his employment patterns. Using the same five cases, we will try to find answers to a few basic questions. First, what are some of the individual's ceremonial and/or leadership role obligations that are centrifugal to the occupational commitments? Second, to what extent can they be accommodated to the requirements of the job without doing a disservice to either? Lastly, what modifications in both ceremonial and occupational roles are effected as a result of this apparently incongruous meeting of social demands?

Alonzo Jose

It is difficult to trace a ceremonial network for Alonzo Jose since his return to the reservation for the past seven years have amounted to only a few days each year. He recently made a trip over to Nolic village to attend the rosary and funeral of a grandson. Since he has no car, and since Mr. Barnes, his employer, does not permit off duty usage of the pickup truck, the only other way he can get over is to pay one of the local Indians to take him, and Al says he cannot afford that very often. He reports that on the very few occasions he can leave his place at the Barnes' farm, he likes to take advantage of a day or two off and visit his children. Even his participation at fiestas appears to be very limited, since there is usually some kind of job to do at the farm during the most important ones. His loyalty to his job is what makes Al such a worthwhile farm hand to his boss, who has a lot of trouble with

Indians running off in the middle of work or not showing up at all. As Al points out, "People usually lose their jobs because they don't come to work when they are supposed to and don't tell anybody. A lot of people lose their jobs because of drinking. They do not realize that they owe their time for getting paid to the man they work for."

This is not to imply that ceremonial obligations are not important to Al. A hypothetical situation was put before Al in order to ascertain the value of ceremonial obligation in the case of a man's job standing in the way of celebrating a friend's wedding. A man's friend asks him to come and play in the orchestra and join in the celebration, but he also has to work at the same time. Al was asked what the man should do.

I guess he ought to play for the wedding since he's a musician and they want to have a good party. Maybe he wants to go over and play for some beer. I guess he'll go over and ask for a day off. If the boss says no, maybe he'll want to go anyway since he has to play. Maybe if the guy says he has to work, maybe he can say, "Well, I'll ask my boss about it. Maybe he'll let me off." I think if the boss let him off, he'd come back. It is his friend and his wedding. If it's evening, it's all right to go but in the daytime it's different. The boss will let him off for things like that.

Al says he just does not get to go much of anywhere anymore, so he just stays at the house when he is not working. When the Father from San Xavier puts a sign up at the Sahuarita store announcing a mass, Al tries to take the family when he can. However Al says, "I don't go much anymore because I work so much. Mr. Barnes likes to go to church every week, but all we are to do is work, work, work. I can't go to church because I have to work most of the time on Sundays."

Despite such expressions of mild displeasure, Al does not permit his discontent to affect his job or his relationships with his bosses, and if there are other pulls to get him away from the farm, he does not seem to give in to them. It does not seem to bother him that he does not have any way to get around.

Al still maintains a voice in the affairs of his home village and likes to make sure that either himself or one of the boys is there to represent his position on a certain matter affecting his own household. There is no indication, however, that Al has any special status in decision-making other than as a householder and resident of the village. If Al has ceremonial obligations, they are largely familial in nature, such as attending a *velorio*, or a funeral, or perhaps getting back to light some candles for the dead. He says he used to like to attend the fiestas, but now he just stays around his place on the Barnes' farm and watches T.V. or does chores when he is not working.

Raymond Victor

Raymond Victor grew up with the anticipation of leadership and active participation in his village, largely due to the influence of his father and a brother-in-law, a Pima from Sacaton. Raymond's father had been recognized by the people of the village for his ability to make speeches, a role that the priests and government workers recognized as useful to their programs and interests. As Raymond reflects,

That was one thing my father was always telling me: "sooner or later you will have to stand up before a crowd and make speeches and interpret." He would always be the speaker at all the gatherings – he had the voice to and he made it strong, too. When he was telling me all this I kept thinking, "Nope, I'll never do all that; no I can't do it." But if I didn't no one would. . . . Charles Valenzuela [brother-in-law] was trying to teach me, especially how to be a good interpreter. At that time I was very bashful and didn't care about it then. When Charles was gone, my father got me to interpret the priest's sermons. That was very hard and I was always nervous. Most of my close relatives always chose me to give speeches when someone died. I did this at Covered Wells and was asked to do it at Santa Rosa, too. My father had always done this; he was an expert at that – making speeches. At Covered Wells another man chose me to make speeches and I got compliments on it – I guess I said the right thing. There is always a leader that would give out information to the people of his village. Right now it is pretty much like it has always been.

In addition to this responsibility as village speaker, Raymond has inherited the leadership in giving the Feast of the Sacred Heart at Covered Wells. The feast falls on different days in June and involves people from Santa Rosa, Sikul Himatk, and Covered Wells. Raymond describes the affair:

This last one [June, 1965] we estimated for about 600 people to feed but maybe it was more. We butchered three steers and it was almost all eaten up. The fiesta begins on Friday and goes all night. Many people come from all over just for the feast. Whoever happens to be there helps out, maybe five or six men and of course the ladies also do a lot of the work. I am the one in charge. We skipped last year [1964] because it was hard for the few people there and I have to be over here [Ajo]. So it will be every other year. My father was in charge of it and I promised him I would take it.

Raymond is an important person to the people of Covered Wells because of his ability to make speeches, his understanding of procedures, his ability to deal with Anglos, and his ability to organize things. He makes it clear, however, that he is not the chief: "Someone gave the wrong information once and said I was chief over there. That was wrong. He is at Santa Rosa, but there is a councilman from Covered Wells. It is too hard to do this with my job over here. Narcho [cousin] tried to get me to do this but I couldn't."

Raymond has also been functioning as a councilman on the Ajo Indian village council since it was established in 1961. Regarding this position, Raymond says, "I am not too active here because I go back to the reservation every chance I get but they insist that I stay on the council, so they put my name on the ballot every year." Some of the main concerns have to do with company housing, village improvements, or stepping in to work with parents whose children are presenting a problem in the larger community of Ajo. Raymond seems to be dissatisfied with the functioning of the council and thinks it is sort of standing still.

It seems that Raymond has been acknowledged by people in both his kinship village and the Ajo Indian village for his ability as a leader and speaker. It is rather clear that leadership roles in each setting tend to weaken his contribution in either. In the first case, he is drawn away, by occupational necessity, from the relationships about which he feels the strongest; in the second case, he lacks interest, but his more frequent presence obligates him to occupy the status since the people insist that he do so. While the two situations would seem to demand that he divide his loyalties, he seems to have accommodated them in a satisfactory way. His leadership at Covered Wells is still called upon, but his lack of availability has made it necessary that he give way to younger men who can give more direct attention to village concerns. The ceremonial calendar has had to be altered by Raymond's occupation at Ajo, and the feast is now held only every other year until another leader emerges who can take charge. At Ajo, Raymond, as do most of the other councilmen, has trouble getting enthused about the council's activities, largely for the same reasons — their obligations and interests in their kinship villages.

Paul Antonio

Paul Antonio, contrary to Alonzo Jose, seems to take advantage of many festive occasions. Through the course of a year, Paul manages to get in on a number of smaller family festivities as well as the larger ones, such as those held at Magdalena or at San Xavier. In June, 1965, Paul told me that he was on a committee at San Xavier to plan for the Feast of Corpus Christi dance. He was obliged to be there, so he indicated, for the entire weekend to help in the planning and preparation. However, Paul was scheduled to work for Mr. Barnes the whole weekend, since it was in the peak of the irrigating season. Paul made his intentions very obvious: "I've got to work days . . . and have to be at the committee meeting, too. I guess I'll just have to make that meeting."

As it turned out, he was able to divide the time with some of Mr. Barnes' other irrigators and managed to get off until one p.m. the following Monday. It was his intention that if he could not get the time off, he would have to take it anyway. One of the foremen actually saw to it that Paul was hauled part way to the mission, an indication of the farm's consideration of the importance of the event. From all indications, he made it back to the farm on time after the festivities.

On another occasion, later in the summer, one of Paul's fellow committee members met with an untimely death, and the wake was scheduled. Paul asked for a couple days off, both to attend the wake and because his infant daughter was in critical condition at the County Hospital. Paul purchased two large bottles of wine and some groceries from two different markets in Tucson and took the "gifts" to the *velorio*. The wine was hidden in some bushes off the road to be retrieved later in the evening, and Paul located the house where the festivities were being held. Paul at first was not sure if he would be staying; but after joining a group of Papago men assembled outside the house of the decedent, Paul was able to identify his relationship to the dead man and delivered his food contribution to the ladies tending the kitchen. It is presumed that the liquor was later retrieved as further assurance of his esteem for his deceased friend. Again, Paul seems to have made it back to work at the designated time.

In October of the same year, Paul took two days off to make a visit to the feast at Magdalena. He had just purchased a used station wagon with some money obtained through a sale of some of his father's allotment at San Xavier and was able to drive down to Mexico and make it back in time for the San Xavier feast to San Francisco all on the same weekend. Due to the continual festivities, Paul was pretty well intoxicated on the night of the procession at San Xavier. This was the same night his daughter died in the home of an Anglo lady who had been caring for the child. The police tried to locate him but could only find Margaret, as Paul was off somewhere drunk. Paul was finally located, and while he was sobering up, his wife made most of the funeral arrangements. On the following Tuesday, the day of the funeral at San Xavier, Paul and many of the male relatives were still showing the signs of the past weekend's festivities. Nevertheless, Paul directed the funeral procession to the church and to the cemetery, and took charge of the burial proceedings. Even during the processional to the cemetery, most of the male members, all relatives, dropped off into the brush to get some more to drink. It was after this experience that Paul disappeared from his family and failed to return to his job at the Barnes' farm.

Except for the last occasion, complicated by the daughter's death, Paul seems to have sought permission from his boss, arranged so much time off, and returned to his job at the specified time. There are several other occasions, not involving important festivities, where Paul failed to get time off or to return when he was expected to be at work. These will be discussed later.

For at least three major festive occasions, it appears that Paul needed merely to tell his boss, trade time with other employees, and be sure to return after the events were over. This he seems to have done, with the exception of the last occasion, an acknowledgment that he was aware that he had both an obligation to his job and to the ceremonial occasions. The boss was able to tolerate his absence on these terms, and Paul seems to have made every effort to meet both commitments.

There were undoubtedly numerous other occasions unknown to me, but the readiness of his boss to grant him the chance indicates that Paul had exhibited some degree of dependability. The boss seems to have understood the ceremonial interests of his employee but could not tolerate the numerous other occasions when there was no explanation for his absence. Thus, while certain festive and ceremonial commitments were acknowledged, the occasions of social drinking in Tucson, at San Xavier, or in Sahuarita, wherein they prevented him from fulfilling his work, could not be tolerated.

Christopher Xavier

Christopher Xavier, contrary to what may seem to be the case, has nothing to resolve with regard to ceremonial roles and occupational roles. While his case is the most difficult to understand from the standpoint of psychological motivation, Chris's pattern of behavior is the most predictable. His spot jobs, his seeking out associates, and his frequenting of the downtown bars inevitably lead to extreme intoxication, arrest, and confinement. It is difficult to see, at the present stage of his progressive alcoholism, where ceremonial and occupational roles are strongly enough established to conflict. Such an area of conflict, if it did ever exist, would need to be reconstructed through some form of clinical technique. Until such a reconstruction is attained, it is far too presumptuous to explain his progressive alcoholism in terms of some past conflict between ceremonial and occupational roles. Perhaps there is much in Paul Antonio's current behavior, however, which might characterize some of Chris's past difficulties in organizing his social personality.

Anthony Cypriano

Other than his responsibilities at the Tucson Indian Center, I can find no other activities which conflict in any way with the demands of Anthony Cypriano's job. As is characteristic of middle class society, there is a clear demarcation between occupation and leisure hours. Anthony knows that in order to keep his job and, thereby, the benefits of his socio-economic position, he must meet the demands of the job. Once the working hours are over, his time is his to use as he pleases.

Anthony spends much of his leisure time working at the center or, perhaps, just staying home. With long weekends and evening hours of leisure, any activity, ceremonial or otherwise, can be scheduled to conform to these hours. A christening, a church gathering, a council meeting of the Indian association, or any festive occasion can be planned to conform to the work week. If there is a conflict of interest, it is not whether to go to work or to attend a particular event; rather, the problem to be resolved would be whether to use the leisure time to stay home, rest, and watch television, or go to the event.

This is a remarkably different kind of decision than Al, Paul, or to some extent Raymond, have to make in resolving the course of action they will take. On the farm, Al and Paul, as steady hands, have to work every day of the week and usually from ten to twelve hours a day. If they want time off to attend an important ceremonial event, they either have to ask, hoping they can get off, or take time off anyway and risk the reaction afterwards. Raymond, who works 26 days straight and then gets a few days off, can at least plan ahead for his leisure time, although it is less frequent.

With this contrast in the philosophy behind the various occupational institutions, it is readily understandable why Anthony seems to face very little of the kind of dilemma confronted by the others. First, Anthony has little or no orientation to reservation ceremonial activity which pulls him away from his occupational responsibilities. Furthermore, his leisure time, a concomitant of his occupational status, provides no basis for a conflict. The activities of which he is a part have long since been geared to the philosophy of industrial society.

DRINKING GROUP ROLES

Wherever I went and to whomever I talked, whether farm operators, mine administrators, or nursery managers, there were comments about Papagos and drinking. The following remarks, coming from a variety of sources, constitute only a few of many such remarks gathered in the course of the field work.

A Mexican farm foreman near Continental: "There are some real good workers who are Papago . . . but I have seen other Papago who were not worth hiring. They would work about four days and even come to work drunk, then leave without any notice and leave me without any men."

A Chinese farm operator near Marana: "Why don't you people do something for them [Papagos]? They just don't want to improve themselves [the discussion was about drinking] ."

An Anglo farm operator near Casa Grande: "Clement [a young Papago machine operator who was fired] was a darn good man to have around; but his problem, as for most Indians, was the booze. Drinking actually was behind much of the trouble."

A Franciscan Priest at Ajo Indian village: "The other big problem [besides common law and cohabitation marriage] is liquor – drunkenness of both adults and juveniles is getting more frequent."

An Ajo juvenile case worker: "As far as I can perceive the community's feelings, the biggest problem with the Indians is their drinking habits."

The Ajo Mine Employment Agent: "When it used to be that Indians could not buy liquor at the bar, there seemed to be more trouble than now. The Indians did not respond to the privilege to buy liquor as any other man. They continued to get their liquor from other sources and did not come to drink in the bars. They drank at home or at dances but were real slow in coming to the bars. . . . It has gradually picked up."

An Ajo elementary school teacher: "Parents are very permissive. Little children are often seen drinking at funerals and weddings. . . . I have had some first graders come to school with mild hangovers."

An Ajo attorney: "Of course they drink quite a bit, but they [Papagos] aren't any trouble to anyone."

A Casa Grande police sergeant: "Sometimes we have as many as 150 Indians in jail during a week's time. We can't be too tough on them if they run off from a work detail in the city. After all, we'll see them again."

A Tucson nursery owner: "You almost have to expect that after a payday, the Indians will end up in jail; and if you want them to work, you have to go the bail or just wait for them to come back."

It would be a serious oversight to ignore the "drinking problem" in a study of Papago occupational adaptation. Until the cultural values underlying Papago drinking behavior are more clearly understood, such catch-all stereotypes as "drunk Indian" or "irresponsible wino" will suffice only for those who find it convenient or practicable to pigeon-hole; they do not explain why a man comes to work drunk or why he does not show up at all. Bahr's (1964) initial work in this area is most encouraging, wherein he relates drinking behavior of Papagos to reference group behavior and the values that operate through the medium of the reference group.

The present discussion is the outcome of an attempt to explore the impact of drinking behavior on the occupational activities of some Papago informants. For purposes of our immediate concern, i.e., the relationship of drinking behavior to occupational adaptation, it seems helpful to look at drinking role behavior in terms of four different frames of reference: (1) the psychodynamics of the individual's drinking history, (2) the social contexts in which drinking most frequently occurs, (3) the effects of drinking behavior on occupational performance, and (4) the individual's efforts to engage corrective facilities to bring his drinking behavior into greater conformity to the demands of his job. Because of the difficulty involved in getting data relative to this touchy area of personal behavior, the discussion will reveal the great disparity in the individual cases as far as what could be learned about drinking attitudes and habits. Where conversation proved unproductive, observation and involvement sometimes filled in the lacunae. This area is a problem unto itself, and a great deal of clinical work is essential to investigating the dimensions of drinking behavior and cross-cultural adjustment. The following, however, is suggestive of an approach and should prove meaningful for the problem at hand.

Alonzo Jose

Although he does drink, Alonzo Jose seems to have encountered little difficulty with regard to alcohol. He thinks he has been able to avoid the trouble that others, such as the young people, including his sons, are experiencing. Al attributes much of it to his early instruction: "My father and my mother and also my grandfathers talked all about that. They said, 'You won't have any money and starve to death. If you work and do something to work, then you can work and sell when people come around and you won't have to starve.' "

Al remembers the time, when he came back from mission school, that he rode over on horseback to Vainom Kug and Big Field just to see the wine ceremonies. As Al recalls,

You ought to see them there. . . . Oh-h-h, the ladies, kids, and everybody, they drink. They come in those wagons from all over and then sit in a circle. Then an old man who sings and passes a basket of wine around . . . to make it rain. . . . Since I come to work, I never go back. That Sahuaro wine the Indians make is maybe like the other wine they get now . . . maybe not so bad. Besides they don't do that but once a year.

Al was away at the mission school for all but two weeks, from the age of 14 to 21, and thus was under the strict supervision of the priests, brothers, and nuns. He likens the experience to the kind of discipline one gets in the Army. It is very unlikely that Al established much of a drinking pattern there except on occasions when the boys might sneak out to get it. Considering his parental instruction, his long experience away from the reservation under the supervision of church personnel, and the infrequency with which bootleg liquor was being peddled on the reservation, the wine ceremonies seemed to be the most frequent occasions for drinking.

Al never claims total abstinence but rather seems to have balanced training, early established habits, and features of temperament into a style of drinking that has caused very little difficulty in terms of his occupational functions. His pattern has some social ramifications, but he likewise seems to have adjusted his personality to these pressures. Perhaps Al's own words will best portray his attitude:

Guys come by and say, "Let's go get something to drink." I'd say, "No, I got to go to work." That's happened to me [referring to a picture with two men seated at a bar]. Sometimes the boss gets mad when people are drinking; they come by and mess up my work. Sometimes the guys get mad at me. Lots of the guys go over to the store, then they come by at two or three in the morning and want me to take them home. Most of the time they come by on payday and want me to take them home in the pickup. The boss says no, not to do that . . . the truck's not for drunks. Those guys down there [Barnes' camp], sometimes they drive around in the truck while they're supposed to be irrigating or working, and they go over to that little bar with the truck. Boy, the boss gets mad! . . .

They won't go for one — they just keep going [laugh]. They *want* to get drunk, else that guy'd say "go on" when the other guy came by. Sometimes I drink one or two cans but that's all and never when I am working. If that one guy wants to go home [again referring to the picture], the other guy would get mad at him, I think so; that's the way those Indian boys are. . . . Sometimes they try to bum money off somebody else. . . . They will go somewhere to get 50¢ or 60¢ more, They don't go for a 35¢ can like I can get down here at the store; they go for that wine. . . . I never give the money like he likes.

Al was asked why he thinks the Indians drink so much if they know it might cost them their jobs or cause them to lose time and money:

'Cause their friends do drinking, too. They come and ask them to go to all these places like Nogales or maybe Tucson. They all start younger and younger, maybe 13 or 14. They have to get somebody to buy it just like we did out there on the reservation . . . have to get some Mexican or somebody else to get it. They have those road blocks at Sells at fiestas and sometimes they take whole cases away from them, those young Indian boys. What do they [police] do with it? Maybe they sell it or drink it themselves [laughter].

Al is very much aware of the problem as it affects the man for whom he works:

Like at the big camp . . . sometimes they take bulldozers or tractors and trucks and go park them in the fields, then run off and get drunk. Just like the irrigators over there; they drive off at night and park and drink. Mr. Barnes tries to stop it but they won't do it. It's worse and worse all the time — they don't care; they say they can find some job someplace else; they don't care 'cause everybody does it. Just like my boy. Oh, sometime they run a truck off the road and ruin it; he [Mr. Barnes] lets them off a week and puts them back to work at the same place. That's why I like to work alone. Over here I work alone.

Al likes to avoid the social complications of this kind of behavior, which seems to be one of the benefits of his house being isolated from the camp by more than two miles.

Regarding his present job and his responsibilities toward it, Al can give this estimate: "They like my work over here. They used to have people up there — they used to get drunk and all that stuff down there and not show up. I don't do that." His present boss and the man he worked for in Coolidge speak highly of Al as a worker and regard him an exceptional case for Papago farm hands in general.

Raymond Victor

The wine ceremonies at Covered Wells, Santa Rosa, and Vainom Kug introduced Raymond Victor to his first drinking at the age of 14. At the commencement of the ceremonies, the leader lectured the people, asking them to stay friendly and avoid fighting or arguing. Raymond remembers that he did not know any songs with which to "cover" the basket of wine as it was served, so he just stayed in the crowd and took his turn when the basket came around. His father always admonished him not to get too drunk or he might lose a saddle or horse, and when he started feeling it too much he should go out somewhere away from things and sleep it off.

Raymond went to the feasts with several older fellows who usually wanted to stay until the last drop was gone. After so much wine was offered in the circle, the people would spread out and go to several different houses to continue drinking. He succeeded in getting drunk the first time he began drinking the cactus wine; but it was not until he was about 16 that he was introduced to bootleg liquor, which was less common in those days. He was working on the district fence at Santa Rosa and went to a dance with some older men. A relative of his was bootlegging whiskey and some was offered to Raymond, and he began drinking; he says he got the habit right there. His father was opposed to bootleg liquor and was very strict, but the family was at the cotton farm so Raymond said he got talked into it. By the time he was 19, Raymond was doing a lot of drinking, mostly

in the association of older relatives and friends who introduced him to it.

By the time he was married, he says he really had the habit. At the time, he was driving the school bus but would miss several days at a time because of his drinking.

When he started working at the mine again in 1947, he knew he had to start thinking about stopping, but would go for a period, then start to drink and would have to call in "sick." Raymond seems to have maintained fairly reliable working habits through the years, both on the farm and at the mine. But the drinking did threaten his jobs on several occasions.

Raymond says that his first drinking as a young man was definitely provoked by his curiosity, the pleasure it gave, the aftereffects it produced, and to maintain the good feelings of those who offered it. He never thought of it as a problem. After he was married, and he was under obligation to support his family, his drinking began to interfere with his jobs. Yet he never, at the time, took his drinking as a serious threat, since he was not thinking about steady jobs then. Drinking was still a habit that brought pleasure in the company of relatives and friends.

It appears that Raymond's drinking habits shifted from a social context and the pressures of friends to a point where he was able to see his drinking presenting problems. While the same kinds of situations compelled him to drink, his awareness of new problems as a result of the demands of a steady job produced a conflict, a conflict that is not yet completely resolved.

While Raymond was president of a local union in 1959, the union was throwing beer parties every night to compete in membership drives with other unions. Raymond admits that the pressures took him to his rock bottom, and he ended up staying away from work for two weeks. He went back to Covered Wells but finally returned to Ajo to see if he had been discharged. Because of his good record Raymond was given a warning slip and reinstated on his job.

Earlier, in 1955, Raymond had been facing some problems relative to his drinking and his absence from work and decided he needed to do something. Some other Indians told him of a Mexican lady who made occasional visits to Mexican town and who offered prayers and different curative treatments. Raymond says she offered to help but that she could not at that time so the problem went "uncured." Raymond continues: "From then on I would drink for two or three days, then when I got over it I would wait about a month, then start all over again. I would miss work and call in and tell them I was sick and couldn't come in — I'd find all kinds of excuses."

After his 1959 layoff due to his drinking, he attended a Sells celebration and talked to a priest who advised him to contact the Alcoholics Anonymous group in Ajo. After fighting off his fear about going to a strange group, Raymond built up courage and attended. The friendliness of the group and the frankness with which they talked about experiences similar to his got him interested in the program. Because of the awareness of the problems Indians were having with drinking, he decided to get an Indian group going, but it did not succeed; they could not see the sense to it and found it hard to follow, except for a couple of individuals.

An Anglo from the outside alienated Raymond from participation in the AA group since Raymond did not like the way the new man tried to make it so official. Raymond says he does not go to meetings anymore, but he tries to live by the big book. It is interesting how Raymond has had to modify both the philosophy of AA, which says that once an alcoholic always an alcoholic and one cannot take the first drink, and his ceremonial participation in the wine feast, which invites continuous drinking. Raymond describes the dilemma:

We had a serious problem back at the village [Covered Wells] two years ago [1963]. It was at that time I took a drink again at the wine feast and followed the custom. This one man and the priest failed in the feast and there was some ill feeling. This man came to me and said he had some wine made and asked me to come and have some. I did it out of obligation and had a good time to bring us all close together again. But it was just for that occasion. My mother agreed with my decision — she is still accustomed to this — she tried to get me to come and drink with my relatives so I wouldn't hurt them. I told her to tell them for me because I couldn't control it and was afraid and this time I didn't want to turn away. I did go and had two drinks and told them, "I had some of your good wine but I have to go to work tomorrow and if I stay, you know how I'll end up." They understood and told me they were glad I could come.

Raymond has developed an insight into his drinking behavior and is able to relate it to his successes and failures in other contexts. It appears that he has

accommodated an Anglo-oriented therapeutic and philosophical program to his own life style, but his ceremonial relationships are successfully compartmentalized so that he can depart from the AA philosophy in order to participate, in a modified manner, in the wine ceremony. His occupational and kinship commitments have made the accommodation necessary. Raymond seems to have been sufficiently motivated and capable of doing so, something that other Ajo Indians, with a few exceptions, have found more difficult, if not impossible.

Raymond, due to his insight and his participation in the AA program, talked frankly and freely of his drinking and provided a rather extensive history. Other informants have been less prone to talk about personal drinking habits, so I have had to employ the techniques of the hypothetical situation and direct observation to supplment the inadequacies of personal interviewing.

Paul Antonio

The readiness with which Al and Raymond talk about drinking is not characteristic of Paul Antonio. Only after the personal relationship had been well established and he had become aware that the complications of his drinking became obvious to me did Paul begin talking about it at all. Even now, he has not been able or willing to relate much regarding his drinking history; but his statements and behavior in the context of drinking situations make up for this lack. In the course of taking Paul's occupational history, over an extended period of interviewing and reinterviewing, he would pass off questions as to why he left a job or was laid off, either by purposeful silence or with a statement to the effect that he had nothing to say about that.

My first encouter with Paul reflecting his drinking situation occurred when I had gone down to the camp to talk with him one morning (summer, 1964) after he got off work. When I got to his house his wife told me that Paul's brother and some other friends came to the camp the day before, and they had been down at the Sahuarita bar drinking since then. He had only been with Mr. Barnes a couple of months after being "laid off" at the large Sahuarita cotton corporation. It was several days before Paul was again in any condition to talk to. I had seen him driving his old car around in circles on the highway; and when it stalled, several of the other Indian fellows got out and tried to push. They were all very much under the influence. Paul managed to sober up soon enough to maintain his job and managed to keep in fairly good graces with his boss until the season's irrigating was all over.

Since he did not like to pick cotton, Paul went to Tucson several times a week, after irrigating had stopped, via the Greyhound bus that stopped right by the Barnes' camp four times each day. He managed to get some yard jobs for people who had called on him before and who would drop him a post card when they had work for him. Some of the time was spent in the Tucson jail for drunkenness in public places. The water was running shortly after Paul got out of jail for the last time that spring, and he was back to work at the farm irrigating.

In July, 1965, Paul's wife called me to ask me to help locate Paul and try to get him back to the farm in time to go to work in the evening. They had come to town to do some shopping, bring the youngest boy to the clinic, and if time, to go to see their infant daughter in the hospital. While Margaret was at the clinic with the child, Paul started drinking with friends in the West Congress Avenue bars near the bus station and failed to meet her at the station to catch the bus back to the ranch. She had heard from other Indians that he was quite drunk at the Silver Dollar Bar around the corner, but he had since disappeared. Margaret said that someone told her that he spent what little money he had and was now getting others to buy drinks.

I combed a four-block area, checking every tavern, and succeeded in finding many Papagos in all stages of intoxication, some dancing with bar girls, some slumped at the bars, others huddled in booths and corners, and a number "sleeping it off" — but no Paul. I finally located him sound asleep in the dark corner of a Congress Avenue pool hall. After some difficulty waking him, we got Paul to the car and to the camp before he was due to start to work. We stopped for groceries at a Chinese market on the Nogales highway and Paul strolled over to a contractor's bus parked there and shared some more beer with some of the crew who were on their way to Tucson after a day's work. Paul went to work that evening although not fully revived from his day's drinking.

As Margaret indicated, with some embarrassment, "He always claims that beer will wake him up, but it just makes him drunker. I'm surprised he didn't ask for some old cheap wine." On another occasion,

Margaret mentioned that "Paul doesn't talk much or say anything when he is sober, but when he has been drinking, you can't keep him from talking. He is O.K. until he goes to Tucson and meets some of his friends. But he should be O.K. now since he doesn't have any more money to take him to town."

My first effort to get him back to the farm after he had been drinking quite heavily led to a host of other similar situations and disclosed to me a new side of Paul's personality. In a number of these situations Paul was gregarious and sullen, resentful against his employers and Anglos in general, and full of nostalgic remorse for the way things used to be so much better for Indians. These situations also became his means for testing the veracity of my avowed friendship: "Say, Jack, is it all right if I have a drink? I have my own to drink so it's O.K., eh, Jack [pulling a bottle of cheap wine from under his shirt]? As my friend, you have to take a drink." In these periods, when he was braced by alcohol, he wanted me to ask him "those questions," but he was usually so incoherent that he could not stay with any one thing, frequently shifting from English to Papago.

On one occasion after I took him home, he went out again around midnight and eventually ended up at the Sahuarita tavern with some other Papagos, where he stayed much of the following day. His money had run out, but someone in the group still had money for drinks. Margaret mentioned that when the money ran out they would all disperse, if they could not find anyone else with money, and head home. Paul made it home and slept for a few hours, then got up and hopped a ride to San Xavier, where, once again, he started drinking at a friend's house, where he finally fell asleep. There was a period of about a week in which Paul seemed to be on a continuous drunk, but when he sobered up, he went back to work and stayed at it steadily for around three weeks with no sign of drinking. His resources, and those of his Papago friends around Continental and Sahuarita, had been temporarily exhausted.

The next occasion for more drinking came at the end of the month, after a payday. His infant daughter had been rushed to the hospital because of a respiratory complication, and he also received word of the funeral of his fellow committeeman at San Xavier. It was on this occasion that Paul bought two bottles of wine and stashed them in the brush in the desert, where he and his friends could converge at the proper time during the funeral festivities. This did not turn out to be a prolonged drinking bout, and he was back to Continental for work at the time he said he would be.

In the course of the field work, I was able to discover that most of Paul's difficulties with the people he had worked for and continues to work for has been his drinking and the erratic behavior it produces. He was fired from the Ajo mine for coming to work drunk; he has been dismissed from at least three farm jobs for the same reason or has been laid off for several days as punishment; he has had altercations with nursery proprietors involving differences over his drinking and its effect on his job responsibilities.

Paul usually pinpoints the problems differently: "All he was letting me do was chop weeds so I quit; me and the boss got in an argument so I quit; the work was too hard and the hours were too long. I just got laid off; there is hardly any time to be with the family or do other things; I don't like long hours and small pay; some foremen are mean." These are undoubtedly considered justifiable complaints in and of themselves, and they tell a great deal about how he feels regarding his work status. Perhaps they have some relationship to his periodic irresponsibility and undependability toward his jobs and his bosses.

By the same token, the employers I have talked to would like to have a sober Paul around all the time, for they are very pleased with his hard work.

The kinds of work Paul has done the most, namely, farm work and nursery work, seem to have institutionalized means for dealing with a man who is a good worker but who is beset by drinking. Mr. Barnes penalizes by laying Paul off for several days when he gets on one of his drinking sprees. When Paul sobers up and comes down to the shop and shows signs of really wanting to get back to work, the boss is quick to take advantage of a good irrigator like Paul. There is a tolerable limit, of course, and Paul extended it once too often and found himself without work.

The nurseries in Tucson have also institutionalized a means of utilizing the services of some of their good Papago employees who are, nonetheless, chronic drinkers. One nursery proprietor expressed that they become attached to certain Papagos who have worked for the nursery, despite their drinking habits and undependability in showing up when they are supposed to. Regarding Paul, this proprietor said, "He was a good man as far as work is concerned, but like all Indians . . . you have to count on days when they won't show up or end up in jail; you have to put up with a few bad days and try to work them when you can, when they show up."

These institutionalized ways of utilizing low wage, unskilled Papagos, and programming the work activity around these occasional expressions of occupational irresponsibility very likely contribute to the persistence of occupational stereotypic roles. There are certain desirable features, despite low economic rewards, to which workers become accustomed. These institutionalized procedures make the employer's behavior toward the worker somewhat predictable and seem to be indications that the employer occasionally expects and is able to tolerate his employee's periodic absence without total censure. This has become very obvious in Paul's relationships toward his employers.

Paul finally expressed to me — after I met him at the jail and took him out to the nursery where he had been working — his inner feelings about a recent series of arrests for drunkenness:

I guess I didn't do so good. This is why I lost my job with Mr. Barnes. I know whenever I come to town with my friends and relatives I drink. I know I have too many friends in South Tucson, like the one that bailed me out. I went out drinking with him and got in again. I try to be kind and remember my friends and relatives, but sometimes it doesn't work out so good. It's not so good to have friends sometimes, maybe, but I try.

When they told me they will let me come back to work, I said I would try but I can't really make any promises. I can't tell how it will come out. I try to explain to them but I can't give them my life's story and how it is. They told me I have a job if I can stand on my own two feet; I know that but it's hard because of my friends and relatives.

I know I got trouble. It was my car and I got it fixed. Now it is me who has the trouble [laughter]. I know I've got to try. I told the judge I had a job and I would try, but I can't promise too much. He was good to me. I know I did bad but I do good things, too. I never was too lucky. I will get my car out and go straight to the reservation so I can go to work in the morning. I've got to try and keep my job since they give me a chance again. I don't know — it won't be easy to stay away from all my friends but I guess I'll have to. But here in South Tucson, they have all those Mexican policemen and that's not good for us Indians. Maybe I should stay away even if I have no friends.

Needless to say, Paul worked several days in a row, then ended up in jail again after drinking with some South Tucson friends. He has continued to work intermittently for the same nursery.

Less attention has been given to the other two cases with regard to drinking, since Christopher Xavier's chronic alcoholism and prolonged jail periods do not permit him, in the short time available, to provide much meaningful information about how his pattern materialized; and Anthony Cypriano, from all indication, has no apparent difficulty with drinking as it affects his work. The field contacts with these two individuals have been less intense and less prolonged. The case studies presented do reflect some of their attitudes.

OCCUPATIONAL ROLES

One of the hypotheses underlying this study is that there are other demands, besides the demands of fulfilling occupational roles, which are relative to the occupational adaptation of Papago workers. The discussion up to this point has dealt largely with a few nonoccupational roles that occupational situations bring into play. Perhaps there is a danger of overdoing this emphasis and ignoring the simple and obvious fact that perhaps there are features in an occupation itself which are compensating and personally satisfying or unrewarding and personally unpleasant. In this section, the discussion will focus strictly on aspects of work roles that are central elements to acceptable job performance in our five case examples.

In evaluating a Papago worker in relationship to his occupational roles, there are six principal features that are considered most significant. (1) The central and peripheral role elements of the particular occupational status must be identified. What are the specific work demands that the worker must carry out in the satisfactory performance of his status roles (central elements)? What are the extra expectations and expediencies, related to the job but not necessary to the technical performance of the job, which tend to enhance the worker's prestige in the eyes of his employer and other people? (2) What is the worker's relationship to supervisors and other official personnel in the institutional structure of the occupations? (3) What preparations and abilities does the worker have in the carrying out of the required work task? (4) What are the worker's aspirations, ideals, values, maximum satisfactions, and most desired work alternatives evident in his cognitive apparatus? (5) What complaints, disappointments, and discontentments are expressed or apparent in his behavior regarding the status he is occupying? (6) In the course of his occupational career, have there been any shifts, changes, or modifications in either his attitudes or his values, and what effect have these had on his employment patterns?

Alonzo Jose

With the exception of the period in the late 1930s and early 1940s when he worked on government projects, Alonzo Jose's occupational activities have been with commercial farms. As noted, up to the time he was 35 years old he had tilled his own soil and raised a few head of cattle. Since coming off-reservation to work, Al has done machine operating and irrigating exclusively.

Since coming to work for Mr. Barnes in 1960, Al has been doing mostly irrigating and driving a dump truck during the hay thrashing in the late fall. His major responsibility is irrigating the large plot of land which lies directly north of his house, although on occasion the boss needs him elsewhere. For the last few years he has taken turns with a "cousin" from Komelik village, alternating day and night shifts. Al works from 7 A.M. to 6 P.M. for one week, then gets a half day or, more seldom, a full day off, then works a week at the night shift from 6 P.M. to 7 A.M. There is a slack period extending from the last of November into February, depending on the weather, but Al sticks around in case Mr. Barnes has some work for him.

When not irrigating, he may be asked to mow weeds with the tractor, clean the irrigation ditches, or any other task that needs to be done. The foreman comes by every morning or evening and instructs him in the work for the day. While he works from 10 to 11 hours a day each day of the week, Al says Mr. Barnes is pretty good about giving him a day off when he needs it. A full pay period (every two weeks), when it has not been necessary to miss any time, nets about $115 gross, or roughly $230 a month. In the past ten years, 1961 was the most rewarding economically when he grossed a yearly income of nearly $2,600. The last two years his yearly income has fallen to about $1,800.

Al usually starts the pumps and then controls the flow of the water to the proper section and rows of the field. He constructs and demolishes crude dams at proper intervals in the irrigation ditches as a means of controlling the water flow and for providing a sufficient pressure to permit water diversion into the fields by means of rubber tubes. He must keep an eye on the dams to make sure that the ditch itself does not overflow into the field. In this manner Al moves around the field, constructing a dam to hold back the water for siphoning into the desired section, and to permit the construction of another dam for the next section, after which the previous dam will be demolished. In all the operation, Al works alone except for an occasional check by the foreman for further instructions. Concerning this kind of work, Al says,

I like to work alone. Sometimes they get too many on a job, then they get mixed up and don't do it the right way. Sometimes they put me in on day and night — sometimes they put me on night too, after I have worked in the day. I work all day, then sleep from 7 to 11, then I work all night. Maybe I should get a little more money; I think maybe they pay enough but maybe I should get more. Irrigating! That's a long time for not so much money. I have to buy groceries and everything.

Al's job is his total involvement, and any peripheral role requirements are difficult to detect, although Al's care of the house and farm property and his conduct off the job have a significant bearing on the favorable relationship he has with his bosses. These extra-work aspects influence the bosses' preferences for Al doing the work when there is extra work to be done. Responsible behavior off the job is important in the farm operator's overall evaluation of his employees as people. However, the primary concern is the dependable performance of the assigned tasks or the central role requirements of the job.

Al knows that his foreman does not like all the drinking that goes on among most of his Indian workers. Al says, "He's pretty hard on them about that, but he is good to me. The other people complain he is too hard on them and they quit."

Al was given a hypothetical situation as a means of probing his attitudes about the relationship between an employee and his boss. The situation presents a worker being bawled out for a job that the boss claims the worker did wrong but that the worker thinks he did right. The following dialogue reveals Al's perception of the situation:

Al: Maybe he's drunk, that's why he don't do it the right way. He'll have to sober up.

Q: What if he *is* sober?

Al: I don't know [shrug of shoulders]. Just walk off I guess. Maybe he should tell him he thinks he did it right.

Q: What if the boss gets mad?

Al: Well, maybe just like Mr. Barnes. He'd get mad. Just do what he says. Like those people over at the camp — he scolds them and they just don't say anything. If they talk back, maybe they get more trouble. Do what the boss says and hope it's right.

Q: What gets the boss mad?

Al: Maybe they don't do the right work. That makes him mad. Sometimes when the boss says to do it and I think it's wrong — maybe I don't do it. If the boss gets mad, well, maybe he don't know you do it different. If the boss wants it that way still, then go ahead. Last changing day [shifts] this boy told me that Mr. Barnes told him to go back and start the water all over again. I started at the second tarp [dam], not the third tarp. I said that the other man told me. "Goddam, he don't do what I say. That's the way it is with all them down there [Indians at the camp]. He don't understand nothing in English! I said, "Mr. Barnes, that's not right [show of emotion in voice]. They do hard work for you and they try to do it right. You shouldn't feel that way."

Al has had some trouble, particularly at night when he gets sleepy:

Sometimes you can get pretty sleepy. I don't try to sleep at nights because you have to watch the pumps and you also have to be sure the ditch doesn't run over. One time I just got sleepy and fell asleep and when I woke up the water had run over the sides of the ditch into the fields. The boss doesn't like that too well [laughter]; that's why I gotta try and keep awake.

Al's relationships with his bosses over the years have been pretty good. On only one occasion did he leave a job because of a disagreement. Al describes the situation:

I left Andover Farms [Coolidge] that first time because they got a man who was a rough foreman; he didn't like us to work for him. We just pulled out. He was gone the next time we went up in 1955. His name was Dixon and they told us he was gone and wouldn't give us trouble any more. He [Dixon] just said, "Maybe you should cultivate"; then he'd follow us around all the time and he'd always complain the way we do it. He wanted to follow us around all the time. If it was a white boy or colored boy, he'd just stand and wouldn't follow them around. He did us. It was the same way irrigating — sometimes he came by at two in the morning and watched us. Mr. Smith [operator] okayed everything but this man told us to do it another way. Then I would say, "But the boss said to do it this way and we did it." So then he would complain and have us do it over again his way.

Al seems to have worked out satisfactory ways of dealing with the controversies that could develop and has managed to maintain harmony between him and his supervisors. He has gotten angry and gets emotional about injustices to his fellow Indian workers, but his relationships with the boss and foreman appear to be stabilized to the point that Al can say, "They treat me pretty good."

In explaining the ease with which he has been able to get and maintain farm jobs, Al thinks his work building roads on the reservation, which taught him to handle all kinds of heavy equipment, has always helped him to get steady farm jobs. When he went to the harvest, he was always asked if he could drive a tractor. "They like to have people who know how to handle heavy machinery in case they need you." This has been the case at every farm on which he has done work.

Al is aware of his lack of training for other kinds of work and admits that he is too old to fret over the work he never had the chance to learn. He can identify jobs that, were he starting over, he might like to do, but when given the choice among a whole range of jobs, disregarding his actual preparations and pretending he had the chance to pick just the one he wanted, Al selects those that have been the most familiar to him. Al selected tractor driving and irrigating as the jobs he likes the most:

I choose this one [picture of man on tractor] because it's the one they want all that land cleared — discing. Because it's for everything on the land — it's best to drive, cleaning the land. ... I think I pick tractor driving and irrigating best of all. ...

... Mr. Cook came to me [1944] and asked me if I could drive a tractor and I said, "I guess I could." So he stood on the back and showed me. It was one of those old tractors and always gave trouble. I leveled land and cultivated for him; sometimes I plowed. I always stayed on the tractor. I never chop cotton, just drive the tractor. I wasn't irrigating then either. I

didn't do any of that 'til later. It was just like I was working for myself. He said you go do this and this and that and I would do it, all by myself. He was a pretty good old man.

It is not difficult to see that his present job permits him to work alone much of the time, something he seems to highly value.

When Al is asked about the hopes that he has for his children and grandchildren, he is able to see them participating in some jobs that Al has never had the chance to perform. Yet when presented with a range of occupational activities in which he would most like to see his grandchildren participate, Al's choices run something like the following:

Maybe they will learn how to hoe. It would be all right. It pays 75¢ an hour [laughter]. That's what they'd get. I think hoeing — that'd be all right. I think they maybe have a chance for all of them. They just have to go down and find out. All they need to do is stick around the cotton fields.

Al feels the father is the head of the family and should see to it that the boys stay in school if they are still young. However, he claims he was not very successful with his own boys. They said they wanted to drop out of school and go to work, but they would only work a little while, then run around and not work.

When Al was asked what a father should say to a 15-year-old boy who says he wants to quit school and go to work, Al answered in this manner:

"You're too young to quit and go to work." Maybe he should try to finish up another grade instead of go look for a job. He might be satisfied with work but what kind of work can he get? Maybe easy work, like maybe — well, field work is too hard — maybe on a farm like herding cows, maybe that would be all right. Maybe 15 is too young, maybe it is just right for farm work. It might help him to finish high school *if he would like to do that,* maybe he would learn more about some kinds of jobs. If he were a man he should tell him to go back to school because boys don't like to go back to school; that's the way it goes.

If they go looking for work, for some kinds of jobs maybe their school helps better than others. Sometimes if a man goes to work and doesn't understand English, like when he goes to work for a white guy, he has to learn it or he can't work very well. It's the same way with Mexicans and Spanish. Maybe school will help. I tried to get the boys to stay in school but they never said anything about that and just go to work. Maybe 24th or 25th [years of age] is better for looking for jobs. Maybe he should be in school if he's 15.

Raymond Victor

Raymond Victor, in his 20 years with the Ajo mine, has gradually ascended through a series of pay levels starting at track labor at the A level and moving through a series of advancements as a member of a pipe gang. He became a mine pipe laborer at the B level in 1947, was advanced to a mine pipe man at the D level in 1950, became a mine pipe lead man at the E level in 1962, and in 1964 Raymond was advanced to mine head pipe man at the F level. He is now anticipating an advancement to the G level.

A pipe gang lays the water and air pipes in the mine pit and removes them when operations have shifted to a new spot or when repairs are necessary. A pipe line crew consists of a lead or head pipe man and three mine pipe men or laborer helpers. There are four crews that work day shift only, while the p.m. and graveyard shifts have two pipe men each. Some of the pipe men are involved in alternating shifts, but Raymond is not. All the pipe line crews are under the supervision of a general pipe line foreman. There are not more than a half dozen Papagos who are pipe men, although more are helpers.

There is a main four-inch water pipe line going all the way down the three percent grade, and then there are from one- to eight-inch water lines and three-inch air lines for the jackhammers at every level of operation. If a line gets too far from an operation, the crew has to move the pipe line closer. When drilling and the operation at one spot are through, the lines are moved elsewhere; or when the pipe needs to be moved out for blasting, the crew moves the pipe. Clamp pipe is now used instead of threaded pipe and makes the operation much easier, demanding fewer men to a crew.

When Raymond started as a helper in 1947, he received $7.68 a day; the same position today offers $20.24 a day. As head pipe man Raymond gets $23.28 a day, which amounts to close to $8,000 gross for a year. He works a straight day shift (7:30 a.m. - 4:00 p.m.), but the operation varies from time to time. In 1963, the operation was an "11 and 3," meaning 11 straight work days, then three days off for a mine shutdown; for those on alternating shifts, a shift change occurs and operations are resumed for another "11 and 3." Since 1964, the mine has been on a "26 and 2" for much of the time. August usually brings a shutdown when most employees take their vacations. Raymond's seniority allows him a three-week paid vacation plus paid holidays.

In addition to his regular work roles as a crew head man or supervisor, Raymond has been active in union affairs. Raymond and one other Papago, also at one of the higher pay levels, have been the only Papago leaders in the local AFL-CIO chemical workers' union, although it has the largest Indian membership. The pressures of the position were just too much for Raymond:

I was president but I got out of that. It took every evening. I was president just at the time of a lot of squawking about not posting bids and discriminating in promotions. I got out of that responsibility. I would worry about the competition with other unions for members. The only way we could hang on was to meet every evening, and we drank along with it. I got so down — I tried to back out of my union responsibilities — it was pulling me down. The man from the international would encourage me to stick with it, telling me that "you have more Indian members than the others, and they are attentive to you. What would happen to the union and the Indians you lead if you step down?"

While the central role requirements of the job can be performed without the extra-work obligation such as union leadership, Raymond's influence with other Indians, his manifestation of responsibility, and his ability to deal with non-Indians on the job have placed peripheral role demands on him in the form of union leadership. Much of this responsibility was assumed under the persuasion of others, including Anglo union leaders; Raymond found many of the demands excessive and emotionally unsatisfying. Due to the pressures, he eventually relinquished the responsibility.

The company reports contain few adverse comments on his record as an employee. Raymond has a good record of work performance except in 1953 and 1959 when he was issued warning slips for unauthorized absences, but no final warnings were necessary. In my first contacts with Raymond, he never told me that his position was a supervisory one, nor did he talk of it as a skilled job. The Employment Agent told me later that Raymond occupies a supervisory position, since he directs the activities of other men in his crew and therefore has a responsible position. In 1964, the agent indicated that Raymond had actually been offered more responsible positions but refused them. The agent's opinion was that Raymond's position was a desirable one with some responsibility but not too much, and he was therefore quite content with it. Raymond had, at that time, the lead over a gang but primarily passed the orders down from the general pipe line foreman. Since most orders came from above, his position, with regard to his relations with his crew, was a rather secure one.

Raymond mentions that when he first went on a pipe gang, he did not know a thing about it. The old man who led the crew of four showed him how to lift and remove the pipes; once the routines were learned, they have pretty much remained the same. Raymond's own comments perhaps best reflect his feelings about his job and his responsibilities:

When I came back to the mine after the war, I was offered my old job at the mill. Instead I went to the track for four months, then to the pipe gang. I've been here ever since. It was for more pay, not what I wanted but better than track man. A pipe line man's not so bad. I like it where I am now. I would like to have taken up mechanics but didn't have a chance after dropping out of school. I have had many opportunities but I feel like I don't have enough education. I took a foreman job for two months. I went on it and then left it. Now the foreman tells me and I direct my men. I don't feel sure of myself. The next contract [1965] asks me to be sub-foreman at another pay level [he was lead man at level E at the time; the new contract provided a level F position of head man]. I won't take it. I'm happy where I am. I have some responsibility; I don't want any more responsibility. I like it where I am now.

While Raymond has ascended through several pay grade levels and has been given some supervisory responsibility, his work routines have varied but little all the time he has been a pipe man. He works right along with the men in his crew, performing essentially the same tasks.

While in 1964 he refused a more responsible position and indicated he would reject the new contract offer as a sub-foreman, Raymond has since accepted the position. Raymond relates the circumstances behind this change of mind:

I think one of the things that made the most difference in my life was about my job. When I started working for the mine here, . . . I guess I just wanted a routine job without any responsibility. I wanted the same thing all the time. That's the way I felt all the time. I was scared to go to a different level; I didn't want to be responsible. The head man for pipe line got sick and they wanted me to take it. . . . but I didn't think I could handle it. The head man is different than a lead man — I was a lead man then. It was at a higher level and I was afraid to try it. I took it and still had the feeling I shouldn't have it, but after three days I just made up my mind that I could do it

and told myself that I could do it. I just told myself to put myself in his place and do just as he had done. That made a change in me. It was an accident that I got it. Now I tell my boys on the gang the same thing. . . . Before that I just wanted the routine job. I was wrong then and I didn't know it until this experience happened. I worried for three days how this was going to turn out, and I couldn't sleep at night thinking about it. Then I had a change in feeling and it made a big difference in how I feel about my work.

The contentment and security which Raymond expects and feels regarding the responsibilities attached to the carrying out of the central elements of his occupational status are pretty clear. There are certain jobs that he would have preferred, had the opportunities availed themselves, such as being a churn drill operator or a welder; but "you can't start all over again now." He is a little worried about some of the recent labor trends at the mine:

People with 20 years are getting cut from their experienced job levels and getting cut back to the pit, right where they started. They don't get to keep their present pay levels but also get a reduction in pay all the way down to the lowest unskilled levels, just like those starting. They worked their ways away from those jobs 20 years ago and all because of automation they are right back where they started except that they get more money than they started with then. But it costs more to live. Nothing can be done about it but that's the way it is going and the unions can't do much about it. There are some really unhappy people right now. . . . I feel that I'm kind of way up to where if I get down this low, I don't know how I would like it. . . . If it does happen I won't have any choice but I would still have to carry on. It [track labor in the pit] is harder and there are too many bosses on the track.

Raymond's relationships to his fellow workers are still very important and seem to lie behind some of his apprehension toward assuming too much direct supervisory responsibility. Yet he wants things easier for his children and grandchildren:

I want them to have an easy job so they won't have to do what we're doing. I want them to be advanced in school so they won't have to labor and do hard work for their money. . . . First they will have to have their education. We will have to try to get them through college. They will also have to learn to be open with people and active in their districts and communities.

There have been some concrete changes in values and attitudes, as Raymond admits:

My brother Fred stays on the reservation. He doesn't have a steady job. He wants to stay on the reservation, get a little money from cotton picking, buy a few groceries. I used to be that way. I felt that way myself. Fred worked over here at the mine a couple months, then went back to Covered Wells. Like they always say to us. We're given good jobs and can't hold on because of drinking. I almost lost mine once. They give us good jobs and so many chances and we always mess up — it is true!

Paul Antonio

Paul Antonio performs both farm labor and nursery or yard work. The main nursery for which Paul has worked off and on since 1950 gave him the job when he answered an ad in the Tucson paper. Paul describes his work at this nursery:

It was about 1950 that I started for Andy Larson at the nursery. . . . I stayed there 'til 1953. I started to work there first, then my brother Juan started there. There were some other Indians there but they took off. Just us two were the only Papagos there when I worked there. We went all over working for homes, working in the yards. We planted shrubbery, pruned and trimmed trees, and other things around the yards — whatever they told us to do. We went out on crews to different homes. This was a pretty steady job for about four years — I think I was there in 1954, too.

Paul worked at this same nursery for short periods in 1958 and again in 1965. It was also the means for getting on at the nursery where Paul now occasionally works, since Mr. Larson contacted Paul's present boss about Paul's work and what to expect. Paul tried working for Mr. Larson one week in February, 1965, while he was waiting for work at the Barnes' farm to resume, but he quit long before the farm called him back. Paul gives his explanation for leaving the nursery after only a week: "I guess there were lots of reasons for it. He wanted to get things done too fast."

The work at the present nursery is much the same. Paul sometimes works in the back of the store watering plants, replanting them, and loading and unloading them. At other times he goes out to assist on the deliveries and helps in the planting. On one occasion the boss was going to have Paul start making deliveries on his own, but he never showed up and ended up in jail instead.

While Paul was maintaining his rural residence at the Barnes' farm, he would occasionally catch a bus going by the camp and go to Tucson to do yard work. This was work he contracted on his own as a result of his many contacts over the years while doing nursery work. People would either drop him a post card, or he would go to town and contact them on his own. None of the jobs have been for more than two or three days. Since Paul has few tools of his own, he has had to rely on the tools of the people for whom he has worked. Most of the work has consisted of cutting grass and trimming hedges and bushes.

Until the beginning of 1966, Paul's dominant occupational pattern has been oriented toward steady farm labor (the past seven or eight years), with the nursery, and yard work only to tide the family over during the winter months when there was little or no irrigating. Paul was with Mr. Barnes for about 15 months and, before that, he worked for the Sahuarita Cotton Farmers Company for about six years. For Mr. Barnes he irrigated only, but for the Sahuarita Company he also did some cotton chopping and picking in addition to irrigating. For both farms the irrigating usually begins in February and extends through August and perhaps into September. Paul's duties as an irrigator are pretty much the same as those described for Alonzo Jose, but Paul is not quite as steady a hand as Al and is not called on to perform as many other tasks in addition to irrigating. At the Sahuarita farm he worked from 6 A.M. to 6 P.M. seven days a week, but he could get a couple days off if he asked for them. All his orders each day were given to him by a Mexican foreman, with whom he seemed to get along quite well. Paul would then start the pumps, run the water, and divert it by means of rubber hoses to the proper fields.

His work for Mr. Barnes was pretty much the same except that his day did not begin until 7 A.M. and ended at 6 P.M. Also, he had to alternate to a night shift every other week. He explains the reason he left the Sahuarita farm and went to work for Mr. Barnes: "I left the other job at Sahuarita farms because all I was doing was chopping cotton; they had a lot of irrigators there; well, I don't know what happened but I got laid off. I think I can stay here [Barnes'] as long as there is a job."

While Paul's work has always been commendable, it has not always been dependable. He seems to run into difficulties with those for whom he works. Some of Paul's real feelings about his work did not become evident until he voiced his complaints while in an intoxicated condition. On one occasion he had been off work for several days and somewhat apprehensive about whether he still had his job or whether he should start looking for another. The boss had evidently talked to Paul's wife about Paul's situation, because she mentioned to me that Paul had done this before, but they only laid him off a few days. She was of the opinion that in a few days everything would be all right and Mr. Barnes would put Paul back to work. Margaret indicated that if they did not want Paul to work there any more, he would just have to go to find some work in the yards in Tucson like he had done before. As long as the oldest son was working, they could stay in their house; so there was no immediate danger even if Paul was fired. Paul's apprehension about his relationship with the boss and his foreman is evident in the following remarks. Again, Paul was under the influence at the time.

Maybe Mr. Barnes will fire me or maybe I will be out working or maybe out looking for a job. . . . I don't know whether I'm fired or not. Mr. Barnes never told me. I worked the other night and the other three irrigators would just ride around in the truck and don't do anything. I walk around where I am supposed to do the work and the foreman asked me when I worked. They don't do anything and I do my work and the foreman asks me that while the other three ride around and don't do anything they are supposed to.

I was going into the mission this morning and the boss asked me where I was going and got mad at me. I told him I was going in to see some of my friends — you know how that is; you are my friend, right Jack? Mr. Phil [Mr. Barnes' son-in-law who manages the farm] is nice but Mr. Barnes is crazy. I know all about irrigating. I'm not bragging or anything, but I can do it good; but they act like they don't trust me. The other three guys just drive around, and they don't do anything; but I have been doing it for ten years [Paul then began weeping and muttering in Papago] . . . . I don't want to complain, Jack. They yell at me but I don't want to complain back at the foreman. That wouldn't help, but they treat me like shit. That old man thinks he's so damn smart. Why, Jack, I don't understand it [again getting emotional, on the verge of tears]. I do a good job but they don't think so.

After three more days of drinking among friends in Sahuarita, Tucson, and at San Xavier, Paul, still quite inebriated, asked me to take him back down to Continental to his place. His remarks to me when I finally got him out of the car at 1 A.M. were, "I'm going to sleep now, and I told Mr. Barnes for sure that I will work days for him tomorrow and I will. I

went down to the garage today [the day before] and told them I will work tomorrow ["tomorrow" was just six hours away] all day. They didn't tell me I would but I will."

I made it a point to check to see if Paul did report back to work, and he did at 7 A.M. that same morning. I was at first doubtful that he would be able to "sleep it off" in time to make it back to work.

From what Paul has mentioned, he has frequently been provoked by comments or criticism about the way he did certain tasks that were assigned to him. Even when Paul felt he did his work as it should be done, he chose not to say anything back. This seems to be characteristic behavior on the part of Papago farm laborers, if the comments of the farm supervisors themselves are considered substantial for supporting this generalization. It was a frequently heard comment from foremen or operators that Papagos are highly desired, because they do not argue back when they are corrected or when they are given a task to do. Later in my interviewing, Papago informants themselves have supported this generalization by their admission that, while they might be extremely provoked or irritated, they silently acquiesce rather than verbally resist. Most statements made by my Papago informants regarding this form of yielding behavior have some note of futility — it does not do any good to try and change the "white man's" mind since he insists on being satisfied according to his own terms. Notwithstanding this somewhat general pattern of acquiescent response to criticism, there are indications in Papago statements of a great deal of repressed hostility, which manifests itself in moments of insobriety and among friends who understand.

Paul was somewhat resentful of Mr. Barnes' mistrust of him as a person. The farm has a policy of not permitting employees the use of trucks or other vehicles for private utilitarian purposes, likely because of the large number of Indians at the farm and the implicit misgivings management has about the Indians' ability to be responsible for the equipment. One of the foremen regularly provides truck service to do shopping at the Sahuarita store or to get mail. Other requests might also be individually met if the request is legitimate and if there is a trustworthy driver available at the time to provide the service.

Paul was disturbed that some of his requests for help could not be met: "I don't know why that Mr. Barnes don't want to help me out [he had asked for the use of a truck to deliver a washing machine he had purchased in Tucson]." On another occasion his baby daughter was having breathing difficulties, and he could not get a truck or anyone to bring them to the emergency room in Tucson. Yet when Paul's wife had to be rushed to Tucson to have her baby, Mr. Barnes' son-in-law drove her all the way to Tucson at 3 a.m.; and on another occasion, a foreman saw to it that Paul was transported to an important San Xavier fiesta. Paul's main source of bitterness appears to have been related to their mistrust of his personally being responsible for a truck. It is understandable, on the other hand, that Mr. Barnes and his supervisory personnel could not establish the precedent of meeting every request from every employee, because the demands would exceed the farm's ability to meet them. Thus, a *patrón*-like arrangement between farm and employees provides a system of institutionalized services for employees and limits other requests for services. This provides a basis for knowing what one can expect from management and what one has no right to expect. Paul was dependent on a kind of patronage that Mr. Barnes could not adequately fulfill, and thus Paul was hostile toward him for not meeting many of his requests.

Paul had done farm work in 1937; after getting out of the service, he tried his hand at a number of jobs in Tucson — at three different nurseries and a cement block plant. How much he might have depended on farm labor during this period has not come out in any of the many conversations, so it is presumed that he performed little or no farm labor. In the latter part of 1953, Paul went to Eloy to work on a farm, mostly to chop cotton but while he was there, he learned how to start the pumps and to irrigate. As in all of his jobs, Paul has learned the techniques and operations directly from trying to perform them.

As mentioned earlier, Paul has a preference for nursery work, but in order to take such work, it almost necesssitates living close to his work in order to make it on time. In addition, it would mean renting a house in town, something which Paul felt he could not afford to do. When he was fired at the Barnes' farm, he moved the family to the reservation with the intention of working at a farm there. Instead, he got the job at the nursery where he has most recently been working [1966] and frequently has had difficulty getting to and from work. In the light of his past pattern and the greater security that

he seems to exhibit in the farm situation, it would seem fairly safe to predict that Paul will have occasion to turn to some kind of farming work again. It is quite clear for at least three different times (1953, 1958, 1965) that Paul, although established in some form of work in Tucson, turned to farm labor, always using Tucson as a subsidiary source of work but maintaining an essentially farm labor pattern. It is difficult to infer the values behind this kind of selective behavior. It is not as if his job source is depleted and he is therefore compelled to look elsewhere. Instead Paul makes the move even when work might still be available to him in town.

Thus far I can only infer a few possible value orientations which might prompt the shift back to farm labor: the desire to avoid too frequent harassment by South Tucson police and a too continuous period of jail confinement; the desire to escape the routines of a current job or to avoid the embarrassment of returning to the job after a series of unexplained absences; the desire to compensate for the complications in transport to and from the job; a desire to escape overextended obligations to his drinking set; a nostalgic sentiment for the countryside; the economic advantages of rural residence; the opportunity to work with other Papago men in familiar surroundings and tasks; a desire to feel he is meeting the needs of his family; the desire to break the present routine, etc. These areas need to be more thoroughly explored with Paul in order to establish the basis for his oscillating pattern. There are suggestions in the data, but they need to be pursued further.

Paul seems to sense the need for work, for as he says, "a man has to work." The problem seems to be in finding an occupational arrangement that can speak to the multiplicity of his psychosocial needs in a satisfying way. Paul does not seem to have found such a situation. On his two previous jobs, Paul said that he was satisfied "until a better one comes along," but it is difficult to chart out with him what constitutes a better job.

Paul has shown an attitude that he is more valuable than he thinks any of his employers have given him credit for, but he accepts their assessments and has an almost paranoid reaction toward them. It seems to have characterized almost all of his past relationships with his employers. The need to offset this negative evaluation of himself in turn tends to make him inwardly defensive. The fact is that most of his employers have praised his ability and hard work (perhaps not in his presence), regretting only the damage that drinking does to his reliability.

Christopher Xavier

Christopher Xavier's present occupational roles are practically nonexistent, although his overall career shows the familiar range of occupational experience characteristic of the off-reservation work found in the careers of many other Papagos — Ajo mine, railroad section gangs, farm labor, bus driving, CCC work, and yard work.

His most recent claim to work is as a trustee assigned to various tasks at the jail, such as checking clothing in and out, laundering and pressing it, and stacking it in storage until prisoners check out. He says he has also done some work in the kitchen. When he gets released, Chris, if he needs to get some quick drinking money, may hop a cotton contractor's bus and go pick or chop for a day or two. Chris also makes the rounds to some of the homes within walking distance from the downtown area and may pick up some yard work for a few hours' pay. If these sources fail, he resorts to mooching or trying to locate relatives or friends in the familiar drinking places in hopes of getting someone to set him up. With this pattern of spotty work, Chris has no commitments to a single employer but simply operates alone in performing the work required at the time. The closest he comes to a recurrent occupational role relationship is with an old lady on North 4th Avenue in Tucson for whom he occasionally does some yard work.

Chris dropped out of the Topawa mission school before finishing the seventh grade and has had no preparation for any kind of work other than ranching. All of his jobs have been in contexts that demanded a minimum of skills and provided familiar tasks by virtue of their being traditionally characteristic of Papago occupational interests.

Chris expresses some concern about his classification as a drunk and jailbird but seems to stick to the familiar groove. He is cognitively aware that he will not be able to keep a job on the outside if he cannot do something about his drinking, but he seems to lack intrinsic motivation for doing something about it. Drinking does provide a way out, and the end result (jail) of a drinking bout is actually not a bad arrangement. It is a relatively secure one.

The officers and custodians of the jail are quite attached to Chris and speak of him as a model inmate. They take it on themselves to advise him about his drinking and what he might do, but Chris keeps coming back.

There is no evidence that Chris will ever hold a basic occupational orientation; instead, if any stable pattern exists at all, it is in terms of a correctional institution setting. Any other spot job is performed to get money in order to buy drinks — and this leads inevitably to jail for a period. When Chris was asked how much he makes during a year, he could only say, "I have no idea. People like yourself can keep track, but people like me who don't make much money or don't have steady jobs don't worry about how much a year. We make what we can and spend it."

Anthony Cypriano

Anthony Cypriano has been a crew chief or supervisor since 1949. There are eight men under him. His only specific responsibility is as a supervisor over the work that his crew has been asked to perform, but he is familiar with all the work that he now only directs. Anthony's 18 years of experience on the flight line and his aircraft mechanic work in the service have long familiarized him with all aspects of this kind of work. The particular work is referred to as process "N" in which his crew works to repair incoming Air Force aircraft. Prior to working on process "N" his crew worked on the flight line.

Anthony's relationship to the members of his crew is important to him, and he tries to keep on the good side of them by pitching in on some of the work and by not trying to take advantage of his seniority. For example, Anthony has a four-week vacation but does not decide on when to take it until everyone on his crew has decided when to take theirs, although he has seniority privilege for first choice of vacation. Anthony is particularly concerned about keeping on the good side of his crew, since he is conscious of his Indian ancestry and is the only Indian on the crew.

Anthony's is a 7:00 a.m. to 3:30 p.m. job for five days a week, paying $3.50 an hour. His good wages are characteristic of a bureaucratic industry, and once he leaves the base, his time is his until the starting whistle the next day. The paternalism to Papago employees that characterizes the relationship of the farm, the nursery, private homes, and to some extent the Ajo mine, is significantly absent in Anthony's relationship to his occupational institution. Whatever institutionalized services available to him and whatever institutionalized demands placed on him by virtue of his occupational status are in terms of him as an individual in a bureaucratic structure. There are no prevailing institutionalized procedures for accommodating the goals of the air base to the cultural patterns of individuals; the individual either performs according to demand or he will be replaced.

This is a quite different employer-employee relationship than we have seen in such practices as temporary layoffs to permit sobering up, hauling personnel to the store, providing rent-free housing, or advancing a man some salary as in the case of the commercial farm. Or compare it with the mine that provides special Indian low-rent housing, special clinical facilities and recreational facilities, and permits Indians to take employment tests twice, or permits three warning slips for unauthorized absences in a year's time to accommodate to the occasional drinking sprees to which Indian employees are especially prone. Also, compare the institutional demands of Anthony's job with the expectations of nursery operators that their Indians will be worked whenever they happen to come in, or the occasional efforts put forth to advance a man some of his salary to bail him out of jail and get him back to work.

There are clearly differences in institutional values, and some occupational institutions' values are more tolerant of apparent cultural behaviors and even reinforce the patterns by institutionalizing ways of dealing with them. It is not surprising that low-income occupations are geared to this kind of *patrón* relationship with members of cultural or ethnic groups, but even a high wage (minimum pay is $19 a day), union-oriented, more bureaucratic institution such as the Phelps Dodge mine at Ajo has fostered a form of paternalism toward all its employees, but particularly the local Indian population.

Anthony Cypriano came to his job by an apparent stroke of good fortune in that his entire sheet metal class at a Tucson night school was called to the air base to help in the war effort. It was actually Anthony's plan to finish the course in sheet metal working and then go to Los Angeles for a job. The significant thing is not that he was lucky but that he had already acquired a sufficient combination of exploitable skill and motivation to stay with the job once it was offered. The Anglo sense of work and industry was a part of his home training and particularly his formal education. One does not find any evidence of resorting to traditional or sterotyped occupational roles as a means of getting along. Instead, Anthony jumps a tramp freighter to get a new kind of experience. Once he had been introduced to aircraft mechanics at the base, it had some bearing on his importance to the military. Further, the military experience as a mechanic reinforced his value in a civilian occupational role.

That Anthony has incorporated some basic Anglo values relative to his own job and the occupational futures of his children is clear from the case material presented earlier. While he hopes for better things for his children and admits that he had even higher aspirations for himself than he actually has been able to achieve, Anthony seems most satisfied with his job. It was not necessarily a total success story in his family of orientation; for while Anthony speaks of his mother's influence, a brother, now dead, was never able to stabilize his work pattern. According to Anthony, it was because his brother lacked such an experience as he had at Sherman. Anthony is not very quick to discuss his job as a baker's helper at a Tucson hotel and brushes it off as if it were just a kid's job that he outgrew. In addition, I have been unable to get much discussion about Anthony's father or the kind of work he did in Tucson. All Anthony told me was that his father died while he was still quite young.

SUMMARY

In this chapter, I have concentrated on providing data that indicate the occupational adaptations of five individual Papago men. There is no pretense that these five cases can tell us all that can be known and needs to be known about Papago adaptation to off-reservation work in general, nor can they tell us a great deal about the broader aspects of cultural change. In fact, it has become increasingly clear that there are many highly relevant unanswered questions pertaining to the cases I have developed. I have concentrated largely on the basic assumption that role compatibility, or accommodating culturally diverse roles to each other, is essential to occupational adaptation. The underlying hypothesis I have sought to test can be stated something like this — the inter- play of contrasting social roles in the social personality of a Papago worker is an important determinant of the kind of adaptation the worker can make to a particular job context. This has seemed a plausible working postulate to guide my investigation and, perhaps, an obvious and simple one.

Yet after spending a great deal of time and space in discussing the significance of certain relevant social roles, it is necessary to ask if looking at social roles tells all about the occupational adaptation of Papago workers. Or must the analysis probe deeper into the cognitive, affective, and normative aspects of individual personalities than has been done in order to really find the answers? Does occupational adaptation or stabilization really hinge on the interplay of occupational roles with other social roles, and has this been demonstrated in the five cases? Undoubtedly the deeper psychological aspects that pertain to individual adjustments need to be considered as highly important and need to be explored in a more highly controlled manner than has been possible in this study.

The focus has been largely sociological, however, utilizing role and institutional theory in attempting to reveal a few significant role relationships and institutional involvements within relatively discrete social fields in which individuals operate and have had to adapt their behavior. There are actually as many kinds of adjustment and adaptation to jobs as there are individuals involved in a particular occupational complex. But this is another kind of operation that would restrict the investigation to a completely psychological, or at the most, social psychological, frame of reference. This study is concerned, on the other hand, with gross sociocultural features of discrete occupational structures that provide relatively equivalent social fields for individuals participating in them.

The study has attempted to construct adaptational environments, or occupational complexes, and has sought to employ a method of role analysis to establish how an individual might adapt his role behaviors to the demands of his particular occupational-social field. From this, on the basis of participation in broadly similar adaptational environments, it becomes possible to project adaptational features that might be assumed to similarly affect larger population segments.

A social field becomes a source for extrinsic motivation of certain forms of standardized behavioral expectations; and an individual, depending on the nature of his psychological propensities and his cumulative personal experience in confronting particular social situations, is intrinsically motivated or unmotivated in the performance of certain roles in accordance with the satisfactions or displeasures the roles afford him. Role adjustments are, in this sense, innovations and, if experienced by many other Papagos on a broader social scale, may become a basis for perceiving the dynamics of social and cultural change. The case analyses do seem to offer suggestions for Papago culture change and the significance of occupations in the direction the changes seem to be taking place.

Alonzo Jose's occupational situation seems to call for little modification of social roles. For one thing, for the past several years Al's residence and occupation have been off-reservation, and he has only very infrequently returned to his home. His reservation homestead of three adobe houses, somewhat removed from other similar compounds in his village, is not a significant contrast to his present off-reservation arrangement. Just as his fields at his home could be easily approached each day, so can the fields in which he is presently working. Despite the fact that his job at the Barnes' farm places him under the supervision of an Anglo, most of his time is spent alone, working in the fields pretty much at his own pace. While his children and their families are scattered more than they were on the reservation, Al's facilities at the farm serve as a nucleus for members of his family, just as I am sure his village home would do if he were living there full time.

Al seems to belong best in the Native Modified Papago category. From what Al has related, his family of orientation could qualify as Native Papago. On the other hand, Al's experiences at the Franciscan mission school on the Navaho reservation, his work for the Bureau of Indian Affairs, his prolonged experience working on commercial farms, and his contacts, mostly economic and recreative, with Anglo towns have called for modification of some Native Papago traits. Al, however, is deeply tied to past cultural values, and he does not appear to be under the same kind of strain as is Raymond Victor, who is definitely straddling two orientations. The essential features of Al's customary kinship arrangements are not severely threatened by his occupational situation, although some modification has been necessary. There has been a reduced participation in social and festive activities as a result of his occupational demands, but he does not seem to count this as a significant deprivation. His long hours on the job, his acknowledgment of his obligation to his employer, his isolation from the main camp of Papagos, the fact that his age does not pressure him into the tight drinking group behavior that is so important to the younger men, and his highly satisfactory adjustments to a number of farm employers over the years are all significant indications that Al has been able to accommodate his personal behavior to an occupational role in which he feels relatively secure and satisfied. In Al's case, it does not appear that an Anglo[1] Modified Papago orientation is necessary to successful adaptation to a satisfying occupational experience.

Al has a strong belief in the function of the *makai* and their medicines. He also participated, until he was past 30, in a traditional Papago economy of flood farming and cattle raising, and made periodic trips to sell products to Tucson and San Xavier consumers. He participated in the traditional foot races and relays in competition with other villages and frequently made the rounds to wine feasts and other festivities. Al is also tied to the past through stories and Papago legends, which he still delights in recalling and reciting. He talks freely and emotionally of places, things, and experiences that have been a part of his early days in the shadow of Baboquivari. And Al looks for the day he can return to his home, which has run down some from his extended absences.

While he has had an orientation to Anglo institutions in the past, I see no extensive involvement nor any desire for involvement. If anything, Al exhibits a naive ignorance toward those that do, to some extent, come to bear in his life. When he first received a W-2 form, he tried to cash it as a paycheck; he needs help to understand and comply with regulations relative to drawing social security; and without an available representative of the agency, I have aided him in these procedures. I detect no great attachment to nor an understanding of the values that characterize our urban, industrial, highly mechanized society. His past

instruction by parents and grandparents toward industriousness seems to explain his present attitude toward his job more than does the explanation that he has inculcated Anglo values with regard to work. I have found Al, in many respects, to be the "most Papago" of any of the five cases, and perhaps this has as much to do with his occupational dependability as anything. He does not seem to be unhappily straddled between two different orientations but, rather, employs the virtues of his Papago socialization to the best advantage in a favorable and not too contrasting occupational setting.

Raymond Victor can be classified in the Anglo Modified Papago acculturative category, following Voget's scheme. This can be done on the basis of the strong influence of Anglo institutions in Raymond's life, such as the Roman Catholic Church, as represented by Franciscan priests reared and educated in the Anglo tradition, the Bureau of Indian Affairs, as represented by Indian Service personnel who are strongly oriented in Anglo values, the mission schools, the United States Army, commercial farming enterprises, and a host of institutions as found in prevalently Anglo towns and cities. The case material gathered in the course of the field work reveals the significance of these institutions in Raymond's personality configuration, although it has been difficult, and largely unnecessary to the interests of this study, to provide detailed discussion of these influences here.

It is the influence of these Anglo institutions on a Native Papago and a predominantly Native Modified Papago cultural orientation that makes it possible to typify Raymond as Anglo Modified Papago. It is possible to pinpoint rather precise Papago cultural features that were integral to the enculturative experiences of his formative years within his family of orientation. To name only a few, there were the kinship village with the extended family compounds, common kitchens, and eating groups; the traditional stories and games; wine ceremonies and social and religious feasts; singing, curing, and medicinal practices. His father functioned as a village speaker, a keeper of the smoke; and the family engaged in the traditional Papago economy of flood farming, cattle raising, cactus fruit harvesting, moving from mountain to field villages, and periodically utilizing the commercial farms for supplemental wage activity.

Raymond's father's family of orientation was, without much question, essentially Native Papago in

---

[1] Voget uses the term American. Anglo is used here because it is believed more descriptive of the western European sociocultural tradition than the more ambiguous term "American."

the sense of the features discussed above; but Raymond's father as a young man was strongly influenced by the Franciscan fathers and government officials and rejected the efficacy of the Indian medicine men for a period. While some of the Papago elements of culture came under more severe skepticism due to the staunch competition of non-Papago institutional values (medical practice, wage work, and formal religious instruction for example) and were abandoned or modified to fit the demands of the new institutions, there was much of Papago culture that remained intact (kinship organization, ceremonial activities, and certain economic activities, to name a few).

A Native Modified Papago cultural heritage is characterized by a strong adherence to an aboriginal or Native Papago cultural system that has come to individuals through processes of socialization in units functioning as instillers of native values, but which, in the course of adult socialization, has been modified by participation in non-Papago systems. One can sense, despite the many native and modified aspects of Papago culture that are still obvious in Raymond's mazeway, that his more "progressive" attitudes relative to future expectations are in terms of a contemporary Papago tribal culture that is strongly inclined toward and influenced by Anglo Modified Papago values. Some of the case material clearly points this out.

The important concern is how Raymond's occupational commitments have affected his Papago cultural heritage and also how that cultural heritage has functioned to affect the nature of his occupational adaptation. The Ajo situation has challenged, but not eliminated, Raymond's ceremonial and social leadership in his reservation village by virtue of the extended periods he must be away on the job. The mine operation, however, is geared to reducing this handicap by allowing sufficient time off at shutdowns to permit frequent returns to the reservation.

His participation in the wine ceremonies and other social festivities has been significantly influenced by the demands of his full-time job; since, if he wants to maintain his good job, he has found it necessary to drastically alter his drinking behavior. This has turned him toward an Anglo-oriented philosophy of group therapy, and his dedication to its principles conflicts with his equally strong desire to share festive activities with his reservation kin. His relatively high-level job (as far as Papagos at the mine are concerned) and

his personal qualities for leadership draw him into political activity in the more "artificial" Ajo Indian village, for which he lacks any strong sentiment. Raymond's rejection of attempts by the company to elevate him to more responsible positions, or to get him to accept one of the newer, more modern company houses, reveals his desire to maintain his loyalties to his kinship village and to the majority of his cultural group rather than to concern himself with the ostentatious living that Anglo officials hold out to him in the Ajo village. He longs to return to the reservation to stay for good, among kin and in the familiar surroundings of his home village.

Yet Raymond has accommodated his job and his activities in his home village to each other by compartmentalizing them. Ajo and Covered Wells constitute two separate but interdependent social fields; and the nature of the mining operation and its proximity to the reservation permit Raymond to live in each independently although not totally uninfluenced by each other. Social roles related to his participation in the Ajo mine complex are made compatible with social roles in kinship contexts by a rather clear compartmentalization of each social field. However, his experiences in one field (efforts to quit drinking in order to maintain his job) are not easy to employ in the other field (sharing in the good feelings promoted by reciprocal drinking behavior at the wine ceremony), and modifications are in order.

If the same kind of analysis was employed for each member of the extended family, using occupational activity as a key variable, it likely would reveal a wide range of individual adaptational experiences. This appears to be so in Raymond's case, yet the extended family compound functions as an integrator of the several adaptational types and a preserver of certain Papago cultural features that all family members share.

It has been rather difficult to get much from Paul Antonio about his early experience at Pan Tak village. With the exception of a couple of brief periods, Paul's father's economic pursuits were largely of a subsistence character; although he came in to the Tucson vicinity on occasion to sell wood and seasonally came to San Xavier to share in the wheat harvest. We have to presume a Native Papago family orientation for Paul in the absence of any further data. In terms of his present grouping, Paul would seem to be best typified as Anglo Modified Papago. There are a number of reasons why this is so.

First, the kinship connections have been significantly rearranged, and although there is a "home-base" at Pan Tak where his elderly mother and an older brother still live, it functions very infrequently as such. The economic interdependence of members of Paul's family of orientation is considerably less significant than in the cases of Alonzo Jose or Raymond Victor. Paul maintains his nuclear family as an isolate unit on the farm (more recently at San Xavier), while one brother stays on the reservation and takes care of the mother (he lives largely off her welfare check) and another brother maintains his nuclear family in South Tucson; a sister has married into a Pan Tak ranching family and lives in her husband's household. Each unit appears to function somewhat separately and is pretty much dependent on its own efforts.

But kinship has functioned as a medium for introducing family members to jobs held by other members; and certain experiences, such as deaths, bring the family members together. Since Paul's nuclear family functions as an isolate, it has come to depend on a number of non-Papago relationships for additional services. The isolation appears to have necessitated nonkinship extensions and not vice versa.

There is still a strong orientation toward participating in festive gatherings, particularly at San Xavier and Magdalena. These are important functions in Paul's pattern, whether or not his occupational commitment permits him to go. Part of this is due to responsibilities he shares in planning, but much of it is related to his affinity to what these social and ceremonial events offer in personal and social satisfactions.

Paul's drinking behavior conflicts even with the institutionalized expectations of farms and nurseries. He seems to be considerably "overdrawn" in his social and drinking obligations — he leans on others to provide the money for drinks but must also let others reciprocate and lean on him. This prompts a less than satisfactory performance of the minimal requirements of certain jobs, and employers eventually either have had to give up on him or he on them.

Like Alonzo Jose, Paul's work on the farm demands long hours with far less latitude for taking time off than the nursery work. The nurseries seemed to have programmed much of their labor demands around this Papago "weakness," and Paul can get by with more delinquency at the nursery than he can on the farm. At the farm, Paul was very close to the

Papago camp, which was a constant threat to his work performance. But he seemed to be less prone to get into drinking with Papagos there than he has been with Papagos in Tucson, 16 miles away. Unlike Alonzo Jose, Paul has not found what could be called a well-established or stable relationship to a particular farm, although he has been doing relatively steady farm labor for over ten years. During this period, he has done work, other than seasonal, for seven different farms, interspersed with periods of work in Tucson.

Psychologically, Paul exhibits a defensive attitude about his high turnover, providing meaningful but not pointed excuses, and feels that employers pick on him or mistreat him. I can find no situation where his relationships with his employers and foremen have been adequate or emotionally satisfying; this he finds, instead, in the circle of Papago friends.

In terms of Papago culture, Paul's orientation to dances, feasts, and social festivities stands out as significant. His experience in a traditional Papago economy has been limited. Paul recalls helping his father hoe weeds in his father's fields, cutting wood and hauling it in to town to sell, working on government projects, and participating in the San Xavier wheat harvest; but many of these activities were dissipating by the time Paul had grown to manhood, and Paul's generation was looking increasingly to off-reservation work.

Paul exhibits a familiarity with the aboriginal culture and has complained to the point of weeping, when drunk, about the loss of what Indians used to need to know to get along. It has been difficult to engage him in conversation about these aspects of Native Papago culture. It has therefore been difficult to surmise whether his reticence to discuss these things is due to a lack of socialization in them, whether he has at some point abandoned them in the course of his own unique experiences, or whether he holds to more of these traits than he will outwardly admit.

Paul's connections with San Xavier and Tucson have exposed him to more acculturated Papagos, or those who have felt the impact of Anglo culture most intensively and over the longest time. Other than his periodic participations in festive events, mostly at San Xavier, I can isolate hardly any cultural participation in which Paul is involved that is distinctively Papago. The attitudes he holds and the role he performs within his drinking group may be more typically

Papago, but even here it is hard to distinguish his drinking behavior as necessarily a distinctive Papago characteristic.

Paul utilizes hospital and public clinical facilities for his children (his wife sees to this, although he frequently accompanies her) and relies on patent medicines in treating what ails him. His children have attended predominantly public schools, and for his first four years Paul also attended a rural public school. It has also been difficult to get Paul to talk about the impact of his military experience and its effect on his personality and his behavior. In the cases of Alonzo Jose and Raymond Victor, it has been possible to isolate discrete cultural domains either in terms of sentiment or in terms of actual participation. While I have had perhaps more overall contact with Paul, the cultural domains are much more fuzzy. This may be due largely to Paul's being much less verbal about his life as a Papago rather than his lacking such sentiments and behaviors. His contacts with many Anglo institutions (hospitals, welfare agencies, law enforcement facilities, sundry commercial establishments in Tucson, Tucson homes where he does yard work, etc.) reveal his immersion in Anglo-oriented activity. Paul and his wife know how to utilize welfare and community services to the maximum when financial difficulties arise, as they frequently do.

Paul's wife, who is very much Anglo oriented, is a contrast to the more quiet, less involved spouses of Alonzo Jose and Raymond Victor. Many times Paul's wife is the initiator and medium of contact with Anglo institutions, while Paul's role is more passive. The exact opposite is true for Alonzo and Raymond, whose wives usually remain at home or, when they accompany their husbands in predominantly Anglo settings, play the more passive and aloof roles.

Paul certainly is not Anglo Marginal Papago, although much of his behavior is immersed in Anglo contexts; and he clearly identifies himself with "us Indians." Yet it is difficult to isolate what are clearly Papago modes of thought and behavior, lacking any psycholinguistic data or lacking any substantial basis of comparing his thought and behavioral processes with those of other Papagos. It does seem somewhat clear that Paul is marginal "something." His distress over the loss of what used to be adequate guides for conduct for Indians and his sensed inferiority and failure to fit into Anglo expectations have been obvious on a number of occasions. Perhaps he might

best be characterized as a native modified Papago-Anglo modified marginal, suggesting a distressing straddle situation in which his experiences in a modified Papago or a modified Anglo sociocultural system are far from adequate. This would make the drinking group of individuals in similar states of mind an especially important group, because it provides a way of dealing with the psychological discomforts of marginal status. Marginal instability in a sense becomes culturally patterned and persists as a way of life.

Paul's oscillating occupational pattern is not the exclusive cause of his psychological stress and the social ambivalence that is created by his immersion in non-Papago ways of life. Rather, the stress is likely reflected in his somewhat erratic occupational pattern.

Christopher Xavier, through his immersion in jail-house and floating subcultures, has long abandoned his active roles in Native Modified Papago and Anglo Modified Papago sociocultural orientations. His present values are those that prompt him to mingle with other floaters such as himself in the downtown area and end up in drinking situations. Chris is currently marginal to both Papago and Anglo values and activities, although we might look for a more intense confrontation of the two cultural orientations at some point earlier in his life.

He has worked in a variety of the usual range of Papago off-reservation occupations without ever achieving a clear occupational commitment for any extensive length of time. His chronic drinking pattern, perhaps partly stimulated by situations similar to those we have seen in Paul Antonio's case, was beginning to emerge well before any stabilized job commitment. Jobs became even more infrequent as drinking with friends increased; and Chris was completely separated from his wife and children as the drinking crowd and the effects of drinking became more important than family responsibilities.

Perhaps Paul Antonio's case illustrates a possible earlier phase of Chris's increasing identification with an urban floating subculture. The ensuing remorse, stemming from awareness of family neglect caused largely by his drinking and his inability to produce a reliable income, may have been one of the factors pointing to chronic alcoholism for Chris.

Anthony Cypriano's enculturative experience seems to have been, in Voget's scheme for classifying

Indian populations according to acculturative type, largely an Anglo Modified Papago orientation. The efforts by his mother to get him away to school, his lifelong experience in the South Tucson Indian community, his enrollment in Tucson public schools, his experience at the government Indian school in California, his ambition to enroll in trade schools and seek relocation, his prolonged experience in a bureaucratically structured industry, his military experience, and his eventual movement away from the Indian section of town all indicate an increasing de-identification from activities and behaviors that generally characterized the life patterns of South Tucson Papagos. As the de-identification crystallized, a movement toward middle class Anglo values was well underway.

His Papago self-identification, however, is not solely an admission of Papago biological ancestry but represents a reflection of his concern for the betterment of Papagos as individuals in urban society rather than for a perpetuation or revival of Papago culture or certain features of Papago culture. Many such features are acknowledged as detrimental to satisfactory adjustment in today's world, such as parental permissiveness, lack of competitive aspiration, and lack of successful occupational experience, to name a few. There is, in this sense, a clear de-identification with features (as Anthony sees them) of Papago culture that have been antithetical to successful identification with the rewards and satisfactions of Anglo culture, such as economic improvement, occupational advancement, and emotionally rewarding social relationships in Anglo institutions.

Anthony's occupational adjustment appears to have been preceded by enculturative experiences that successfully introduced him to Anglo-oriented values and behavior and were reinforced by recurrent successful experiences, such as at school, on his job, or in his social relationships with non-Papagos. Once the occupational experience proved to be rewarding and fulfilling, it became easier to incorporate other Anglo values or sustain those he had already incorporated.

If the Papago traits (parental permissiveness, lack of competitive aspiration, lack of educational and vocational values, etc.) that he acknowledges as being detrimental to Papago improvement, were at all a part of his earlier heritage, there finally came a time when there could be no place for some of the values or behaviors evident in many other Papagos in the Indian community in South Tucson. In this respect Anthony could well be classified as Anglo Marginal Papago, having successfully assimilated Anglo values but retaining his Papago physical identity and, perhaps, some marginal areas of Papago custom.

This chapter has covered some data that appear most pertinent to the understanding of how five occupational types might have adapted or failed to adapt their particular social personalities to the demands of particular occupational-social environments. It is acknowledged that a much larger and more carefully chosen sample would provide a much more lucid picture of the dimensions of Papago adaptational behavior.

8. CONCLUSIONS: ROLE COMPATIBILITY, OCCUPATIONAL ADAPTATION, AND PAPAGO ACCULTURATION

An individual participating in an occupational system not only possesses a job, he becomes oriented to a system of social values that characterizes a complex industrial society. Chapter 1 begins with the statement that assimilation of members of ethnic groups and their social mobility in the United States are positively related and that the United States sociocultural system functions to integrate diverse strata and cultural or ethnic groups. In this sense, acculturation, or more precisely assimilation, refers to the process of aligning personal and cultural attitudes and behaviors with the prevailing cultural orientations of the sociocultural system in the United States.

However, the interplay of contrasting cultural values and social roles in particular Papago personalities is significant, not in terms of adaptation to some grand system of national values or an absorption into or rejection from a socioeconomic status in the general, overall class system of the United States, but in terms of particular manifestations or variations of the general orientations at regional or local levels. This is why the identification and delineation of discrete occupational fields is of importance; they become localized social media for the interplay of cultural demands on personalities found within them and dependent on them.

Particular personal responses to occupational fields have already been presented as illustrative of how specific Papago individuals might organize their social personalities in response to occupational and other social demands. Although far short of establishing the range of variation for idiosyncratic adaptations, some general principles about the relationship of occupational activity to Papago adaptation and acculturation can be established from the data. These propositions will be formulated on the basis of both the structural features of particular occupational fields and the responses to the structural features as evidenced in the patterns of individual Papago informants.

The discussion will first attempt to specify what might be termed the Anglo American cultural maximizers (Henry 1965: 31) and the Papago cultural modifiers which seem to be operating as sometimes oppositional, sometimes complementary, and sometimes neutral social forces in the lives of Papago individuals within each of the occupational complex types hitherto presented. These maximizing and modifying "forces" are essentially the Anglo versus Papago social structures, value orientations, and personal agents of change or resistance to change that can be identified in each occupational-social field. This should provide a better understanding of the direction of assimilative change within each complex; that is, what are the significant features of certain occupational complexes that have major bearing on the achievement and/or maintenance of relatively secure personal live styles (adaptation)?

The Anglo maximizing institutions, values, and personal agents and the Papago institutions, values, and agents that modify these maximizing influences constitute two kinds of structural models for individual behavior. Maximizing influences are those Anglo institutions, values, and individuals that operate locally to encourage maximum social and economic participation of Papagos in particular occupational complexes. The interplay of social roles that originate in the two different sociocultural systems modifies the demands of the occupational orientation in terms of essentially Papago interests. Attention will now be directed toward the structural and normative features of the particular occupational complex types, how they function as maximizing influences on the social personalities of Papago workers, and how they are modified by Papago workers.

ANGLO CULTURAL MAXIMIZERS

Commercial Farms

A Papago farm hand who relies on relatively steady work on a southern Arizona farm is involved in a hierarchy of social structures that provides a progressively diminishing intensity of contact and interaction with fellow Papagos as he extends himself beyond the farm. That is, the commercial farming enterprise is so structured that the most intense and direct social experiences are in terms of other Papagos in the farm setting, with a minimization of contact with other Papagos as social relationships are traced outward from the farm setting to non-Papago involvements in towns and cities.

Most farms with which I have become familiar have made provisions for their farm laboring families to live in the many adobe, wood, or block dwellings that have been constructed on farm property over the years. Within such encampments, it has been possible for Papagos, particularly the ones more regularly attached to the camp or farm, to appropriate the dwellings in accordance with changes in the numerical structure of the household. A nuclear household may either be relatively isolated from all other nuclear or extended households at the farm, or it may be adjacent to other nuclear households. In the cases where there are close relatives, adjacent nuclear households may actually function as a form of extended family and utilize common cooking and eating facilities and manifest other forms of cooperative interdependence. A number of individuals from a number of related nuclear families may rely on the stable incomes of one or two individuals plus whatever other members might contribute from occasionally joining chopping or picking crews.

It is a general characteristic of commercial farm organization to segregate the homes of farm laborers from the residences of supervisors. Papagos can further semi-isolate themselves, within farm camps, through the manner in which they occupy certain sections of them. The camps usually have ample buildings to permit a kind of Papago farm community or neighborhood of relatives to develop, although the larger camps are more complex since a number of ethnic groups may be represented. Even in this case,

Papagos usually can maintain the integrity of their corporate households. The most intense and direct interaction is with other Papagos, usually related, in adjacent sections of the camp. Lesser contacts with members of other camp households, including those of other ethnic groups, also occur. The tendency of certain farms to have high concentrations of Papagos tends to be reinforcing and Papagos know where to go in order to find certain concentrations. After all, many of these are built up and sustained by a flow of relatives over several generations or seasons.

Although there are irrigating teams, cleaning crews, and other occasions for group work and informal contact in fields among Papago workers, I would generalize by saying that the formal requirements of farm jobs are performed largely in relative solitude — driving a tractor, irrigating a field, or chopping or picking in a crew that is spread over a cotton field. Any informal contacts between employees usually take place without the knowledge or concern of supervisors.

Other significant relationships provided by the farm structure and organization are the formal and informal interactions with foremen and farm operators. A foreman or an operator usually makes initial contacts to explain the nature of the day's work or to get the worker started, making periodic checks throughout the day. Occasional informal contacts with a foreman seem to be significant; since it is common for the foreman's house to be near the camp, and the foreman may become the channel through which personal requests for services such as transportation are made. The foreman's children may play with children in the camp, and he may have a familiarity with informal activities in the camp because of its proximity and his more direct relationships with the laborers.

The structured relationships are largely due to the organization of the farm itself but subject to the greatest amount of Papago modification. A next level of structured relationships would consist of those that occur within the rural farming town center. The store becomes the focal point for informal contacts with Anglo, Mexican, or Chinese store managers; but

Papago farm hands' relationships with the general stores are essentially economic in nature.[1] In some places, such as Stanfield, Marana, and Sahuarita, for example, the store becomes the source of contact with other Indians from other farms and reservation villages in the vicinity. These meeting places provide an additional source for sharing the present state of the farm labor market in terms of jobs available in an area.

Public drinking by Papagos in the town centers usually takes place in rather well-known establishments. The names of particular taverns where Papagos go are well known in Gila Bend, Casa Grande, Coolidge, Florence, Marana, and Sahuarita. Thus, the town centers, through their taverns, also become media for drawing together Papagos scattered throughout the farming region. In this way, rather than breaking down Papago contacts with other Papagos, rural towns — through stores, taverns, jails, and other congregating places — actually function to integrate Papago informal activities and thus contribute to ethnic maintenance and cultural identification.

I found that a number of my informants had occasion to go to Sells to consult with a representative of the agency about income tax reports, the handling of money, or some welfare problem relating to some member of the family. The state, county, and BIA agencies are not always together as to which has jurisdiction in particular cases involving off-reservation Papagos, since Papago families off-reservation may be in touch with a number of such agencies. My general impressions are that Papagos whose experiences have been predominantly off the reservation do utilize the services of BIA agencies but with less frequency. The modified kinship settlements on farms orient individuals and families to the more immediate rural town centers or urban areas for the services of state and county agencies or to Anglo individuals for the personal advice that might have formerly been performed by the Indian service representatives.

There are other Anglo structures that extend into the countryside to link Papagos to the larger social order. Protestant and Catholic churches attempt to minister to individuals and families within the camps; state agencies, through public health nurses and welfare case workers, pay visits to families within the camps; selling agencies send traveling salesmen to call on homes with their products; and law enforcement agencies have official business in camps. These contacts are, however, most meaningful largely in terms of the individual agents representing the various institutions.

Figure 17 summarizes the structural features of the farm complex type in terms of the significant Anglo social structures that influence Papago life on the farm.

There are significant cultural values relating to industrialized commercial farming that are extremely relevant to Papago participation in a non-Papago social environment. The fact that commercial farms are concerned primarily in producing market crops that will result in profit implies that farm management must employ whatever instrumentalities best ensure this kind of production. Whether to exploit machines, human effort, or both largely hinges on this.

The immediate effect of this production-profit value on Papago and other unskilled laborers consists in the rationalization of industrialized farming that there are great risks in producing for a market. The farm must battle against unforeseen losses due to inclement weather, bacterial infestations, fluctuations in national market economy, the uncertainties of a labor force, etc. As one way of offsetting this risk, it must rely on a largely unskilled labor force to which it cannot pay, nor need it pay, very substantial wages.

As further rationalization to offset this apparent "inhumane" practice, the farm operator can claim a number of "humane" practices that are not found in urban industrialized labor appropriation. The farm can claim that it provides rent-free facilities to its employees. Likewise, it provides wage opportunities for those who would have difficulty marketing their unskilled abilities in other kinds of work. Even more significant is the rationalization that farms are more tolerant of Papago life ways in that the demands of the job actually alter Papago social organization, activity interests, and other values very little. There is a form of institutionalization, which I call condescending institutionalization, in which certain operations of an industry are actually geared to the behavior patterns of the particular people being

---

[1] Store operators are usually selective in offering credit and usually do so only for the more established families. Some store operators I have found to be very helpful in assisting Indian customers in interpreting the meaning of letters, making out money orders, or answering other questions. There seems to be a wide range of difference in attitudes toward Indians manifest by different ethnic store operators. This would be an interesting subject for future investigation.

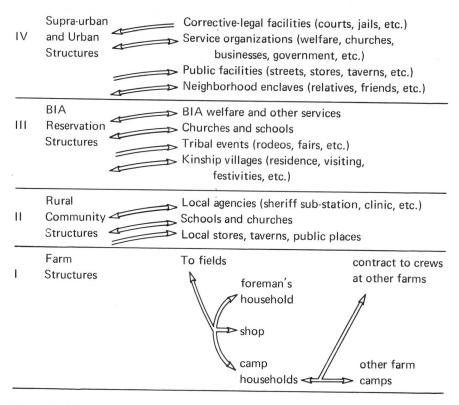

Figure 17. The Structural Basis of Social Interaction in the Commercial Farm Complex

The most prolonged, direct, personal, informal, and self-initiated interactions occur at level I, primarily with other Papagos; the most curtailed, indirect, impersonal, formal, and other-initiated interactions occur at level IV, primarily involving Anglos. At each level, the most intense social relations are with other Papagos, although less intense than at level I. The arrows indicate the source and direction of initiated interaction.

utilized by that industry. This form of institutionalization contrasts with what I call bureaucratic institutionalization, where operations are not geared to or dependent on the habits of a particular group of people but, rather, are standardized to utilize only those who qualify and continue to meet the job requirements.

Farms condescend in institutionalizing their dealings with Papagos in that they are cognizant of family ties, aware of festive occasions that take Papagos away from their jobs, acknowledge that the jobs they provide fall within traditional and well established activity interests, and can adjust occupational rewards and punishments to Papago drinking patterns without losing access to this labor resource. I call it condescending institutionalization because it admits the availability of an inferior, subordinate group of workers whose very deficits are exploitable and can

be appropriated to the best interests of commercial farming goals. Several operators and foremen have complained about the erratic and undependable behavior of their Indians but at the same time choose to depend largely on Indians for their sources of labor. There is good evidence to suppose that farmers have long come to be as dependent on this kind of institutionalization as have their Indian employees. This is particularly true of some of the smaller, less highly industrialized or mechanized farms.

The extent to which farm operators and supervisors become friends and neighbors to the working force, including Papagos, must be restricted. Homes are provided for laborers; but they are segregated from the homes of management, since the success of the operation depends on a relative amount of social distance. Laborers are kept within reach for use on necessary activities, but social distance is maintained.

Common laborers, with their "different" values and usually "depraved" economic situations, cannot be treated as equals or as friends because equality and friendship would imply mutual and reciprocal manifestations of such status. With unequal economic statuses, if operators treated laborers as friends and neighbors, they fear they would soon be overdrawn in requested favors and the functioning of the farm organization, which depends on employer-employee relationships (not friend to friend relationships), would be seriously challenged. The functional solution, long ago achieved, is a brand of paternalism similar to the *patrón* system, where proprietors and workers alike know just how far to extend themselves in their interpersonal relationships. It is a controlled relationship that may be distantly friendly but not a friendship. The employer may respond to a request for aid or favor, but it is not as a neighbor, friend, or equal. He responds instead, as employer who is seeking to maintain a relationship with a relatively reliable and trustworthy economic commodity — a laborer.

This brand of paternalism is not inhumanitarian; it is, instead, expedient humanitarianism in which both employer and employee understand what to expect and what not to expect in terms of the other. I found a considerable degree of attachment and interest on the part of some farmers toward some of their more steady Papago hands, even when the farmers spoke negatively of Papagos as a whole. The humaneness lies in the rationalization that the farm is tolerant toward what is assumed to be the Papago style of life. Since the arrangement is economically advantageous as well, both farmer and Papago worker can be relatively content. The Papago farm worker whose lifetime has been spent in this kind of relationship to a farm or farms may have misgivings about it; but generally I have found far greater contentment, or better, lack of manifest resentment than I have in those situations where occupational experience has attempted to venture outside of the farm labor market.

Farm life, centered in a camp and involving a limited range of familiar occupational activities currently is not particularly a system unto itself. The countryside, as an extension of more populous, industrialized urban centers, is constantly invaded by the values of the larger system. Perhaps the most influential inroads of Anglo industrial culture into the farm camps where Papagos live are traversed by agents of the welfare complex, that complex of institutions which operates on the value premise that the

people who are out of step with the economic, health, and spiritual benefits of the Anglo technological tradition are in need of directed efforts to aid them in articulating with these benefits. Much of the activity related to this concern is directed by governmental or public agencies and supported by a number of institutions at the horizontal (national) and vertical (local) levels (Steward 1950: 115). Public health instruction, economic services, various other social services, and spiritual guidance and indoctrination are some of the instrumental values to which Papagos on farms are being introduced.

The influence of the various public institutions, however, is largely through individual agents. The extent to which the institutional values are effectively transmitted depends largely on the quality of the particular interpersonal relationships between Papagos and the individual agents of the cultural values embodied in the local and national institutions they represent. The most significant agents, generally speaking, are those that represent the hierarchy of structures depicted in Figure 17.

The agents of Anglo institutions that most frequently have contact with Papago households and camps are school teachers, migrant ministers and priests, public health nurses, deputies, salesmen, and independent Anglo benefactors. While there are the usual formal expectations of their services (special tutoring, indoctrination, performance of rites, health instruction, arrests, sales, etc.), the influence the personal agents have in transmitting Anglo values depends on their personal qualities and the extent of their interest in certain individuals and/or families. Public health nurses, for instance, not only advise in matters of domestic health but, if close to a family, might talk to a young person about saving money or the kind of work for which he might prepare. These influences, since highly personalized, are never evenly distributed over a single camp but are usually centered on the more receptive households. Papago men seem to be far less influenced by these contacts than are the women and children.

Ajo Mine

A Papago miner at Ajo similarly is involved in a hierarchy of social structures in which his interactions with non-Papagos undergo qualitative changes in duration, nature, intensity, quality, and directionality as he extends himself beyond his Papago household and the Indian village.

The Ajo Indian village is a segregated segment of the community of Ajo and consists of a number of individual nuclear households. Households that are related by kinship ties are generally dispersed throughout the village, due to company regulation of housing rental and due to the fact that turnover at the mine does not usually permit acquisition of adjacent houses by related families. There is, however, some informal and uncondoned "swapping" of houses which creates a few neighborhood aggregate households of kin. The overall community arrangements are more favorable to individual nuclear households. During the periodic shutdowns, most Papagos in the Indian village return to their various kinship villages on the reservation; or reservation relatives frequently come to visit in Ajo. The vital kinship links are still largely in terms of kinship villages, not the Ajo village.

Partly due to the complexity of the Indian village and partly as a result of company encouragement, the Indian community is stratified. The smallest and lowest rent houses are usually clustered together and are more frequently occupied by Papagos with the highest turnover and lowest skill levels. Next are clusters of larger houses at slightly higher rent that are generally occupied by employees with greater seniority and occupying higher skill levels. Also, there is one section of the village where homes are owned, usually by Papago families of several generations in Ajo. They are usually the most permanent Ajo Papagos. Lastly, there is a marginal section between the Indian village and upper Mexican town where a few Papago families occupy modern bungalow type houses. The heads of these households are Papagos who are involved in political activity for the village and who generally have stable positions if not higher job levels with the company. The company has been instrumental in encouraging Papagos who it feels could best occupy these better houses. As would be expected, there is a great deal of rivalry and interpersonal conflict that results from these internal status differences.

Other significant structural features of the Ajo Indian community are the several pan-village sodalities. Besides integrating a number of unrelated and independent Papago households in the different "strata," the sodalities seem to contribute to an Indian (primarily Papago) cultural identity that the diverse origins, the wide range of acculturation types, and the stratified nature of the community would otherwise tend to weaken. In addition, the sodalities serve as links to the larger Anglo community, including Mexican town — the Feast of St. Catherine draws Anglos and Mexicans as well as reservation Papagos; a women's club helps plan for "Indian Day" in the schools; the village councilmen consult with personnel of local agencies regarding problems relating to Papagos in the larger community, etc.

Most Papago contacts within the larger community are self-initiated and consist of individual contacts in various facilities in town, such as the stores, recreational facilities, and welfare agencies. There is wide variation in the extent of participation. The mining company, through its cooperative store, its housing authority, its company hospital, its employment opportunities and policies, and its overall influence in the community through its officialdom, functions to integrate the segregated ethnic communities. The structural basis of interaction in the Ajo complex, as it involves Papagos generally, is depicted in Figure 18.

There are some central value orientations that are instrumental in encouraging the behavior and attitudes of Papago miners to conform to certain social and economic demands. The formal occupational structure and the policies relating to the mine operation embody values that are extremely significant; since they largely stimulate the social differences in the village and the town proper, thus having an important bearing on the structure of interaction for Papagos.

First, there is the wage system that is structured according to the level of skill demanded for particular work roles. Even the minimum wage for an unskilled worker is considerably more than even the highest paid farm hand receives. Since unskilled jobs are gradually being eliminated through mechanization, skill and training are becoming even more important. Whether one is hired depends on a high school diploma, and success on a whole battery of standardized tests. While seniority still functions for older employees, skilled competence is the only assurance for advancement to higher skill-pay levels and more responsible and prestigious jobs. The skill levels are still sufficiently spread out to provide a wide range of skills and responsibilities, but it is an implicit feature of the structure that certain jobs and certain performances have a greater value and worth attached to them. The best indication of this worth is in the wage and the job title, and the motivation is directed upward in these terms.

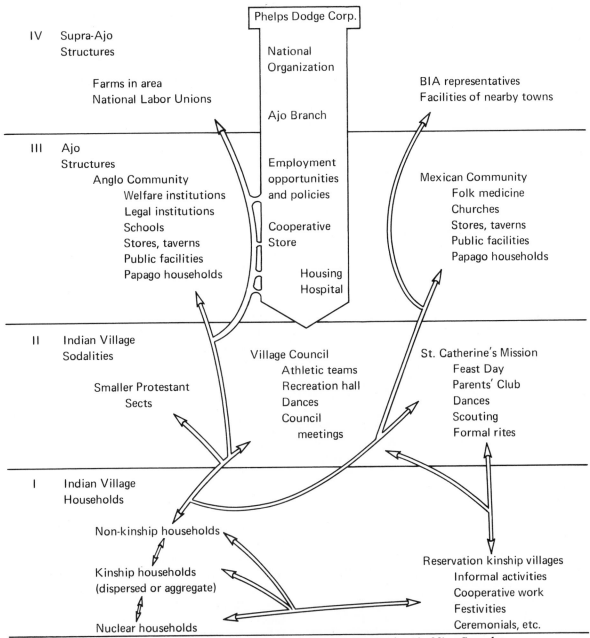

Figure 18. The Structural Basis of Social Interaction in the Ajo Mine Complex

The arrows indicate the source and direction of initiated interaction

Ideally, the structure is bureaucratic in that the many levels are open to all who can qualify for them, and all employees have equal opportunity to rise in the system. Those who cannot qualify at higher levels cannot ascend the opportunity structure, and those who cannot meet minimum requirements do not qualify for a job in the first place. This feature is therefore a very selective one, since Papagos who do qualify are those who either have long-term seniority or who have incorporated the motivational values and the necessary skills to qualify in the first place.

The occupational structure at the Ajo mine, in other words, embodies the values of a technologically and industrially advanced society — namely, the importance of supervisory and administrative know-how; the significance of equal opportunity as an ideal value; the right to organize and express grievances or to arbitrate them; the importance of material manifestations (type of home, clothes, goods, etc.) of one's success in the system; and the importance of formal education as an index of one's ability to do a job.

Notwithstanding these cultural ideals, Papagos and other Indians at Ajo are a discretely identifiable segment of a highly segregated mining community. This is, in part, due to historical precedent wherein the demand for a large unskilled work force in the past and the availability of Papagos drew a large number to the mine. With the rapid changes of the past few decades, the mine's own rationalizations have functioned to further segregate the Indians as something different, while at the same time promoting the ideal of equal opportunity. Some of these rationalizations are that the mine has been understanding by helping to provide the Indians with a community all their own in which they can carry on many of their own activities. At the same time the company has helped to provide better housing and facilities than the Indians demanded for themselves.

The employment office has also made allowances for Papagos as the mining industry has undergone radical technological changes that have demanded new kinds of skills. Formerly, most Papagos who came to work on the track could usually get a job for a few days, and, as turnover was high, these unskilled labor jobs could usually be performed at will. This seems to have been the occupational stereotype supported by both Papagos and the company for many years. This has been radically transformed in recent years, particularly by the company and by some Papagos. It is actually a source of disappointment among some Papagos to see this stereotype eliminated, since it has likewise barred unskilled and untrained Papagos from getting jobs for which they could qualify.

There are still allowances, made largely with Papagos in mind, for irresponsible drinking habits and lack of concern for the time demands of a steady job. The warning slip system for dealing with delinquency on the job is an accommodation of the company to these essentially Indian characteristics.[2]

---

[2] This is the rationalization of the company; that is, it instituted the warning slip system as a corrective device to control the extent of employee drinking and delinquency, a particular problem with Indian employees, although not exclusively.

Another rationalization is that while all are to be treated equally, Papagos must be treated unequally if they are to have equal access to the occupational system. Hence, while all applicants must qualify by passing standardized tests, Indians are given second chances to pass. If Indians do pass the tests, they are usually put to work if possible; while this is not true for other ethnic groups, who may have to wait.

The company also points to figures that indicate how Indians have elevated themselves over the years. One can see in the Ajo mine operation a combination of both bureaucratic and condescending institutionalization. I would suggest that the latter is the earlier manifestation, wherein former mining operations could function adequately by being geared to the habits of the common labor force. As operations changed, demands for greater and more diversified skills led toward the bureaucratization of the industry, whereby competence and skill became more essential than a muscle force. The high complement of Indians with seniority and the continued need for certain lower skilled performances have, nevertheless, maintained some of the condescending attitudes toward Indian employees. The process seems to be in the direction of greater bureaucratization and less condescension. This has necessarily affected many Papagos, both those that are caught in the bureaucratic system and those whose jobs have been eliminated because of it.

Urban Occupations

The urban Papago worker has a considerable range of social experience, depending largely on his particular occupation and the specific kind of residence pattern he assumes. It is possible for a worker to be relatively insulated from intense and direct relationships with middle class Anglos if he attaches to a Papago residence compound in the Papago urban enclave and assumes one or several of the stereotypic work roles in the urban setting. In the residence compound his interactions are predominantly with Papago relatives whose social experiences are similar to his. In the stereotyped work role (i.e., yard work, nursery, railroad gang, etc.), he is party to the condescending institutionalization that reinforces the Indian stereotype for both himself and his employer. Other than economic relationships at stores; socializing experiences in taverns, on the streets, and in recreational facilities; or confrontations with public

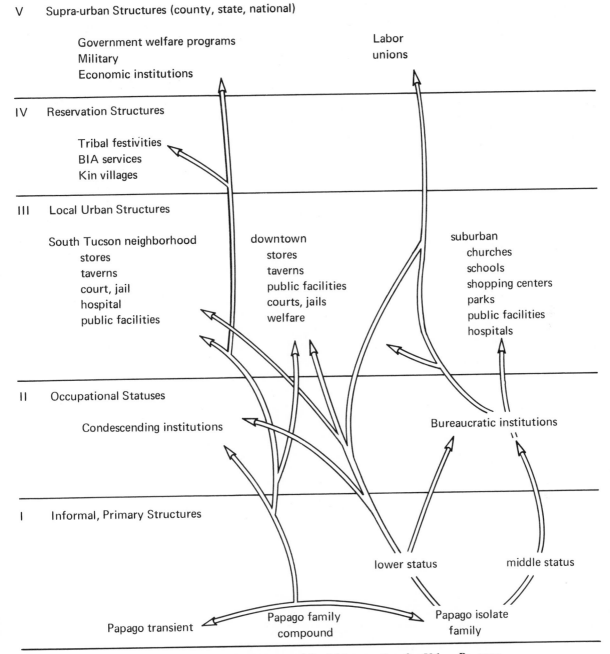

Figure 19. The Structural Basis of Social Interaction for Urban Papagos

The arrows indicate the source and direction of initiated interaction

agency personnel, his interactions are largely in terms of other Papagos or other lower status ethnic group members.

Other urban Papagos, particularly those of second or third generations in Tucson, who have stabilized work roles, although still of low status, may have incentives to be more detached from the cultural group; because they have sufficiently grasped Anglo values to have hopes for their children, even if it is too late for themselves. They may move away from the center of the enclave into homes of their own, interspersed among other ethnic groups, or they may have retained homes in neighborhoods that have been abandoned by the Papago enclave as it has been pressed southward.

Of course, there are many transitory Papagos who do not succeed in attaching themselves to any particular Papago residence unit. These individuals simply float around certain downtown or South Tucson areas, having interaction with other Papagos on the streets but remaining unattached to any stable residence unit.

A last group would be those Papagos who, by their enculturation and training experiences, have assimilated the necessary values and motivations to have experienced some successes and satisfactions in their occupations and in their social relationships with non-Papagos. The values and interests of Anglo society have sufficiently motivated them to the point of selectively de-identifying with much that has characterized social life in the urban Papago enclave or social life in the reservation villages. They are more articulate with Anglos and are capable of articulating the condescending concern toward other Papagos that is characteristic of Anglos. Figure 19 depicts the structural bases of social interaction for each of these four urban social types.

It is difficult to treat each of these four kinds of urban social orientations as a unit, but it seems justifiable to assume that they constitute a vertical mobility structure within the urban Papago "community" in which one group is largely stimulated by Anglo middle-class values. This Anglo-oriented Papago group in turn may function as a reference group for a younger generation derived from a more stable lower status group of Papagos. The latter, in turn, may serve as a reference group for certain individuals originating in the enclave compounds to which certain transitory Papagos may attach themselves and thus use the enclave community as a point of reference behavior.

Central Anglo values, then, funnel downward and become the basis of aspiration for Papago individuals throughout the Papago urban population. The most significant values are economic betterment and material acquisition, educational improvement, occupational preparation and training for higher statuses, better paying jobs, social participation in non-Papago types of organizations and sodalities, home ownership and improvement, and neighborhood affiliation that corresponds to socioeconomic status.

The discussion thus far has centered on general propositions about the social structure of occupational social fields. It has been suggested that these Anglo based sociostructural fields provide the basic social situations wherein Papago individuals experience different kinds and degrees of maximization in non-Papago culture, depending on the particular occupational field and the particular kinds of interactive experiences within it.

PAPAGO CULTURAL MODIFIERS

In addition to the structural bases of interaction in each of the various Anglo dominated occupational settings, there are Papago social structures and values that must be accommodated to the occupational structures and values, through the media of individuals. What are some of the most obvious and significant of these modifying features of Papago culture that operate in the occupational field?

This study has treated kinship and other features of Papago social organization as significant dependent variables. In addition, leadership and ceremonial activities, informal group relations relative particularly to drinking and festive activities, and values about work and leisure activities have been assumed to be important in adapting behavior to the demands of an occupational involvement. Since the research design has concentrated on gathering data relative to these four areas, other significant areas, known and unknown, have necessarily been omitted or neglected in the data gathering stage. The following discussion is an evaluative conclusion as to the general significance of the four chosen areas for answering the question that has been the concern of this study; namely, what are the most significant demands that off-reservation occupational situations place on Papago individuals, and how do Papagos go about adapting their accustomed behavior to these demands?

Kinship and Social Organization

It does not seem satisfactory to unconditionally accept the proposition that the Papago extended family is altered at great psychic cost to Papago individuals when it confronts industrial society, where the nuclear family becomes a functional necessity. In the first place, the nuclear family is a meaningful Papago social unit that exists as one among a number of other relatively contiguous nuclear households made up of relatives. Kinship can be traced to many individuals in one's village or beyond, and domestic life and cooperation within this network of relatives takes many forms. This in no way obviates the nuclear household's importance or precedence, any more than the nuclear household prevents individual members from feeling obligated toward more distant relatives. Papagos speak of their obligations to relatives, relate meaningful experiences with them, and even lump classes of them together terminologically; but the nuclear household residence is a vital element in the socialization of individuals. The structure of kinship villages and their ecological relationships nonetheless provide a Papago individual with a social environment that is completely oriented to interactions with relatives of varying degrees of genealogical closeness.

Some of my data challenge my original notion that occupational mobility is always antithetical to extended family relations. It seems to support Litwak's (1960: 20) conclusion that in contemporary industrial society extended family relations emerge out of different institutional sources and are not totally dependent on geographic and occupational proximity in order for the extended family to be a functioning entity. In some cases the modified extended family relationships are more congruous with certain kinds of occupational mobility than are those of the isolated nuclear family.

The Papago cases seem to point to a number of ways that extended family ties can be modified to meet occupational exigencies. The modifications do seem to be functionally relevant to adaptations in particular occupational fields; and some types of occupational organization are more congenial to satisfactory modifications of extended family ties than are others. The facility with which Papago families are able to accommodate their family organization to certain kinds of occupational situations lies not only in the occupational structure; the Papago family has a cultural history of modification in its structure and in the relationships of its members. Economic expediencies (seasonal movement to mountain and field villages, taking in relatives to support, living in tent camps following construction crews, temporary encampments near sources of labor, etc.) seem to be primary causes for changes in family organization.

Thus, a family can be exclusively nuclear in terms of spatial arrangement (either due to the particular features of the occupational structure or due to internal features of the Papago family itself) and at the same time can be a functioning extended family network in terms of sentiment, economic cooperation, serving as informal channels of occupational recruitment, periodic festive activity, and providing sources of social reunion and leisure. The combination of nuclear and extended relationships is the functioning quality of the Papago family in adapting to the demands of making a living, and it has its foundations in the indigenous system, not exclusively in the more recent wage work complexes. The Papago family seems to be quite flexible in terms of adapting its organization to the facilities available in certain kinds of occupations.

I have been impressed by how widely distributed in space members of the Papago families with which I have become familiar seem to be. The majority of family histories and individual life histories reveal lifetime patterns of this extensive spatial distribution of individual members. It is difficult, therefore, to support the proposition that familiar kinship units and relationships are drastically disrupted by the exigencies of off-reservation occupational environments and thereby make Papago adaptation to jobs more difficult. The cases presented seem to support the proposition that Papago kinship boundaries are sentimental domains in which kinsmen over extensive spatial areas are linked together but that Papago family units and individual members in actuality are capable of considerable modification if the occupational situation is deemed to be an economically expedient arrangement.

The case studies presented seem to indicate that there is sufficient flexibility in the family and kinship structure; that any number of functional modifications in family arrangements are possible, even for the same family; and that any number of these arrangements are adaptive in nature; that is, they are capable of facilitating styles of life acceptable to the individuals involved. While there is expressed dissatisfaction at being apart from one's kinship village or one's relatives, I cannot attribute this dissatisfaction as a major difficulty in adapting personal behavior to the demands of a particular job. While family and kinship facets of role behavior are vital to Papago satisfaction and emotional security, it is difficult to consider kinship, by itself, as the crucial element in adaptive behavior in occupational social fields. The cases with which I have become familiar seem to indicate that Papagos adapt themselves personally to wage systems, despite what these occupations might immediately do to the family arrangements.

A long history of geographical mobility within an extensive but spatially limited area has produced a somewhat malleable form of family organization that is capable of adapting to a number of economic situations and still provides meaningful relationships with kinsmen. I do not see anything in the particular occupational complexes that are overwhelmingly incongruous with indigenous Papago patterns as far as kinship matters are concerned.

The farm organization seems more pliable for incorporating relatives, both with respect to the physical layout of farm camps and with respect to tendencies of farms to institutionalize relationships with related Papagos from certain reservation areas. It is not uncommon, however, to find isolated nuclear Papago households that have little direct relationships with kin; and I have found steady, reliable, and long-time employed Papagos from both extended family rural camps and from nuclear family isolate households largely cut off from a rural farm kinship community. Neither the assurance of extended family facilities nor the assumption of more isolated nuclear family organization is a guarantee of a stable relationship between a family and a commercial farm.

Ajo provides little in the way of a continuous experience for a worker among his many relatives. I found a few families that have been able to skirt company rules and form a neighborhood of related nuclear households into a kind of corporate family, but the majority of households are entirely nuclear arrangements. I found a prevailing lack of interest in Ajo other than as a necessary place to live while work is performed.

The nuclear family organization is the prevailing type within the Ajo Indian village, but the proximity to the reservation and the frequent shutdowns permit those who have extended family commitments on the reservation to fulfill them at anticipated intervals. As the company takes a more direct role in encouraging long-time Papago families to improve their status and living conditions to conform to Anglo values, the greater will be the threats to the workers' relationships with their fellow Papago kinsmen and friends who do not conform. I see Ajo as a much greater influence in stratifying Papago society and altering kinship ties than is the farm. More and more of the less acculturated Papagos are rejected by the Ajo complex and filter back to the reservation or to the commercial farm complex, and Ajo is becoming a selective social base for only the more assimilated Papagos.

The urban setting provides a wide range of family organization, and the type of family organization is significantly related to the extent of Papago vertical mobility in the urban socioeconomic structure. The South Tucson enclave provides a rather persisting base, through its residence compounds of related families, where individuals can find temporary or more prolonged support within an extended family context. Yet there are urban isolate nuclear families with progressively decreasing dependence on relatives and kinsmen as they stabilize occupations and become more socially mobile. It is in the urban setting that the family organization seems to undergo the greatest change, and this is related to the fact that Papagos have come to participate differentially in a socioeconomically stratified urban environment.

A review of the social organization data encourages me to conclude that while kinship may be an important element in a worker's overall adaptation to a job, I must look elsewhere for more pertinent explanations of adaptive behavior.

Leadership and Ceremonial Activities

Another area of social activity that I was initially interested in exploring in terms of its relevance to adaptive behavior in an occupational field was that of leadership and/or ceremonial activities and roles. I wanted to determine the validity of an assumption that extensive participation in the ceremonial calendar and leadership or decision-making responsibilities in kinship villages are antithetical to stabilization of an occupational pattern.

First, in those cases where the informants are relatively steady farm hands or whose residence patterns have been oriented toward prolonged off-reservation residences, I find some variation; although generally there is little evidence to suggest that they have any major functions in the activities of their villages. Of the 11 cases involved exclusively in farm activities and oriented residentially off-reservation, 10 were attached to some form of farm laborer encampment or residence; and the remaining case resided within an off-reservation Indian village. Only one of the 11 had a house in a reservation village while all of them had access to living quarters of either siblings, more distant collateral relatives, or affinal relatives during infrequent visits. The time demands of their particular occupational tasks, the distance to kinship villages, their prolonged periods away from their kinship villages, and their orientations to rural town centers and larger towns and cities indicate little in the way of involvement in the political and leadership aspects of their villages. Most contacts with villages are in the nature of visits with relatives for short periods when the work is slack or attendance at special festivities or ceremonial events involving kinsmen.

As already noted, farms have generally acknowledged the festive and ceremonial activities of their Papago employees. Those Papagos who have had prolonged relationships with farm employers and clearly established responsibilities in the farm operation can usually anticipate that their employers will permit them to take time off for such occasions if it is at all possible. Those who depend largely on seasonal labor and crew type work can leave at will without seriously affecting their chances to make a little money some other time. The former type make the most reliable steady hands, since they pay more heed to the time demands of their jobs and rely on the institutionalized condescension of their employers.

Indian villages off the reservation usually have political structures that are absent in farm camps and have informal leaders who are usually the eldest and most prestigious individuals. In addition there are elected leaders, frequently younger men, responsible for organizing village events and dealing with representatives of the Indian Bureau or other Anglo institutions. Further, there are individuals that Anglos in the nearby towns try to utilize to mediate their concerns; but such presumed leaders may also be sources of intravillage antagonisms. These political aspects are usually quite separate from an individual's occupation, and he can participate in work on nearby farms without his work conflicting in any way with political events in the village. The villages, since they usually lie adjacent to or close to an Anglo town, can gear their political and ceremonial activities to the time demands of the occupations (predominantly farm work) represented by village members.

Data gathered from Papago farm laborers indicate that while kinship village activities and obligations may be important to them, they apparently are not that crucial in determining whether individuals do or do not adapt to relatively steady farm jobs.

The Ajo data have suggested a paradigm in which the interplay of leadership and ceremonial roles, and activities in the occupational and kinship communities can be depicted. The following paradigm classifies the possible types of situations, with the first two types being the most crucial in terms of adapting dual roles:

1. Responsibilities and obligations at a kinship village with none at the Ajo Village.
2. Responsibilities and obligations at a kinship village as well as at the Ajo village.
3. No responsibilities and obligations at either a kinship village or at the Ajo village.
4. No responsibilities and obligations at a kinship village but at the Ajo village.

The paradigm might be explained in another way. Those Ajo miners who have significant duties in their kinship villages and none whatever at the Ajo village are under the greatest pressure because of the time a steady job keeps them away. I do not think there are many who remain in Ajo if their commitments to their kinship villages are too strong. If an Ajo miner has responsibilities to both kinship village and Ajo village, there may be a strong pull toward the home village; but a commitment to the village in which he resides as a result of his steady job leads to a compartmentalization of roles, without which the pull toward the kinship village would threaten his commitment to the job.

No leadership or ceremonial commitments in either village would indicate either a highly transient Papago or one who lives within the village but who is somewhat detached from the activities of the Indian village. Such an individual would have no problem in adapting behavior relative to this aspect of the social field. He may or may not maintain a steady job at the mine, but for entirely different reasons. If there are no obligations at a kinship village but increasing leadership obligations at the Ajo village, an individual likely has the full support of company officialdom and would represent a local Papago elite. This latter kind of individual has the greatest chance of success with the company and thus in his job. A Papago in category two of the paradigm would have difficulty in achieving category four and vice versa. The mine operation's schedule of shutdowns makes categories one and two possible, however; otherwise kinship village activities could not be accommodated to the mining occupation.

The urban data are not sufficient to ascertain other than general impressions. There are individuals from some isolated Papago nuclear households, as well as some in the Papago enclaves, that maintain strong reservation ties and may have responsibilities in their kinship villages. Other individuals, due to long-term residence in the city, are almost totally unattached from any kinship village. There are festive activities and ceremonial events in reservation villages that involve almost all Papagos, especially when they relate to situations involving relatives.

The stereotypic urban occupations are more amenable to participation in many of these social obligations, while the higher status jobs curtail, although do not completely exclude, the carrying out of such obligations. A new kind of leadership role becomes apparent with higher socioeconomic status and among vertically mobile Papagos. It is a welfare leadership, where a Papago appropriates the middle class value of condescension toward the less fortunate and seeks to influence other Papagos through his example.

While kinship relationships and social responsibilities and obligations to kinship communities are significant variables, they still do not provide the kinds of explanations I am looking for in dealing with adaptive behavior in occupational settings. There are adaptations taking place, as the individual cases seem to reveal rather clearly; but taken alone they are not explanatory enough. There are institutionalized supports (farm acknowledgment of festive patterns, shutdowns at mine, and weekends off, etc.) that reduce the conflicts that might otherwise occur. Where there are conflicts, there are alternatives, such as compartmentalizing roles to do what one can as the job permits, or to take off regardless of consequences, or to try one's luck elsewhere.

Except in individual cases, the resolutions of various leadership or ceremonial roles do not generally seem insurmountable for those who have found it necessary to venture into the off-reservation wage system. Indigenous functions do not seem so rigid

that they cannot be accommodated to an economic demand.

Interpersonal Relations and Drinking Behavior

It is in the area of informal Papago interpersonal relations that I have found some of the most meaningful data relative to discovering barriers that inhibit or restrict Papago occupational adjustment and acculturation. This area of investigation has been a most difficult one, however, and is much in need of further investigations. There are some generalizations that can be drawn from field observations and interviews. These generalizations should reveal the direction that further research might take.

There seem to be some rather distinct differences in the patterns of interpersonal relations of different Papago age groups. Also, there are some quite noticeable differences in the structure of interpersonal relations relative to informal group behavior in each of the different occupational complexes. At the same time, there are some general rules or norms relative to interpersonal relations among Papago men that have an important bearing on occupational adjustment. These will be discussed with particular emphasis on drinking behavior.

Older Papago men that I have come to know in various off-reservation settings have generally conveyed the idea that they drink for different reasons and in different quantities than do younger Papago men. In addition, they seem to drink in different places and on different occasions, although I found both young and old to be affected by older Papago values and rules regulating the custom of social drinking. Such a general assumption is, of course, untested and would be a very useful line of inquiry.

Older men, particularly on the farms, are interested in sitting around, after a day's work in the fields, in the cool of the evening conversing and playing games with other men or perhaps, if one is available, watching TV and resting. Younger men are more prone to head for nearby towns or to visit friends at neighboring camps. The steadiest farm hands among my informants were older men (50 or older), while the majority of the youngest of my informants (19-35) were usually part-time irrigators or, even more commonly, almost wholly dependent on a contractor in a chopping or picking crew.

Some of the middle-aged men (35-50) had steadier work but still exhibited a great deal of job jumping within the general vicinities of their usual residence, reflecting some of the pattern of the younger men. Much of this mobility and job-jumping seems to have some direct relationship to the interpersonal relations with those of one's own age group. Joining a chopping crew gives the individual a control over just when he desires to place himself in the wage market, and he can enter or withdraw at will. One day's work may give him enough money to invest in an evening of companionable drinking.

Several of my younger informants mentioned that they liked to keep on the go and not stay in one spot. Older informants (50 and older) have confirmed this general tendency on the part of younger men, and their own earlier patterns give some evidence of the same kind of leisurely attitude toward wage work. This is apparent even in the earlier patterns of Papago workers now engaged in nonfarm labor, such as at Ajo or in Tucson. Older informants have pointed out this difference in behavior to me; but seldom, if ever, did I detect censure or undue criticism of this erratic behavior of younger men. In fact, it seems to be understood as something to expect from younger men.

On the basis of prolonged personal contact with a number of informants representing all ages, types of wage work, and locations, it is possible to conceptualize what have seemed to be rather general norms behind drinking group or companionable drinking behavior. It is of importance because I think the "norms" are highly relevant to occupational adaptation.

Drinking is not a disapprobation even if it occasionally leads to difficulties with legal authorities, although inappropriate excess may be frowned upon by other Papagos. Drinking in Papago culture has stemmed from a ritual-social context and carries with it the power to affirm affections and to seal friendships. Drinking what is offered is equally an affirmation of goodwill just as is offering it.

Drinking groups, therefore, are made up of individuals who reciprocally exhaust the source (money) and supply (liquor available); and each participant, although he may lack resources on one occasion, can still participate, knowing that there will be other times. Since the money resources of drinking friends are never the same, individuals are continuously

obligated to return their gestures of affection on other occasions. Even when an individual has good reason for stopping and may desire to do so, he may run into another similar group of friends and may get involved, either contributing anything he has left or counting on someone else. Several informants have conveyed to me how they are "trapped" in an unavoidable situation; to handle it any differently would be insulting.

There is, of course, a good deal of drinking in which it is the intention of individuals to get drunk; and individuals who start drinking know that is how everyone will end up. Younger men, and older men who have had rather intense experience in non-Papago social situations (military, for instance) and are aware of status differences, undoubtedly use voluminous and prolonged drinking as a way of expressing or airing their status grievances to each other (James 1961: 740-1). Their awareness of their status inferiority among Anglos, while not verbally aired to employers, is expressed in the context of an ingroup involved in extended drinking. The explicit explanation for these drinking bouts invokes the older cultural value that one is supposed to drink with friends, while the drinking itself functions also to air the grievances an individual holds within himself when face to face with an employer or other Anglos.

If drinking and its end results (drunkenness, arrest, and confinement) are bad, they are bad only in the sense that they cross Anglos and their legal and welfare institutions. So a Papago can and does "feel bad" about where his drinking leads him, and he can share the guilt imposed on him by a court or by an awareness that his family has had to do without. But I have yet to find the attitude that drinking in itself is bad. When Papago individuals seek therapeutic assistance, regardless of the agent sought, it is due to a desire to meet the time demands of an occupational task rather than to relieve oneself of a "bad" habit.

It has not been uncommon to find Papagos who could work relatively long periods during the busy season, only to fall into extended periods of intoxication during the slack weeks or months. Even some of the most chronic drinkers I have had dealings with have exhibited this ability to control just how much time they really wanted to give to work or to drinking. I am not suggesting that alcoholism, in the disease sense, is not present; it is important, however, to be sure that "drinking-in-excess" is not just a convenient label based on recognition instead of a well-established definition (Hoyt 1960: 135).

Papagos, like many other Indian tribes, have a long history of being compelled to skirt Anglo legal restrictions relative to drinking, so they are well aware of what is "good" and "bad" or "right" and "wrong" (i.e., bootlegging). They know the Anglo "negative stereotype" (James 1961: 731) of Indians as "heavy drinkers but damn good workers when sober", and some learn to behave in accordance with the stereotype. There are, of course, old Papagos who drink heavily and do not work, just as there are young Papagos who are most dependable in the eyes of employers.

While this aspect of Papago behavior is general for all the occupational types represented, the structure of interaction provided by specific complexes would account for identifiable differences. The Ajo and urban bureaucratic occupational demands show less tolerance for uncontrolled drinking. In order for men to hold jobs, there must be some motivation to utilize whatever means are available to alter drinking patterns.

The farm provides an outlet, through seasonal work and contract labor, for those who cannot or do not wish to modify their drinking behavior. The steadiest of farm hands, however, usually have brought this aspect of social behavior into some kind of alignment with the demands of the job. It is far easier for employees on farms to sneak off to drink on the job, even though there are ultimate consequences as far as the job is concerned. A rationale of some young Papago farm laborers (confirmed by more elderly Papago informants) I have come to know is that one can always find a little farm labor somewhere, so one need not worry too much about where immediate drinking may lead.

Data gathered from my field work seem to support Bahr's (1964: 12,66) observation that there is a *miligan kiidag* (a necessity to work for wages) and an *'o'odham kiidag* (making local resources work for one's good). Companionable drinking is far more compatible with the time and performance demands of the latter than with the former, but *miligan kiidag* is important because it takes money to enjoy companionable drinking as well as to buy food and other necessities.

To commit oneself to steady work demands a modification of one's interpersonal relationships with one's peers. This seems to be one explanation why an occupational pattern takes so long in materializing, if it does at all. Rather than aiding in the adjustment, such things as partial education, partial assimilation of Anglo values, partial vocational training experience, etc., may only intensify the pattern of ambivalence and status inferiority. Individuals partially but unsuccessfully assimilated into Anglo institutional values seem to be even more aberrant in terms of their occupational patterns. These people, particularly, are apt to fall back to the peer group and share in the corporate retreat from social isolation with the aid of alcohol and companions.

Values Regarding Work and Leisure

The central concern in the analysis has been directed toward the disclosure of certain kinds of role adaptations which Papago workers have worked out for themselves in response to the social demands of particular occupational complexes. Adaptation in this sense refers to the process of learning to modify Papago social structures and cultural behaviors in order to conform to the demands of institutionalized occupational roles and the numerous other social roles that are afforded by the particular adaptational social fields connected with particular types of occupations.

Certain values and certain role demands, related specifically to the occupations Papagos perform, are important in analyzing adaptational behavior. With different kinds of wage work, there are different time demands — the hours and days that a status occupant must put in, both for the recompense he receives for his time and in order to maintain the status. In addition there are performance demands, or the tasks and activities required in the carrying out of the central role elements of a status, as well as the additional expectations an employer may demand, such as certain desired personality traits and social behavior.

Against the time and performance demands there are the ego demands, such as desires for emotional security and satisfactions, recognition by others, autonomy, and a host of other individual personality needs. Further, there are social demands related to the job, such as relationships with bosses and supervisors and associations with other workers. Finally, there are extra-work social demands that may either be compatible with the work status demands, in conflict with the demands of the job, or relatively neutral and irrelevant to the job requirements.

The following are some of the most significant generalizations my data suggest relative to Papago adaptation to certain kinds of work. On the farm, the amount of time a worker has to spend on the job varies considerably with the kind of job. A steady job as an equipment operator or a full-time irrigator demands long hours with few days off and well-established pay periods. These jobs may slacken during the height of the harvest season and may provide the steady hand with an opportunity to pick cotton or to take a little time off to visit the reservation. Very few of my informants who were steady irrigators or tractor drivers liked to pick cotton and usually left this to other members of their families. The picking season becomes a vacation time for steady hands who do not have other tasks to perform. There appear to be status or prestige factors involved if this generalization proves to be quantitatively valid. Only under dire necessity do tractor drivers or irrigators turn to picking cotton.

On the other hand, there are Papagos, particularly young men, who work almost exclusively under labor contractors, even if they live permanently at a particular farm camp. They can select when they wish to join a crew and make a little money for immediate use, as there is usually no need to wait for the end of a pay period. The risk of a few days in jail or laying off work to sober up is no great threat to the job, since the individual can get back to it again when he desires.

The range of farm tasks Papagos generally perform falls within familiar bounds; that is, the tasks, in terms of what is to be done, what kinds of motor movements to employ, and what can be expected in return, are well established by years of routine experience. While interviewing or visiting in camps, I would occasionally observe little children at the edge of a cotton field dragging a paper sack and picking cotton, all in play, or perhaps hoeing with a stick. Parents have conveyed to me that while they worked, their children would be given little sacks or a stick to play with along the field's edge. One Papago tractor driver says his eight-year-old son likes to watch him drive the tractor and hopes he will be able to do it someday, just like his father.

Much of my projective data reveal familiar patterns of work that constitute ideals for future generations. While other kinds of wage work, involving new kinds of experience, are known and of interest, farm Papagos manifest a prevailing selectivity, reinforced by enculturative experiences, for certain kinds of routine farm jobs. Familiar physical environments or surroundings, along with the established features of the work itself, tend to fix some Papagos' patterns in terms of the farm. This inclination for farm work may be due to a lack of preparation for anything else, but the fixed or institutionalized dependence on certain kinds of farm work in turn operates to restrict interest in any other forms of wage work.

Communicating instructions to farm laborers is less complicated, although the channels do get muddled by language barriers or other social habit barriers. Routine work is usually its own instructor. A Papago need not be personally compatible with a foreman or supervisor as long as the time demands are kept within the institutionalized bounds and the tasks can be channeled from supervisor to employee.

The ego demands depend to a great extent on particular individual personality organization, but there are some general tendencies. I found a rather strong tendency to desire a considerable amount of autonomy or to be left alone on the job with little interference from supervisors. Along with this there is the desire to maintain routine work roles and the avoidance of undue responsibility or anything that would require an excessive reorientation of performance demands. Ego demands are also significant for understanding the influence of extra-work social demands.

Some of the requirements of social life that are not directly a part of the work performance may either support or conflict with the demands of one's job. Attachments to kinsmen and reservation villages, discomfort around Anglos, language difficulties, festive events, attitudes about how to spend one's time, absence of other Papagos, complications with Anglo authorities, and a host of other states of mind or social situations that occupational life demands are in conflict with the Anglo cultural requirement to maintain steady work.

On the other hand, having a settlement of relatives, friends, or other Papagos close by with living expense at a minimum, having places where liquor is obtainable and where companionable drinking can take place, being reasonably close to reservation villages, residing at camps where relatives through the years have established certain relationships with employers, living in rural surroundings similar to the environmental ecology of home villages, etc., all tend to complement the farm occupational roles as well as to restrict movement into nonfarm occupations. Failure in securely attaching to nonfarm jobs results in a flow of urban-oriented Papagos back to the rural areas or to the reservation.

At Ajo, there are definite time demands that hold for all employees, Papagos or anyone else. In former days, Indians had to be rounded up on the reservation in order to have a sufficient number of common laborers, mostly track men. It was then possible to work whenever one wanted to put in time, and there was considerable turnover. Now, all employees are on regular payroll, and workers must either report to work with a minimum of unexcused absences or be dropped. Circulating shifts of personnel and a set rhythm of shutdowns for shift changes must be adhered to. There are set vacations, holidays, and sick leave privileges. All employees in the labor operation are paid by the hour, according to level of the skilled operation, at set pay intervals.

Performance demands vary considerably according to the grade or level of skill in the hierarchy of occupational statuses. Indians have tended to cluster at the lowest levels, largely in unskilled routine but important tasks. More recently a few have invaded the semiskilled, intermediate levels; but there has been no change with regard to the highest levels.

Papagos generally have avoided supervisory responsibility, preferring to remain as peers to others in predominantly Indian work groups. Most jobs at the levels where Papagos are most frequently distributed are largely routine jobs, once learned. There is a reticence about assuming new kinds of responsibility, and I frequently found that the biggest reasons given are lack of education and inability to measure up to what Anglos expect. I detected a considerable amount of expressed inferiority and unpreparedness for some of the higher jobs. There is no reason to question the sincerity of expressions of inadequacy, but I perceive that Papagos also see occupational mobility in the Ajo mine structure as a threat to the cultural identity of the Indian community. The higher status Papagos in the newer suburban-type houses are beginning to be the objects of gossip by the other families, and some Papagos decline company offers to move into the bigger and better houses. Their own acceptance of their "inadequacy" helps to confirm that Indians are different and functions to preserve a kind of cultural identity.

The influence of the company, then, is instrumental in compounding a form of factionalism by its policy of stimulating certain select Indian families to "set an example" for the other Indians. There are those who follow the example, some who could but do not, and many more that are not even considered. So there are some additional social demands of a job at Ajo outside of the job itself.

The extra-work demands in conflict with occupational performance are similar to those discussed with regard to Papagos on farms — strong orientations toward reservation kinsmen, activities in home villages, strong sentiment toward their homes, distinctive customs, etc. Compensating features of the Ajo situation, however, are advantageous company housing, predictable shutdowns for periodic visiting in reservation villages, the availability of company economic and medical services, and an Indian cultural identity through a modified Indian community with many of its own activities, to reiterate only a few. An Ajo job is a rather secure arrangement but due to its selective features, many Papagos fail to make the grade in it.

The urban environment is much too complex for so general a treatment. For those Papagos within the Papago enclave and dependent on stereotypic work roles, there are less rigid time demands. The stereotypic jobs are not too dissimilar from those found on the farm, since the individual can usually work at will and does not have to count on anything steady. Close relationships or paternalistic relationships are prone to develop in the stereotyped roles, much like that which occurs on farms.

The urban setting provides greater anonymity for Papagos, but most of the informal relationships are centered in Papago neighborhoods or in familiar congregating and drinking places. As Papagos attain other-than-stereotypic work roles, there are new kinds of social demands involving more intense relations with non-Papagos. Thus, the stratified nature of the urban occupational structure induces a certain amount of cultural de-identification as well as a motivation to rise in socioeconomic status.

DIRECTION OF ASSIMILATIVE CHANGE

Each occupational complex has its own unique social structures and its own form of stratified statuses. It is possible to trace the general direction of assimilative change within each type of adaptational environment. Further, it is possible to see certain relationships of the occupational fields to each other and to trace the direction of assimilative change as Papagos move throughout these complexes.

In the farm complex Papagos find the most accessible means of earning money to live on. For many, seasonal farm labor has been a means of supplementing reservation subsistence economy. As derived needs have accumulated, acquired from directed change programs of government as well as through living adjacent to growing Anglo concentrations, there have emerged new economic necessities that could be satisfied only by some form of wage work. As the reservation has failed in its ability to support a growing population with expanding economic needs, certain families have built on the former pattern of seasonal labor and have come to be totally dependent on some form of wage labor in year around off-reservation settlements.

Some individuals have persisted in the more leisurely attitude toward wage work and participate only in seasonal work, such as chopping or picking cotton. Others have been able to achieve the status of more permanent ranch or farm hands, performing tasks that impose greater time demands and require some degree of revision in leisurely attitudes toward work. For those with steadier work patterns, tractor or equipment driving, cattle punching, and irrigating have emerged as the ideal patterns which influence oncoming generations. The acme of farming as an occupation is reached in the role of a farm equipment mechanic.

With the more recent trend toward mechanization of cotton farming, Papago farm workers are more and more occupying the middle range as steady irrigators or equipment operators. Chopping crews are still widely used, but in many places there is less demand for hand pickers. Thus, those Papagos who become relatively permanent fixtures in commercial farm industries are achieving a certain degree of economic integration as well as conforming to the time and performance demands that industralized farming imposes.

Yet as I review the case studies of farm workers, it is difficult to accept the proposition that the most assimilated Papagos are the most well adapted farm laborers. Papagos who seem best adapted to their particular farm roles, include some who have had no formal education, speak little or no English, and have had no other formal vocational training in Indian schools. To achieve the maximum ideal in the farming complex, these Anglo values do not seem to be necessary prerequisites.

In fact, the most unstable and undependable farm laborers from the farmers' points of view are those who use English well, have had extended exposure to schools and vocational programs, and comprehend the meaning of certain Anglo values. These seem to be most prone to job-jumping and voluntary unemployment. Much of it can be attributed to age and an unreadiness to feel obliged to settle down, but much of the behavior can be explained in terms of dissonance or the inability to articulate the understanding they have of Anglo cultural values with a sufficient motivation to implement these values.

It is not quite correct, therefore, to propose that Papago culture is antithetical to any form of wage labor (*miligan kiidag*), for case studies indicate that younger men who understand the system more completely are often less well adapted than those who are less familiar with Anglo institutional values. Partial or incomplete assimilation is apparently a worse enemy to Papago occupational stability than is the failure to assimilate certain non-Papago values at all. Once the capacity to assimilate the necessary dominant values has been individually demonstrated, there is no assurance that motivation and ability to implement learned values have necessarily been assimilated. It may only lead to greater dissonance.

While we are always safe at this stage of our knowledge about the present Papago cultural system to assume that there are counterexpectations within Papago culture that inhibit occupational and socioeconomic adjustment, much of the present difficulty seems to be a result of what Van Baal (1960: 108) has referred to as "erring acculturation," or the inability of institutions of the dominant society to achieve an adequate acculturation ethos in which changes in a subordinate culture can take place at the least psychic cost to individuals and indigenous social units.

The occupational complexes discussed in this study each provide a different kind of "acculturation ethos" for Papagos. Acculturation takes place largely within relatively stratified Indian communities that are components of a larger stratified system. Excluding those working on commercial farms, however, the Papagos whose assimilation of Anglo cultural values is more complete are generally better adapted to their occupational fields. Social and economic mobility, although largely directed from without, takes place largely within the Indian community, whether at Ajo or in urban Tucson.

In Ajo, although socioeconomic statuses may be shared by the separate ethnic communities, stratification and social status indicators operate largely in the three separate social contexts. Yet the entire Ajo community is a hierarchy of the three stratified ethnic communities, with Anglos at the top, Mexicans in the middle, and Indians at the base. This feature prevails even when a Papago occupies the highest stratum in the Indian community, while an Anglo occupies the lowest stratum in the Anglo community. There is only negligible movement from one ethnic community to another.

Even with a company-induced stratified Indian community, there are many factors that prevent complete Papago assimilation into the Ajo Anglo community, although Anglo values may be largely assimilated, particularly economic values. The Indian cultural identity; the strong ties to reservation kinsmen, villages, and customs; and company rationalizations to give Indians equal treatment tend to restrict complete assimilation of Anglo culture and enhance Papago cultural identity. In the Ajo case, there is occupational adaptation without complete Papago assimilation into the larger Ajo community. Papago culture survives by social segregation in Ajo in much the same way that Papago culture survives on commercial farms through geographic isolation.

Papagos in the process of urbanization are assimilated through the stratified structure of the entire Papago urban segment. Transient Papagos either remain floaters, filter back to rural settlements or reservation villages, or attach themselves to urban family residence compounds in predominantly Papago enclaves. Members of a family compound may succeed in engaging in occupations in which urban Papagos have traditionally participated. As occupations are stabilized, nuclear households emerge that may become detached from the more conservative, lower status residence compounds. As second and third generation Papagos experience relative successes in implementing middle class Anglo values, they break from the conservative community without forsaking their cultural identity altogether. Thus Papagos in Tucson have Papagos as social status reference points at ascending status levels. Whether or not one ascends the structure, that is, uses a higher stratum as a social reference point, is explainable only through the analysis of the peculiarities of particular cases.

Papago social mobility and assimilation seem to operate within the stratified Papago segment. The most significant social status indicators for urban Papagos are literacy and educational advancement, occupational status and income level, area of residence, economic assets and utilization of wealth, the manner in which leisure time is spent, and sodality affiliations. There are considerable differences in these aspects as Papagos from each of the four socio-economic statuses are identified.

There seem to be marginal domains where commitments to one field or another are not clear. A sizable number are assumed to oscillate from rural to urban to rural, etc., due to certain inabilities to accommodate to a single pattern. It has not been unusual to find a Papago's life history revealing a trial in any number of the more familiar Papago occupations during his younger years. Some never substantially crystallize a pattern, while many others fall into a discernible pattern and retain it in later life. Once again, it is the study of individual cases that will most adequately demonstrate the dynamics of adaptive behavior.

The direction of individual Papago assimilation has been determined by a few rather fixed social contexts, where each acculturation ethos has been restricted by Anglo institutional barriers, by barriers resulting from Papago efforts to maintain Papago cultural identity, and by directed attempts to bring the two systems closer together.

SUGGESTIONS FOR FUTURE RESEARCH

In the process of defining a field of research, it is possible to overlook important avenues of approach or methods of accumulating pertinent data. Only after the field operations are well under way and after the data have been collected and analyzed does one clearly begin to see how the investigation should have proceeded. This has clearly been the case in this investigation. It seems most appropriate, therefore, to chart some of the avenues which might have been included as well as to point out some possible areas of research suggested by this particular effort.

First, there is clearly a need for some traditional ethnography that can extend over a period of time and involve many investigators. The lack of ethnographic studies of particular kinds of reservation communities is clearly evident when one seeks to establish an ethnographic base on which to build off-reservation studies. Further, there is a need for quantitatively establishing the range and number of off-reservation Indian settlement types, such as I have rather subjectively or impressionistically tried to do in this study. Related to this is a need for a number of ethnographic studies in a number of different kinds of off-reservation Papago settlements — studies of different kinds of farm camps, Indian villages, planned communities, urban family compounds, town enclaves, etc.

In addition to the ethnographic concerns, there are any number of problem- centered studies that might utilize any of the newer techniques such as "ethnoscience." How do Papagos, in terms of their own linguistic categories, structure their domains of activity, and how do they rate them? This study has almost completely bypassed the use of linguistic methods and has thereby imposed its own serious limits.

There is a need to explore what I prefer to call the ecology of sentiment; that is, how do Papagos see themselves in terms of their relationships to the environment in which they perceive themselves to be living? This, again, would call for sophistication in linguistic technique as well as some refined and tested projective devices. Also, there is an urgent need for further studies in the acculturation ethos to which a category of Papago individuals are oriented. This would call for detailed studies of specific occupational structures, or of welfare and other directed change institutions, or of certain strata within predominantly Papago communities, or of the role of innovators and specific individual agents of change, to name only a few possible studies.

This study has been concerned with cultural changes as they have been experienced by individual Papago laborers representing certain occupational and adaptational environments. It has not been exhaustive, but it has shown that cultural changes do have their most immediate loci in the personality organizations of individuals who are participating in particular kinds of social structures. This study has attempted to follow the procedure noted by Hallowell (1945: 175, 178):

Individuals are the dynamic centers of this process of interaction [between peoples of different cultures]. If perceptible differences in the mode of life of either people result, it means that new ways of acting, thinking, and feeling have been learned by individuals. . . . the analysis of cultural changes always leads us from our initial descriptive abstractions of stabilized cultural forms, through a series of processes involving conditions that have led to readjustments on the part of individuals, and then back again to the socially discernible effects of such readaptation which can once more be described as new or modified cultural forms.

BIBLIOGRAPHY

Ajo, Gila Bend City Directory
   1960

ARENSBERG, CONRAD M.
   1954   The Community Study Method. The
          American Journal of Sociology, Vol.
          60, No. 2, pp. 109-24.

ARIZONA COMMISSION OF INDIAN AFFAIRS
   1957   The Off-Reservation Papagos. *Program
          and Proceedings of the Arizona Com-
          mission of Indian Affairs.* Sells,
          Arizona.

ARIZONA STATE EMPLOYMENT SERVICE
   1960   *Arizona Cotton Production Survey,
          1959-60 Harvest.* Phoenix.

BAHR, DONALD
   1964   Santa Rosa, Arizona. Manuscript in
          files of the Bureau of Ethnic Research,
          University of Arizona, Tucson.

BANCROFT, HUBERT HOWE
   1886   *History of the North Mexican States
          and Texas, 1531-1800,* Vol. 1. The His-
          tory Company Publishers, San Fran-
          cisco.

BARNES, WILL C.
   1960   *Arizona Place Names.* University of
          Arizona Press, Tucson.

BARTLETT, JOHN RUSSELL
   1854   *Personal Narrative of Explorations and
          Incidents in Texas, New Mexico,
          California, Sonora and Chihuahua* . . . .
          Vol. 2. D. Appleton and Co., New
          York.

BEALS, RALPH L.
   1951   Urbanism, Urbanization, and Accultur-
          ation. *American Anthropologist,* Vol.
          53, No. 1, pp. 1-10.

BOHANNON, PAUL
   1963   *Social Anthropology.* Holt, Rinehart,
          and Winston, New York.

BOLTON, HERBERT
   1919   *Kino's Historical Memoir of Pimería
          Alta.* University of California Press,
          Berkeley and Los Angeles.

BROWN, C. B.
   n.d.   *Farming in Pima County.* Agricultural
          Bureau, Chamber of Commerce,
          Tucson.

BROWN, MALCOLM, AND ORIN CASSMORE
   1939   *Migratory Cotton Pickers of Arizona.*
          U.S. Government Printing Office,
          Washington.

BROWNE, J. ROSS
   1950   *A Tour Through Arizona, 1864.* Ari-
          zona Silhouettes, Tucson.

BRUNER, EDWARD M.
   1964   The Psychological Approach in An-
          thropology. In *Horizons of Anthropol-
          ogy,* edited by Sol Tax, pp. 71-80.
          Aldine, Chicago.

BRYAN, KIRK
   1925   The Papago Country, Arizona. *U.S.
          Geological Survey, Water Supply Paper
          No. 499.* U.S. Government Printing
          Office, Washington.

BUEHMAN, ESTELLE M.
   1911   *Old Tucson.* State Consolidated Pub-
          lishing Co., Tucson.

CAPLOW, THEODORE
   1954   *The Sociology of Work.* University of
          Minnesota Press, Minneapolis.

CLOTTS, HERBERT V.
   1915   *Nomadic Papago Surveys and Investiga-
          tions, 1914-1915.* Report submitted to
          Chief Engineer, U.S. Indian Service,
          Washington.

COHEN, ALBERT K.
   1959   The Study of Social Disorganization
          and Deviant Behavior. In *Sociology
          Today,* edited by Robert K. Merton,
          Leonard Broom, and Leonard S. Cott-
          rell, Jr., pp. 461-84. Basic Books, New
          York.

COHEN, YEHUDI A.
   1961   A Question of Approach: I. Theoreti-
          cal. In *Social Structure and Personali-
          ty, A Case Book,* edited by Yehudi A.

Cohen, pp. 3-10. Holt, Rinehart, and Winston, New York.

COMMISSIONER OF INDIAN AFFAIRS

1865 *Annual Report.* U.S. Government Printing Office, Washington.

1866 *Annual Report.* U.S. Government Printing Office, Washington.

1867 *Annual Report.* U.S. Government Printing Office, Washington.

1872 *Annual Report.* U.S. Government Printing Office, Washington.

1875 *Annual Report.* U.S. Government Printing Office, Washington.

1876 *Annual Report.* U.S. Government Printing Office, Washington.

1894 *Annual Report.* U.S. Government Printing Office, Washington.

1901 *Annual Report.* U.S. Government Printing Office, Washington.

1902 *Annual Report.* U.S. Government Printing Office, Washington.

COSULICH, BERNICE
1953 *Tucson.* Arizona Silhouettes, Tucson.

CURTIS, RICHARD F.
1959 Occupational Mobility and Urban Social Life. *The American Journal of Sociology*, Vol. 65, No. 3, pp. 296-8.

DOBYNS, HENRY F.
1950 Papagos in the Cotton Fields. Unpublished Master's Thesis, University of Arizona, Tucson.

1954 Sketch of the "Sand Indians." *The Kiva*, Vol. 19, Nos. 2-4, pp. 27-39.

1955 The Case of Paint vs. Garlic. *Arizona Quarterly*, Vol. 2, No. 2, pp. 156-60.

EATON, JOSEPH W.
1952 Controlled Acculturation: A Survival Technique of the Hutterites. *American Sociological Review*, Vol. 17, No. 3, pp. 331-40.

FITZGERALD, KEN
1955 Tucson, Arizona as a Potential Location for a Bureau of Indian Affairs Field Relocation Office. Manuscript in files of the Bureau of Ethnic Research, University of Arizona, Tucson.

FONTANA, BERNARD L.
1960 Assimilative Change: A Papago Case Study. Unpublished Doctoral Dissertation, University of Arizona, Tucson.

FORBES, ROBERT H.
1911 Irrigation and Agricultural Practice in Arizona. *University of Arizona Agricultural Experiment Station, Bulletin 63.* Tucson.

FORDE, DARYLL
1956 Social Aspects of Urbanization and Industrialization in Africa: A General Review. *Social Implications of Industrialization and Urbanization in Africa South of the Sahara*, edited by Daryll Forde, pp. 11-50. UNESCO, Imprimerie Centrale Lausanne South Africa.

FORTES, MEYER
1936 Culture Contact as a Dynamic Process. *Africa*, Vol. 9, No. 1, pp. 24-55.

GEIGER, MAYNARD
1939 *The Kingdom of St. Francis in Arizona, 1839-1939.* Santa Barbara, California.

GOODE, WILLIAM J.
1960 Norm Commitment and Conformity to Role-Status Obligations. *The American Journal of Sociology*, Vol. 66, No. 3, pp. 246-58.

GREENLEAF, CAMERON AND ANDREW WALLACE
1962 Tucson: Pueblo, Presidio, and American City. *Arizoniana*, Vol. 3, No. 2, pp. 18-27.

HACKENBERG, ROBERT
1961 *Papago Population Study, Research Methods and Preliminary Results.* Bureau of Ethnic Research, University of Arizona, Tucson.

1964 Aboriginal Land Use and Occupancy of the Papago Indians. Manuscript in Arizona State Museum Library. University of Arizona, Tucson.

HAGEN, EVERETT E.
    1961 Analytical Models in the Study of So-
          cial Systems. *The American Journal of
          Sociology*, Vol. 67, No. 2, pp. 144-51.

HALLOWELL, A. IRVING
    1945 Sociopsychological Aspects of Accul-
          turation. In *The Science of Man in the
          World Crisis*, edited by Ralph Linton,
          pp. 171-200. Columbia University
          Press, New York.
    1952 Ojibwa Personality and Acculturation.
          In *Acculturation in the Americas*,
          edited by Sol Tax, pp. 105-12. Univer-
          sity of Chicago Press, Chicago.
    1962 Culture, Personality, and Society. In
          Anthropology Today, edited by Sol
          Tax, pp. 351-74. University of Chicago
          Press, Chicago.

HENRY, JULES
    1965 *Culture Against Man.* Vintage Books,
          New York.

HERTZLER, J. O.
    1961 *American Social Institutions.* Allyn
          and Bacon, Boston.

HINTON, RICHARD J.
    1878 *The Handbook to Arizona, 1877.*
          Payot, Upham's Co., San Francisco.

HOYT, ELIZABETH E.
    1960 Voluntary Unemployment and Unem-
          ployability in Jamaica with Special Re-
          ference to the Standard of Living.
          British Journal of Sociology, Vol. 11,
          No. 2, pp. 129-36.

INKELES, ALEX
    1960 Industrial Man: The Relation of Status
          to Experience, Perception, and Value.
          The American Journal of Sociology,
          Vol. 66, No. 1, pp. 1-31.

JAMES, BERNARD J.
    1961 Socio-Psychological Dimensions of O-
          jibwa Acculturation. *American Anth-
          ropologist,* Vol. 63, No. 4, pp. 721-46.

JOSEPH, ALICE, ROSAMOND B. SPICER, AND JANE
CHESKY
    1949 *The Desert People, A Study of the
          Papago Indians of Southern Arizona.*
          University of Chicago Press, Chicago.

KELLY, WILLIAM H.
    1963 *The Papago Indians of Arizona: A Pop-
          ulation and Economic Study.* Bureau
          of Ethnic Research, University of Ari-
          zona, Tucson.

KING, WILLIAM S.
    1954 The Folk Catholicism of the Tucson
          Papagos. Unpublished Master's Thesis,
          University of Arizona, Tucson.

KINO, EUSEBIO F.
    1954 *Kino Reports to Headquarters, Corres-
          pondence of Eusebio F. Kino, S. J.,
          from New Spain with Rome*, translated
          by Ernest J. Burrus. Institutum
          Societatis, Rome.

LEEDS, ANTHONY
    1965 Brazilian Careers and Social Structure:
          A Case History and Model. In *Contem-
          porary Cultures and Societies of Latin
          America,* edited by Dwight B. Heath
          and Richard N. Adams, pp. 379-404.
          Random House, New York.

LEONARD, JOHN WALLACE
    1954 The Economics of a One-Industry
          Town. Unpublished Master's Thesis,
          University of Arizona, Tucson.

LEWIS, OSCAR
    1959 *Five Families.* Basic Books, New York.
    1965 Urbanization Without Breakdown. In
          *Contemporary Cultures and Societies
          of Latin America*, edited by Dwight B.
          Heath and Richard N. Adams, pp.
          424-37. Random House, New York.

LINTON, RALPH
    1936 *The Study of Man.* Appleton-Century-
          Crofts, New York.

LITWAK, EUGENE
    1960 Occupational Mobility and Extended
          Family Cohesion. *American Sociologi-
          cal Review*, Vol. 25, No. 1, pp. 9-21.

LOCKWOOD, FRANK C., AND DONALD W. PAGE
    1930 *Tucson, the Old Pueblo.* The Manufac-
          turing Stationers, Inc., Phoenix.

LOOMIS, CHARLES P. AND ZONA K. LOOMIS
    1965 *Modern Social Theories, Selected
          American Writers.* D. Van Nostrand
          Company, Princeton, New Jersey.

LUMHOLTZ, KARL
 1912 *New Trails in Mexico*. Charles Scribner's Sons, New York.

MAIR, LUCY P.
 1957 *Studies in Applied Anthropology*. The Althone Press, London.

MANJE, JUAN MATEO
 1954 *Luz de Tierra Incógnita: Unknown Arizona and Sonora, 1693-1701*, translated by Harry J. Karns and Associates. Arizona Silhouettes, Tucson.

MARTIN, DOUGLAS D.
 1963 *An Arizona Chronology: The Territorial Years, 1846-1912*. University of Arizona Press, Tucson.

MASON, LEONARD
 1955 American Culture in Studies of Acculturation. *American Anthropologist*, Vol. 57, No. 6, pp. 1264-79.

MATHEWSON, E. P.
 1933 History of the Ajo District. Manuscript in Special Collections Library, University of Arizona, Tucson.

MAYER, PHILIP
 1962 Migrancy and the Study of Africans in Towns. *American Anthropologist*, Vol. 64, No. 3, pp. 576-92.

MCCLINTOCK, JAMES H.
 1916 *Arizona: The Youngest State*, Vol. 2. The S. J. Clarke Publishing Co., Chicago.

MCGOWAN, JOSEPH C.
 1961 *History of Extra-Long Staple Cottons*. Hill Printing Co., El Paso.

MERTON, ROBERT K.
 1957 *Social Theory and Social Structure*. The Free Press, Glencoe, Illinois.

METZLER, WILLIAM H.
 n.d. Economic Potential of the Papago Indians of Arizona. Manuscript in files of the Bureau of Ethnic Research, University of Arizona, Tucson.

NEW CORNELIA COPPER COMPANY
 n.d. *New Cornelia Copper Company, Ajo, Arizona: Property, Plant, and Process*. R. A. Watkins, Printer, Phoenix.

OFFICER, JAMES E.
 1956 *Indians in School*. Bureau of Ethnic Research, University of Arizona, Tucson.

OPLER, MORRIS E.
 1964 The Human Being in Culture Theory. *American Anthropologist*, Vol. 66, No. 3, pp. 507-52.

PADFIELD, HARLAND I.
 1961 The Papago Farm Worker. A Pilot Study. Manuscript in files of the Bureau of Ethnic Research, University of Arizona, Tucson.

 1965 Technological and Social Change in Farm Industries of Arizona. Unpublished Doctoral Dissertation, University of Arizona, Tucson.

PAPAGO EMPLOYMENT SURVEY
 1965 Field Schedules in Files of the Bureau of Ethnic Research. University of Arizona, Tucson.

PAPAGO POPULATION REGISTER
 1959 Bureau of Ethnic Research, University of Arizona, Tucson.

PEPLOW, EDWARD H., JR.
 1958 *History of Arizona*, Vol. 2. Lewis Historical Publishing Co., Inc., New York.

PIMA FARMS
 1925 *Pima Farms, Cortaro, Arizona*. Acme Printing Co., Tucson.

REDFIELD, ROBERT
 1960 *The Little Community, and Peasant Society and Culture*. University of Chicago Press, Chicago.

REDFIELD, ROBERT, RALPH LINTON, AND MELVILLE HERKOVITZ
 1936 Memorandum on the Study of Acculturation. *American Anthropologist*, Vol. 38, No. 1, pp. 149-52.

ROSE, DAN
 1936 *The Ancient Mines of Ajo*.

SMELSER, NEIL J., AND WILLIAM T. SMELSER
 1963 Introduction: Analyzing Personality and Social Systems. In *Personality and Social Systems*, edited by Neil J. Smelser and William T. Smelser, pp. 1-18. John Wiley and Sons, New York.

SOFER, C.
  1956 Urban African Social Structure and
        Working Group Behavior at Jinja,
        Uganda. In *Social Implications of In-
        dustrialization and Urbanization in
        Africa South of the Sahara*, edited by
        Daryll Forde, pp. 590-612. UNESCO,
        Imprimerie Centrale Lausanne South
        Africa.

SPICER, EDWARD H.
  1962 *Cycles of Conquest: The Impact of
        Spain, Mexico, and the United States
        on the Indians of the Southwest,
        1533-1960.* University of Arizona
        Press, Tucson.

SPINDLER, GEORGE, AND LOUISE SPINDLER
  1965 The Instrumental Activities Inventory:
        A Technique for the Study of the
        Psychology of Acculturation. *South-
        western Journal of Anthropology*, Vol.
        21, No. 1, pp. 1-23.

SPINDLER, LOUISE S.
  1962 Menomini Women and Culture Change.
        *American Anthropological Association
        Memoir* 91, Vol. 64, No. 1, Pt. 2.

SPIRO, MELFORD
  1955 The Acculturation of American Ethnic
        Groups. *American Anthropologist*,
        Vol. 57, No. 6, pp. 1240-52.

  1961a An Overview and a Suggested Reorien-
        tation. In *Psychological Anthropology:
        Approaches to Culture and Personality*,
        edited by Francis L. K. Hsu, pp.
        459-98. The Dorsey Press, Homewood,
        Illinois.

  1961b Social Systems, Personality, and Func-
        tional Analysis. In *Studying Personali-
        ty Cross-Culturally,* edited by Bert
        Kaplan, pp. 93-127. Row, Peterson
        and Company, Elmsford, New York.

STEWARD, JULIAN
  1950 Area Research: Theory and Practice.
        *Social Science Research Council Bulle-
        tin*, No. 63. New York.

THURNWALD, RICHARD C.
  1950 *Black and White in East Africa.* The
        Humanities Press, New York.

TOOKER, ELIZABETH
  1952 Papagos in Tucson: An Introduction to
        Their History, Community Life, and
        Acculturation. Unpublished Master's
        Thesis, University of Arizona, Tucson.

Tucson City Directory
  1958

  1959

TUMIN, MELVIN M.
  1957 Some Unapplauded Consequences of
        Social Mobility in Mass Society. *Social
        Forces*, Vol. 36, No. 1, pp. 32-7.

UNDERHILL, RUTH MURRAY
  1939 *Social Organization of the Papago
        Indians.* Columbia University Press,
        New York.

  1940 The Papago Indians of Arizona and
        Their Relatives the Pima. *Sherman
        Pamphlet* No. 3, Haskell Institute,
        Lawrence, Kansas.

  1946 *Papago Indian Religion.* Columbia Uni-
        versity Press, New York.

VAN BAAL, JAN
  1960 Erring Acculturation. *American Anth-
        ropologist*, Vol. 62, No. 1, pp. 108-21.

VOGET, FRED
  1952 Crow Socio-Cultural Groups. In *Accul-
        turation in the Americas*, edited by
        Sol Tax, pp. 88-93. University of Chi-
        cago Press, Chicago.

WALLACE, ANTHONY F. C.
  1961a *Culture and Personality.* Random
        House, New York.

  1961b The Psychic Unity of Human Groups.
        In *Studying Personality Cross-Cultur-
        ally*, edited by Bert Kaplan, pp.
        129-63. Row, Peterson, and Company,
        Elmsford, New York.

WEINSTOCK, S. ALEXANDER
  1963 Role Elements: A Link Between Accul-
        turation and Occupational Status.
        British Journal of Sociology, Vol. 14,
        No. 2, pp. 144-9.

WILLIAMS, THOMAS R.
  1956 Papago Personal Adaptability as a
        Product of the Culture Contact and

Change Situation. Unpublished Master's Thesis, University of Arizona, Tucson.

WOLF, ERIC
1955   Types of Latin American Peasantry: A Preliminary Discussion. *American Anthropologist*, Vol. 57, No. 3, pp. 452-71.

WYLLYS, RUFUS KAY
1950   *Arizona: The History of a Frontier State*. Hobson and Herr, Phoenix.

ZURCHER, LOUIS A., JR., ARNOLD MEADOW, AND SUSAN LEE ZURCHER
1965   Value Orientation, Role Conflict, and Alienation from Work: A Cross-Cultural Study. *American Sociological Review*, Vol. 30, No. 4, pp. 539-48.